IMAGES
of America

WALNUT RIDGE AND HOXIE

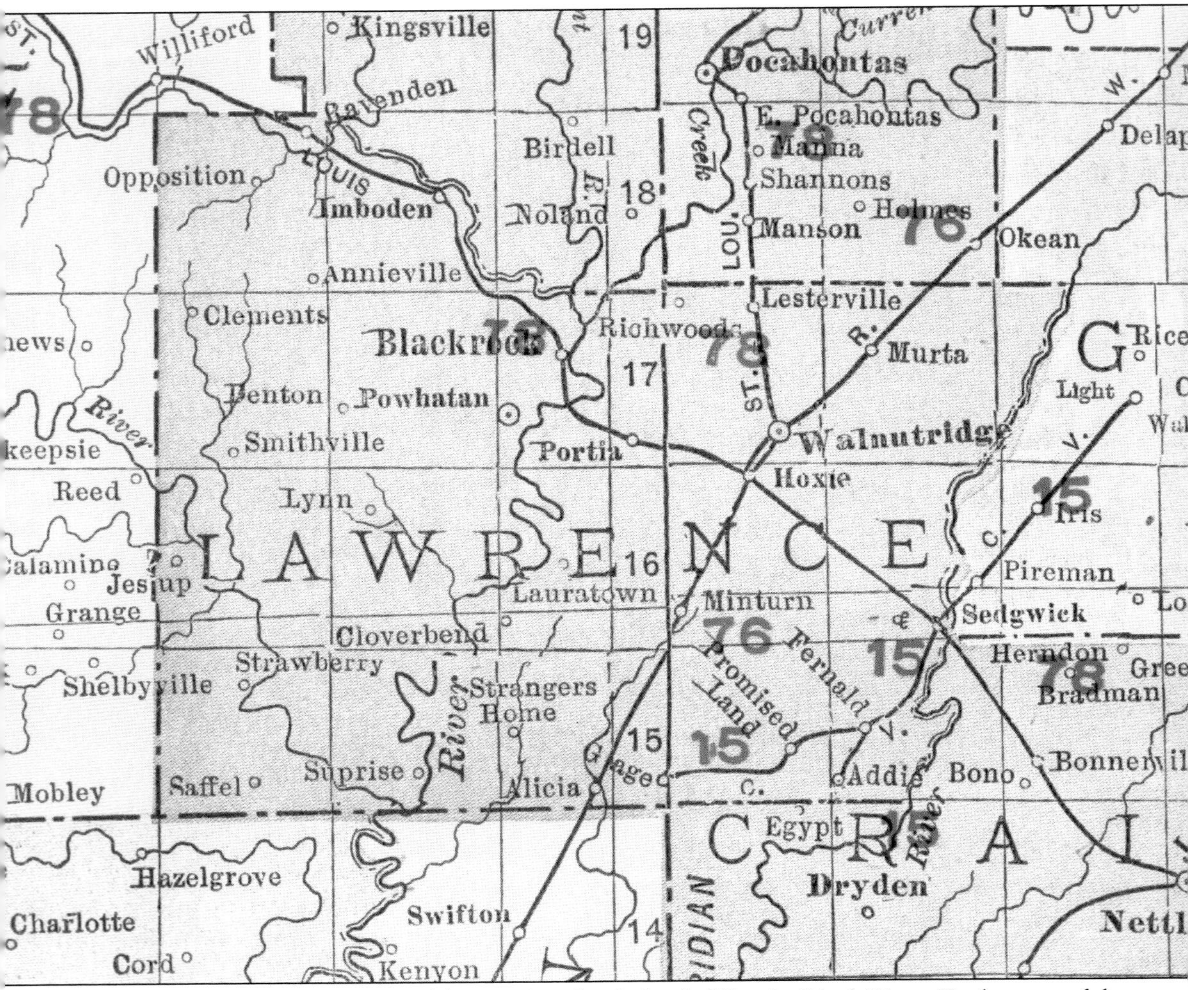

Lawrence County, 200 years old in 2015, is divided in half by the Black River. To the west of the river are the foothills of the Ozark Mountains, and to the east are the flatlands of the Mississippi Delta. Western towns are located near water sources; eastern towns are located near railroads. This 1900s railroad map shows Walnut Ridge and Hoxie at the convergence of three railroads—Iron Mountain, Frisco, and Hoxie, Pocahontas & Northern. (Jim Bohannon.)

On the Cover: Two boys in knickers watch passengers entering the Walnut Ridge and Hoxie streetcar in front of the Hoxie Union Station around 1914. This car, marked No. 3, was built in 1912 by the American Car Company. Cars No. 1 and 2 began service in 1904 when the line opened. These three cars made a round-trip every half hour along two miles of track. (James Whitlow.)

IMAGES
of America

WALNUT RIDGE AND HOXIE

Jon Walter and James Whitlow

ARCADIA PUBLISHING

ISBN 978-1-4671-1485-1

Published by Arcadia Publishing
Charleston, South Carolina

Printed in the United States of America

Library of Congress Control Number: 2015942091

For all general information, please contact Arcadia Publishing:
Telephone 843-853-2070
Fax 843-853-0044
E-mail sales@arcadiapublishing.com
For customer service and orders:
Toll-Free 1-888-313-2665

Visit us on the Internet at www.arcadiapublishing.com

To the visionaries who came before us and to the ones that strive to improve our communities for future generations

Contents

Acknowledgments

This was truly a community effort. We want to thank all the institutions and private donors who provided these wonderful photographs. We are particularly indebted to Evelyn Flippo for saving Lawrence County's abandoned records; Leroy Johnson for his extra help in identifying images; Jeannie Moore Smith for her photographic memory; Sandy and Roger Barrington for allowing us to dig through a treasure trove of Boas family information; the *Times Dispatch* archives on microfiche; and Lesa Walter, Alice Walter, and Diane Midkiff for their invaluable editing job. Special thanks go to Tina Stowers and her staff at the county clerk's office; Lisa Perry and her staff at the Northeast Arkansas Regional Archives; Harold Johnson and volunteers at the Wings of Honor Museum; Dr. Gerald Chaudron and Brigitte Billeaudeaux at the Ned R. McWherter Library, University of Memphis; Lawrence County Historical Society; Arkansas History Commission; Butler Center for Arkansas Studies; and the entire staff of the Lawrence County Library.

The images in this volume appear courtesy of the Arkansas History Commission (AHC), Butler Center for Arkansas Studies (BCAS), First Baptist Church of Hoxie (FBCH), First National Bank of Lawrence County (FNB), Hoxie City Hall (HCH), Kenneth Spencer Research Library, University of Kansas Libraries (KSRL), Lawrence County Chamber of Commerce (LCCC), Lawrence County Historical Society (LCHS), Missouri Pacific Historical Society (MPHS), Regions Bank (RB), University of Memphis (UM), Williams Baptist College (WBC), Wings of Honor Museum (WOH), and private collections from Ben Henry (BH), Boyd Lamb (BL), Billie Lane Brewer (BLB), Barney Sellers (BS), Calvin Allison (CA), Carrie Mae Snapp (CMS), Catherine Richey (CR), Charles Snapp (CS), Dirk Davis (DD), Dennis Flippo (DF), Daniel Mullen (DM), Dan Sears (DS), Fred Weeks (FW), Ginger Spades Milan (GSM), Hannah Roach Stacy (HRS), Helen Weir (HW), Joann Gardner (JAG), Jim Bohannon (JB), James Whitlow (JBW), Jon Walter (JCW), James E. Sauls (JES), Janene Fouts Ashlock (JFA), Jim Green (JG), Juanita Johnson (JJ), Jeff Keene (JK), Julie Kapales Jones (JKJ), Jeannie Moore Smith (JMS), JR Cox (JRC), John Statler (JS), Kellie Allison Yates (KAY), Larry Dobbs (LD), Lenore Belk Doyle (LBD), LeAnne Jones Liscomb (LJL), Linda Parker Linebaugh (LPL), Matt Loudermilk (ML), Marlyn Tate (MT), Norma Jean Smith Shields (NJS), Phyllis Recker Smith (PRS), Roy Osburn (RO), Sandy Barrington (SB), Shirley Johnson Douglas (SJD), Stacy Rice (SR), Sherry Smith Moore (SSM), Tonda Brand (TB), and Tammy Hembrey Jones (THJ).

Introduction

It was the best of times, it was the worst of times, it was the age of wisdom, it was the age of foolishness, it was the epoch of belief, it was the epoch of incredulity, it was the season of Light, it was the season of Darkness, it was the spring of hope, it was the winter of despair, we had everything before us, we had nothing before us . . .

—Charles Dickens, *A Tale of Two Cities*

This opening sentence, arguably one of the most recognized in English literature, was penned by Charles Dickens over 150 years ago to describe an era more than 60 years earlier. The chief settings in this tale are London and Paris, in countries separated only by a narrow channel of water. If you did not know when the above quote was written or to what it pertained, it could refer to many subjects of many eras gone by, as is the case with our two towns. Separated only by an imaginary line, Hoxie and Walnut Ridge are intertwined by histories, stories, times of prosperity and hardship, acts of God, rivalries, marriages, and interesting characters since before incorporation.

It is impossible to tell the rich history of these communities with a little over 200 photographs and their associated brief captions. However, the old adage "a picture is worth a thousand words" is truly the case in this instance. Our attempt is not to write a complete history but rather to give the reader a visual snapshot through the ages of how Walnut Ridge and Hoxie became the towns they are today.

After the Civil War, Col. Willis Miles Ponder came to Arkansas and settled on high ground two miles northwest of the present-day town of Walnut Ridge. Legend has it that he originally named the settlement Paw Paw for the abundant tree but was denied when he applied for a post office, because a town with that name already existed. Research shows the post office at Paw Paw was actually discontinued in the 1860s, so we are not sure if this legend is true, but it makes a nice story. However, it is true there were a great number of walnut trees on the sandy ridge, and a successful application for a post office was filed under Walnut Ridge in 1870. When Colonel Ponder moved east to the railroad in 1873, he moved the name with him, which is why Walnut Ridge is located in possibly the flattest land in Arkansas.

Henry and Mary Boas settled in a town called Moark, Arkansas, in 1871. They built a railroad restaurant there and managed it for two years until the Cairo and Fulton Railroad extended its route through Walnut Ridge. Sometime in 1873, the same year W.M. Ponder moved east to the railroad, the Boases also settled in Walnut Ridge and built another railroad restaurant where the Iron Mountain Depot sits today. In the book *A History of the North-Western Editorial Excursion to Arkansas*, this restaurant is mentioned numerous times by different reporters during their two-hour stop in Walnut Ridge on September 28, 1876.

In 1883, the Frisco Railway made plans to come through this area. The Boases offered right-of-way through their 400 acres south of Walnut Ridge, sold the hotel, built the Boas Hotel where the two railroads crossed, and platted the town of Hoxie. Hoxie was named for Herbert Melville Hoxie, an executive with Jay Gould's Iron Mountain Railroad.

By 1889, there was a mule-drawn streetcar connecting the two towns. By 1904, it was replaced by an electric streetcar line that ran from Walnut Ridge to the newly built Iron Mountain Roundhouse and YMCA in Hoxie, making a round-trip every 30 minutes. This was one of only eight streetcar lines ever in existence in Arkansas; most were in larger cities like Little Rock and Fort Smith. It was gone when the Great Depression hit in 1929, but the tracks were still visible on Main Street decades later.

Walnut Ridge is unique for a small town in Arkansas because of its early Jewish businessmen and leaders. Many of the Jewish merchants who settled in this area in the 1800s started as foot merchants, delivering wares from town to town and rural areas. Some of the surnames of successful early Jewish businessmen in Walnut Ridge were Albertstein, Arndt, Berger, Bloom, Less, Levit, Marx, Neustadler, Pitzele, and Riegler. According to an article written in 1895, it was thought that a Jewish synagogue would soon be built in Walnut Ridge, but that never occurred.

Hoxie is just as unique for its early Catholic presence. Meeting first in the home of Swan C. Dowell and also the Boas Hotel starting in 1881, the All Saints Catholic Church was the first church built in Hoxie in 1886. An exceptionally large painting (four by nine feet) hung above the altar, depicting the Crucifixion. It was one of three successive Catholic churches built in Hoxie; one was destroyed by fire, and the next was too small for the growing Catholic population caused by an influx of workers at the roundhouse and railroad shops in Hoxie. The Catholic church is now in Walnut Ridge but has the original stained-glass windows from the third church in Hoxie.

Walnut Ridge and Hoxie have had their share of "seasons of darkness" and "winters of despair." Fires damaged large portions of Walnut Ridge in 1888 and 1893; both town schools were destroyed by fire—Hoxie's multiple times. Both towns were hit hard by disastrous tornadoes in 1913 and again in 1927. Fires returned during the Great Depression and were rampant in Hoxie and Walnut Ridge; both business districts were described as ghost towns.

Thankfully, there were also "seasons of light" and "springs of hope." Walnut Ridge was blessed with a huge airport, which featured three 5,000-foot runways built for Army Air Corps training during World War II. Over 4,500 pilots were trained to fly here. The population increased by 4,000 people overnight. After the war, this became one of seven aircraft graveyards, with over 10,000 planes flown to Walnut Ridge for sale or disposal. A very nice museum is on-site at the well-traveled airport now.

In 1955, Hoxie made a landmark decision to integrate schools. The 25 new black students at Hoxie were accepted until *Life* magazine came to take pictures for a three-page spread. This caused national segregationist groups to travel to Hoxie and campaign to stop the integration; the attention put Hoxie on the map. Hoxie was the first successfully contested integration in the state, two years prior to the more famous case at Central High in Little Rock.

Some might say all roads lead to Walnut Ridge and Hoxie. They are definitely a crossroads for transportation. Highways 25, 34, 63, 67, 91, and 412 all weave through the towns, as well as the Iron Mountain (now Union Pacific) Railroad and the Frisco (now BNSF) Railway.

Highway 67 was nicknamed "Rock 'n' Roll Highway 67" due to the numerous rockabilly bands—Elvis, Johnny Cash, Jerry Lee Lewis, Conway Twitty, Sonny Burgess, and Billy Lee Riley—that played up and down this stretch of road and in and near Walnut Ridge and Hoxie. In addition, the Beatles stopped at the Walnut Ridge airport in 1964 on their first American tour, en route to a weekend vacation at a dude ranch in Missouri. This is the only time the Beatles ever set foot in Arkansas. Walnut Ridge started a Beatles-themed music festival called Beatles at the Ridge and erected a life-sized sculpture depicting the scene from *Abbey Road*. The music festival brings between 10,000 and 15,000 people into town each year.

Downtown Walnut Ridge is listed in the National Register of Historic Places as an example of a complete historic business district.

One

Early Years, 1870s to 1930s

The population of Walnut Ridge and Hoxie grew slowly at first; by 1890, there were 457 residents in Walnut Ridge and only 102 in Hoxie. The majority of the initial population was involved in agriculture, growing corn, wheat, cotton, and potatoes. Those not involved with farming were mostly lumbermen, merchants, and livestock dealers. Several town scenes show hogs and chickens roaming freely down the main streets. One humorous story involving free-range pigs occurred in 1892 during a fundraiser speech at the Hoxie Catholic Church given by a visiting preacher from Helena:

> On the night on which he was scheduled to speak at Hoxie, a veritable downpour occurred . . . An entire herd of hogs found shelter under the church against the inclemency of the storm. While the people quietly assembled, no one noticed anything. But after the speaker had begun, the "grunters" let out infernal noises so that scarcely any one could understand the speaker. Angrily, Father McQuaid rushed out and succeeded to rout the herd of screaming hogs with the first whip he found and used.

There was not a bank in Walnut Ridge for the first 16 years, until Lawrence County Bank opened its doors on Northeast Front Street in 1890 with Capt. J.M. Phelps as president. The Bank of Hoxie followed in 1903, with John Hill as president.

The tides changed at the turn of the century. The Iron Mountain Railroad established a roundhouse and built maintenance shops in Hoxie in 1901, the Phoenix Cotton Oil Company was built in Walnut Ridge in 1903, and electricity came to both towns in 1904, complete with a streetcar. The population of both towns, stagnant in the 1890s, quintupled in size in a few short years.

In addition to the previously mentioned Jewish businessmen, a list of some of the early leaders of Walnut Ridge includes names such as Andrews, Beakley, Beloate, Benningfield, Camp, Childers, Cooper, Dowell, Followwill, Gibson, Graff, Grimes, Hill, Lane, McCarroll, McClamrock, McDonald, Meriwether, Peters, Phelps, Ponder, Rankin, Rhea, Richardson, Riley, Ruffner, Sexton, Sharum, Sloan, Surridge, Thornburgh, Westphal, White, and Williams. Hoxie's first leaders include the names of Boas, Burrow, Gibson, Goodloe, Hill, Pace, Richardson, and Whalen. Of all these names, Swan C. Dowell was the chief promoter of Walnut Ridge and all of Lawrence County, advertising the benefits of the area nationwide. In Hoxie, John S. Gibson and his wife, Annie Boas Gibson (daughter of town founders), did more than anyone else to make Hoxie an early success.

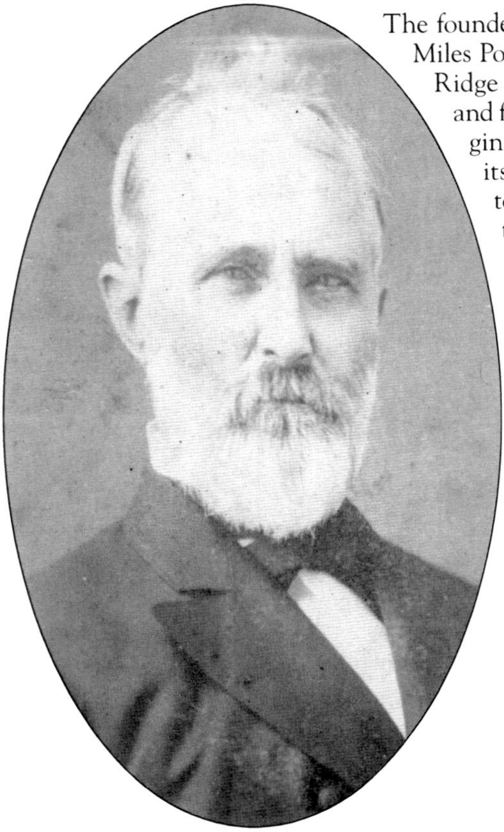

The founder of Walnut Ridge, Confederate colonel Willis Miles Ponder, bought 200 acres near present-day Walnut Ridge after the Civil War. He began merchandising and farming, as well as operating sawmills and cotton gins. When the Cairo & Fulton Railroad announced its plans in 1872, Ponder increased his holdings to 2,600 acres, cleared an area for a depot, built the first home, and laid out the plat for Walnut Ridge. (KSRL.)

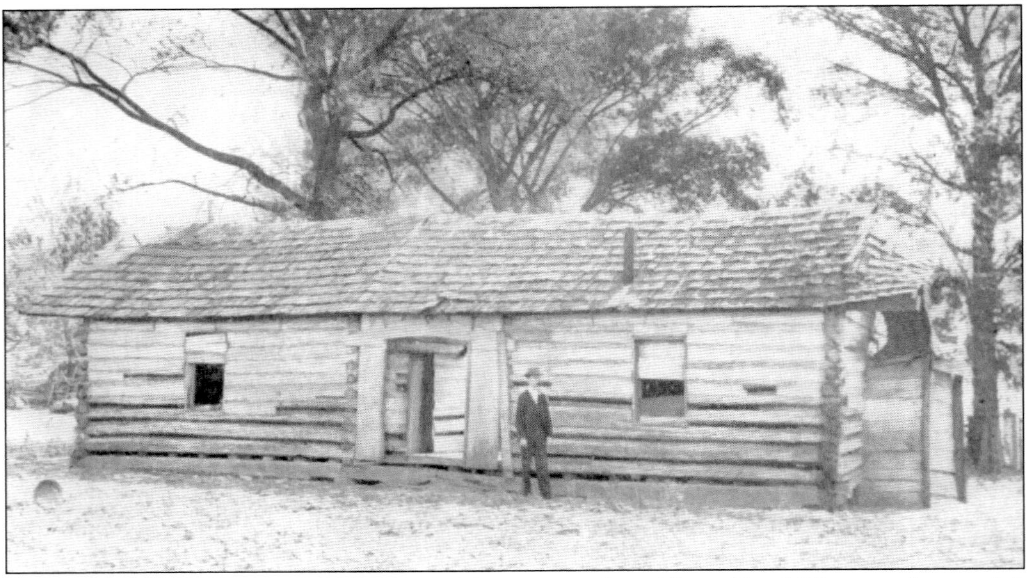

In 1868, Colonel Ponder married Mary A. Montgomery from Clover Bend. This was the couple's home in Old Walnut Ridge, located about two miles northwest of the present-day town. Their first two (of six) children were born here—Andrew in 1869 and Harry Lee in 1873. After founding Walnut Ridge in 1874, Ponder served as its first mayor. He also served as county judge and held one term in the state legislature. (JBW.)

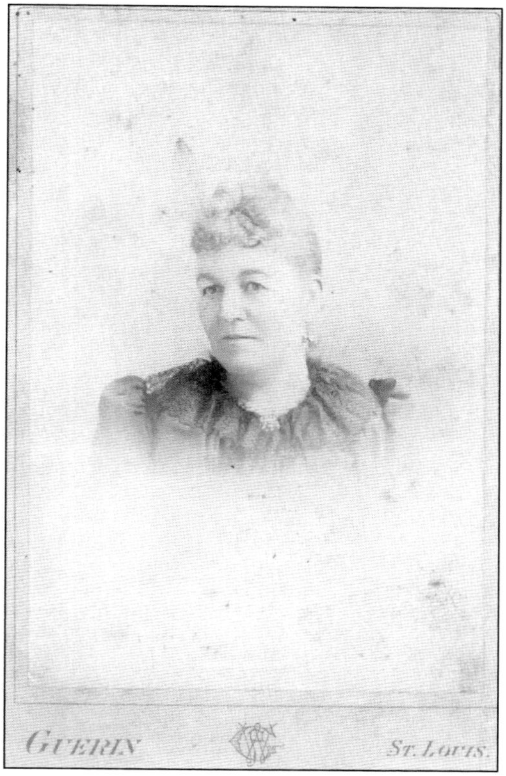

Henry Boas, a Missouri native and railroad man, met Mary Stephens in New Orleans, where they married in November 1864. They settled in Walnut Ridge in 1873 and immediately opened a railroad restaurant where the Iron Mountain Depot currently stands today. They also owned 400 acres of land just south of Walnut Ridge. On March 6, 1883, the St. Louis-San Francisco Railway (commonly known as the Frisco) made plans to build a railroad from Springfield, Missouri, to Memphis, Tennessee. When an agreement could not be reached to lay the tracks through Walnut Ridge, the Boases offered right-of-way through their land and built the Boas Hotel where the Iron Mountain and Frisco lines crossed; Hoxie was on the map. Henry and Mary had three children—William, who died as a young man, Annie, and Harry. (Both, SB.)

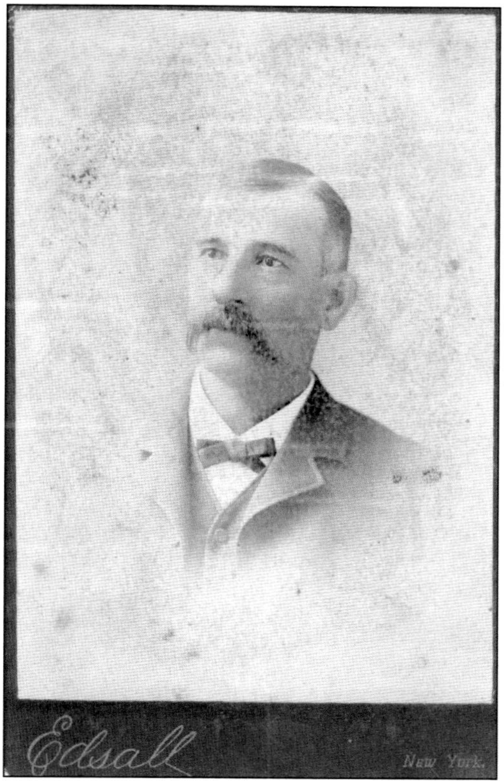

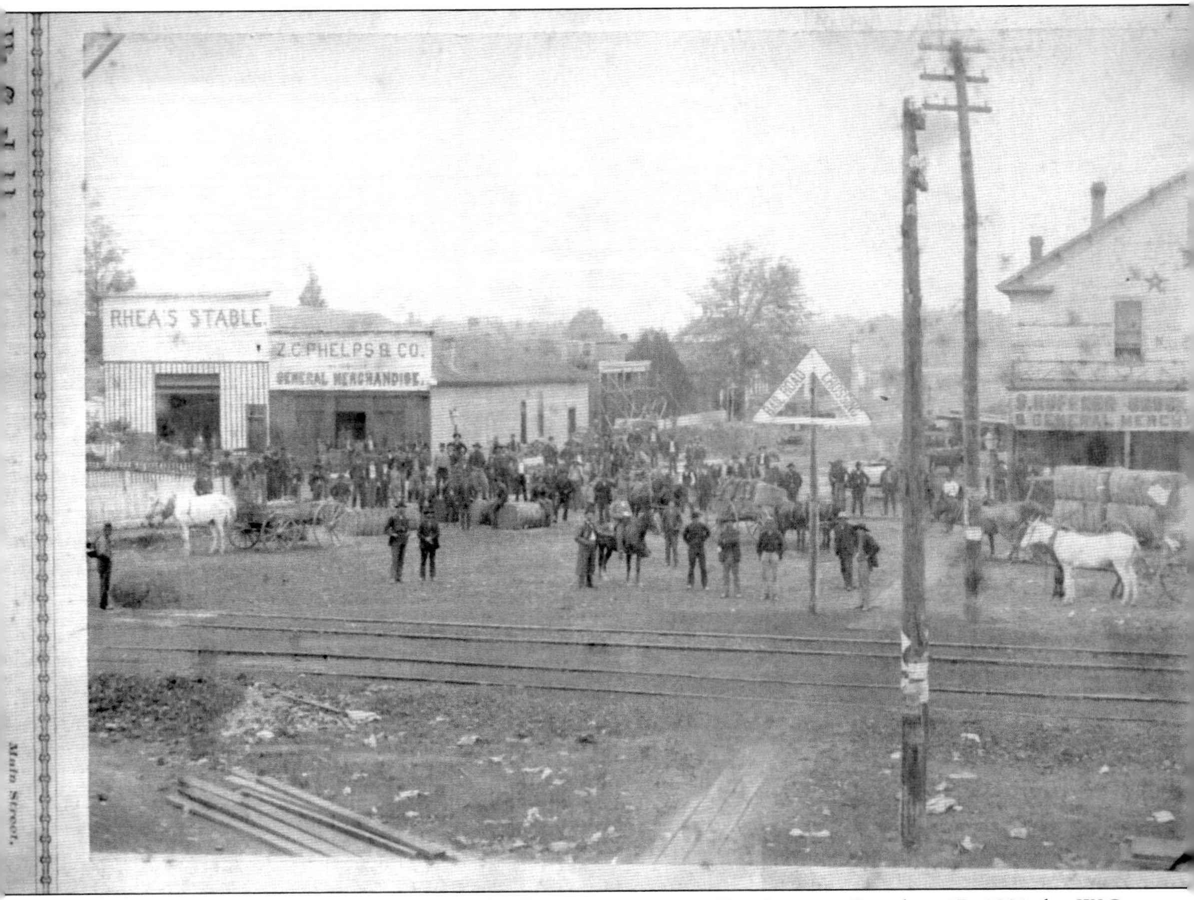

This photograph and the two on the facing page were all taken on October 17, 1891, by W.S. Hubbs. Side by side, these images create a three-block panoramic view along Front Street in Walnut Ridge. The view in this picture is looking down West Main Street at the intersection of Southwest and Northwest Front Streets. Visible are, from left to right, the Rhea Stables, owned by John A. Rhea; Z.C. Phelps and Company General Merchandise; and, partly, the Star Hotel across Main Street, with S. Ruffner's Groceries on the first floor. Behind the Phelps store is a partially constructed building, believed to be the opera house located there in the late 1890s. The majority of businesses in 1891 were located along Front Street. Businesses started migrating to West Main Street after the courthouse was built there in 1900. (KSRL.)

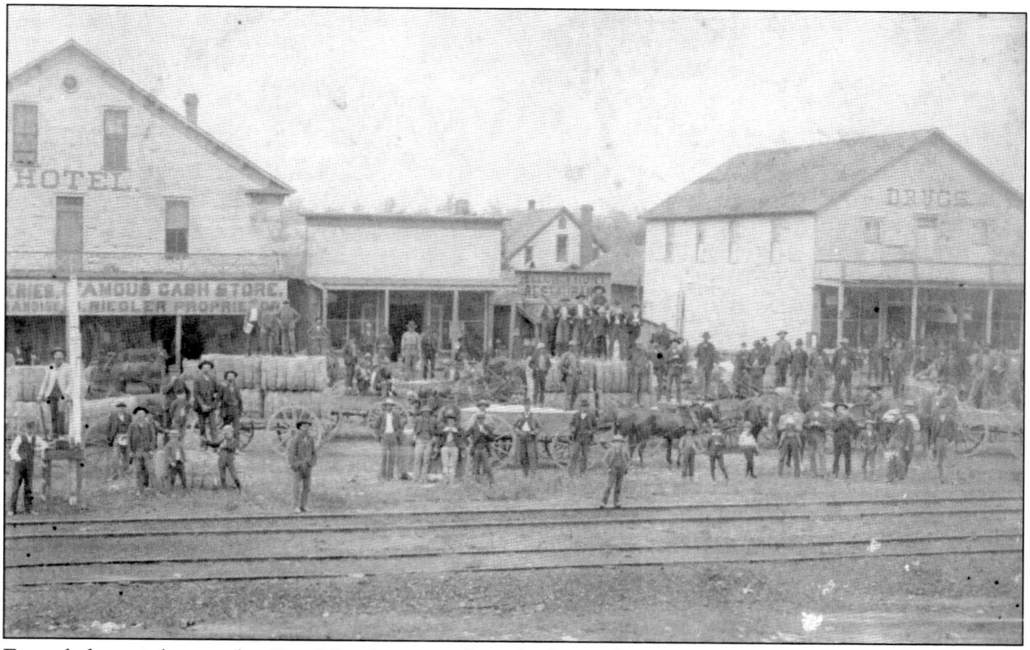

From left to right are the Star Hotel, an unidentified storefront, the Yellow Front Restaurant, and Swan C. Dowell's first drugstore, built in 1880. A fire destroyed all of these buildings 18 months after these photographs were taken. The fire, started by an arsonist, originated in the Star Hotel and quickly burned 13 buildings to the ground. Two people were killed in the hotel. (JBW.)

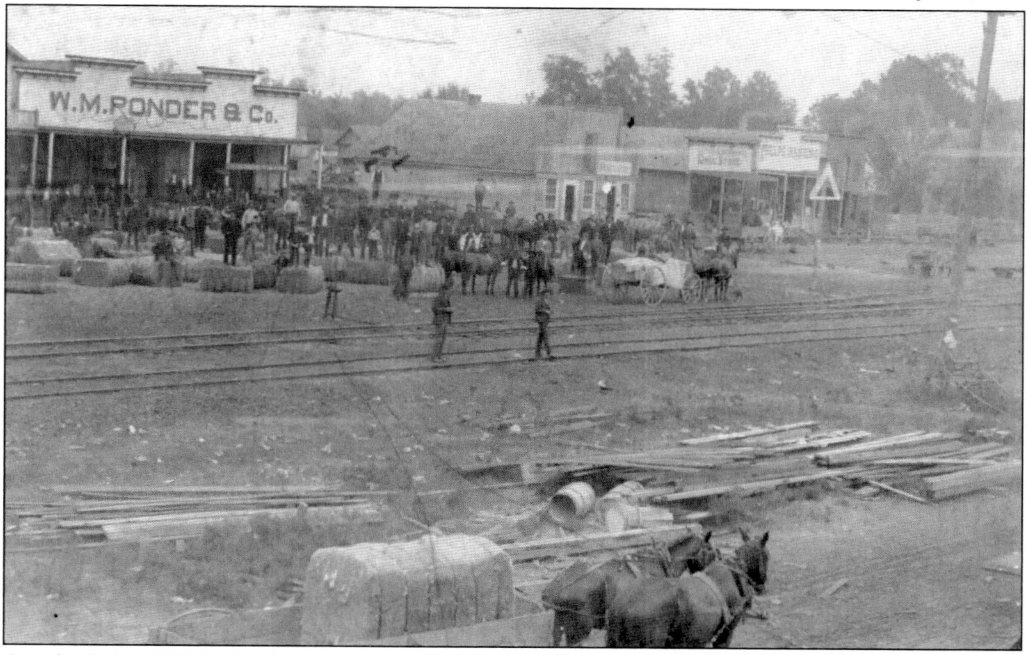

On the left is W.M. Ponder's store, the first business constructed in Walnut Ridge. Continuing to the right are a racket store, Sexton and Andrews drugstore, Phelps and Rankin general store, and an unidentified storefront. Sexton's Drug Store, established in 1886, is still in business today on West Main Street as Sexton Pharmacy. Cotton wagons are visible in this photograph and the previous two images. (JBW.)

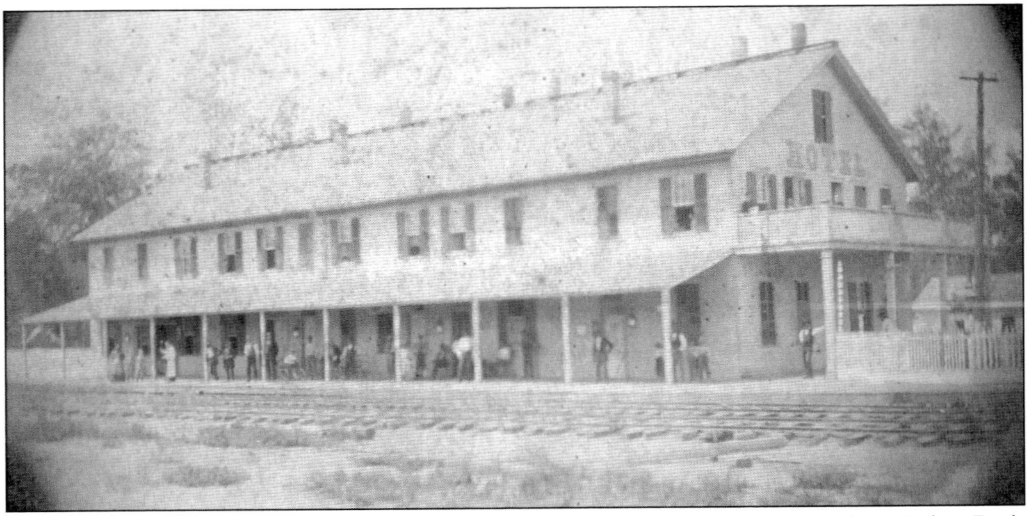

The Iron Mountain Hotel sat where the Iron Mountain Depot sits today in Walnut Ridge. Built by Henry and Mary Boas in 1877, it replaced their first restaurant, which burned that same year. It featured a spacious dining room, kitchen, office, lunch counter, ticket office, two separate waiting rooms, and telegraph office on the first floor. By 1908, the present Iron Mountain Depot was built in its place. (SB.)

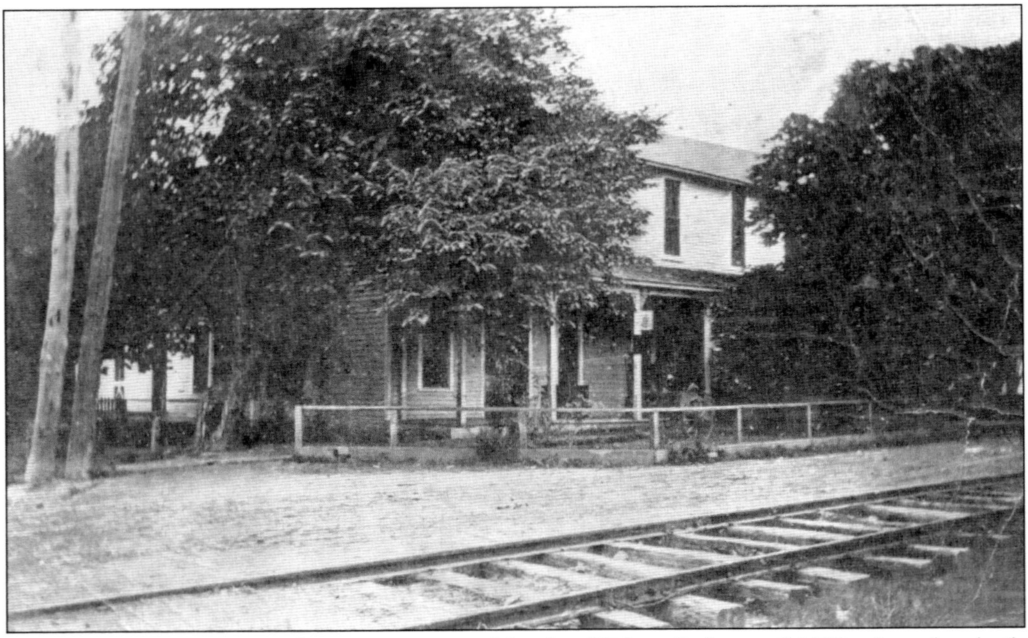

Henry and Mary Boas ran the Iron Mountain Hotel in Walnut Ridge until 1883, when they built the first hotel in Hoxie. Pictured here around 1906, it was a small white frame structure located just north of where the Frisco and Iron Mountain Railroads crossed. The Hoxie and Walnut Ridge streetcar tracks run along Texas Street, later Highway 67, in front of the hotel. (JBW.)

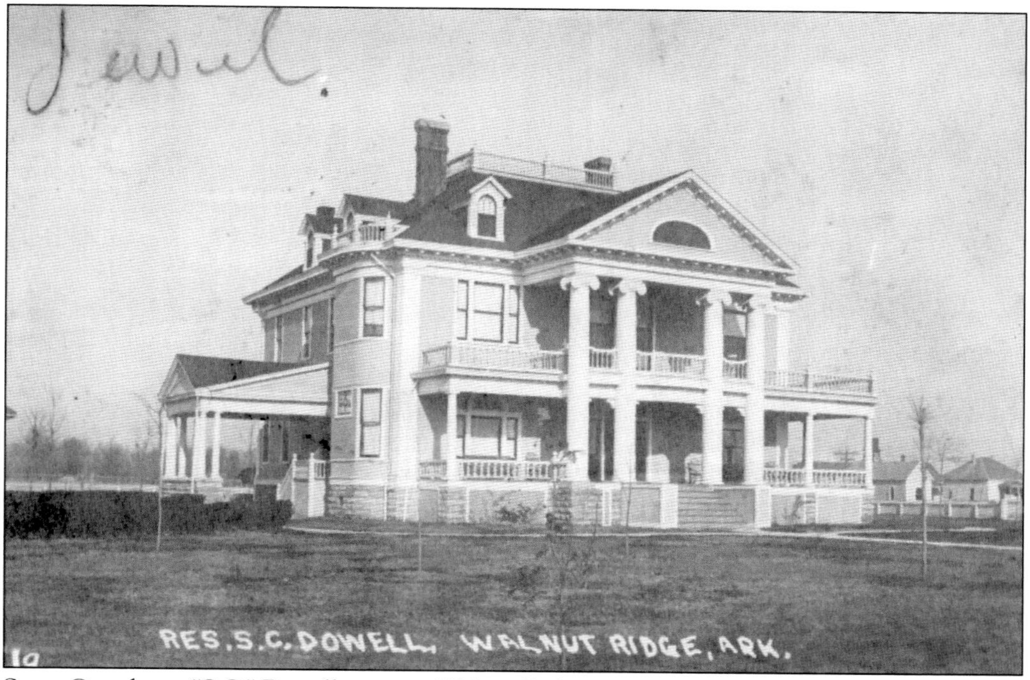

Swan Crutcheon "S.C." Dowell came to Walnut Ridge in 1880 and started a drugstore. In 1890, he entered the real estate and promotion business. Later, he sold his drugstore to Mose and Bob Cooper. Dowell advertised nationwide about the advantages of farmland in Hoxie and Walnut Ridge, successfully bringing many to this area. His home covered an entire block, bounded by Southwest Second, Southwest Third, Ash, and Maple Streets. (JBW.)

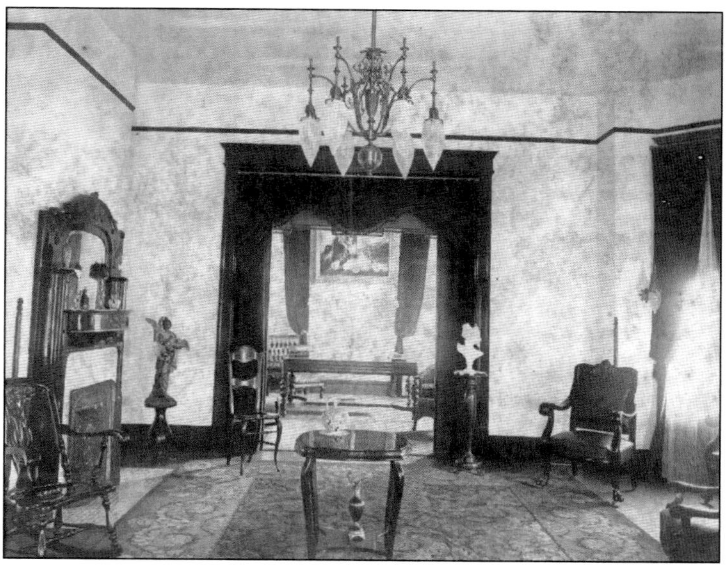

In 1881, the very first Catholic Mass was celebrated in an earlier home belonging to S.C. Dowell. By the turn of the century, Dowell had built his new seven-bedroom home in Walnut Ridge. Decorated here for Christmas, this home was the site of numerous social events and performers. Famous blues composer and musician W.C. Handy entertained here on at least two occasions. (BCAS.)

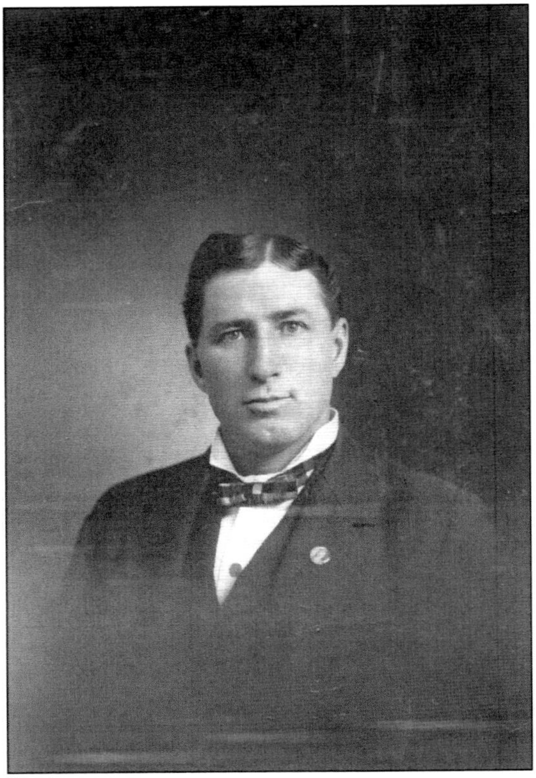

William Royal "W.R." Lane came to Walnut Ridge in 1894 as a medicine salesman. He decided to stay when he saw Miss Duffie Coffey from his train window and was instantly smitten. He became an early chief architect of the city. His major businesses included an ice plant, distillery, bottling works, ice cream factory, cotton gin, broom factory, the Lane Hotel, and the Lawrence Hotel. (BLB.)

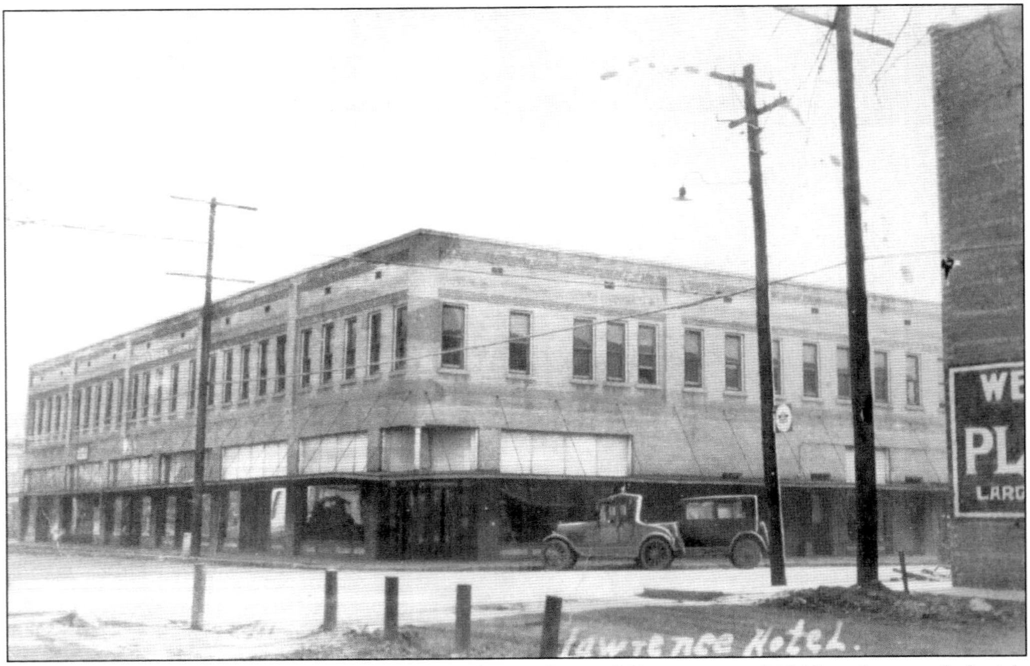

W.R. Lane opened the Lane Hotel along Southwest Second Street around 1910 and expanded with an adjacent three-story addition on Elm Street in 1915, which was razed in 2014. He built an even larger and finer hotel in 1921 called the Lawrence Hotel. Pictured here soon after opening, it was located on the corner of Southwest Third and Elm Streets, where Iberia Bank now stands. (JS.)

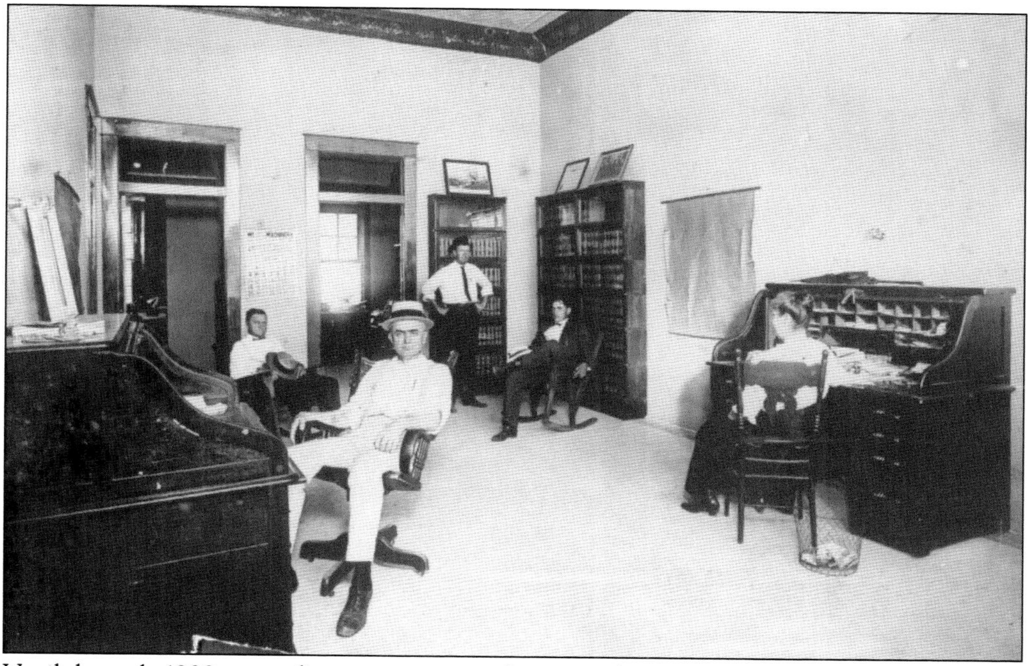

Until the early 1900s, attending a university and passing a bar exam were not required to practice law. So when William Edmund "W.E." Beloate set up shop in Walnut Ridge in 1890, he was a rare breed with a degree from an Ivy League school—Cornell Law. Seated at his desk, Beloate is pictured in his office on the top floor of the Lane Hotel in July 1915. (DM.)

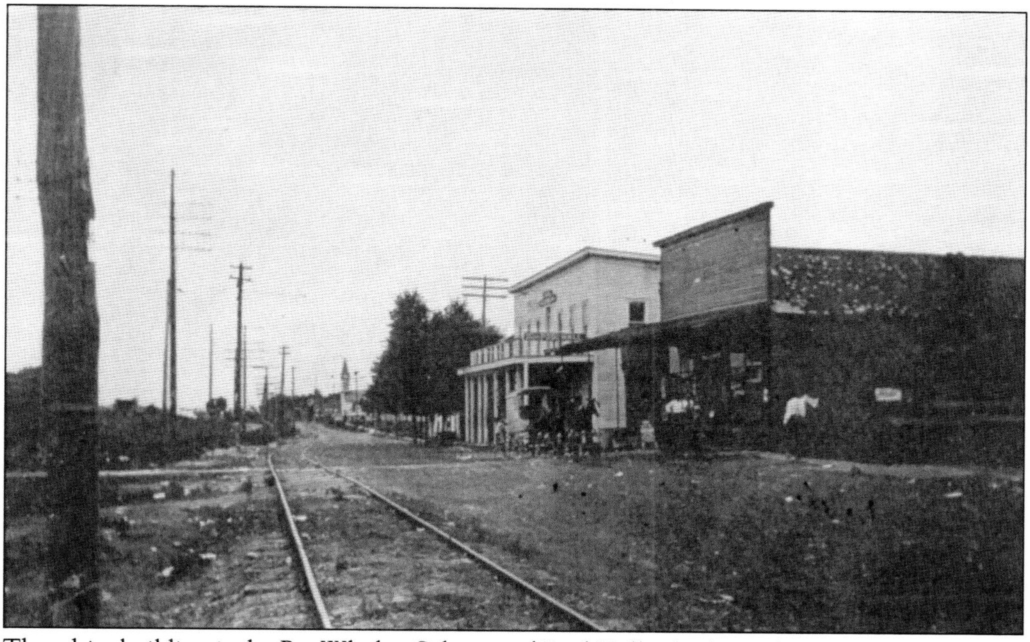

The white building is the Pat Whalen Saloon and Pool Hall, which was located near the corner of Memphis and Texas Streets in Hoxie. The streetcar tracks, heading south to the roundhouse, swerve to the right before reaching the Catholic church, its steeple barely visible. All Saints Church, built in 1886, was the first of three Catholic churches built in Hoxie. It was destroyed by fire in 1913. (JBW.)

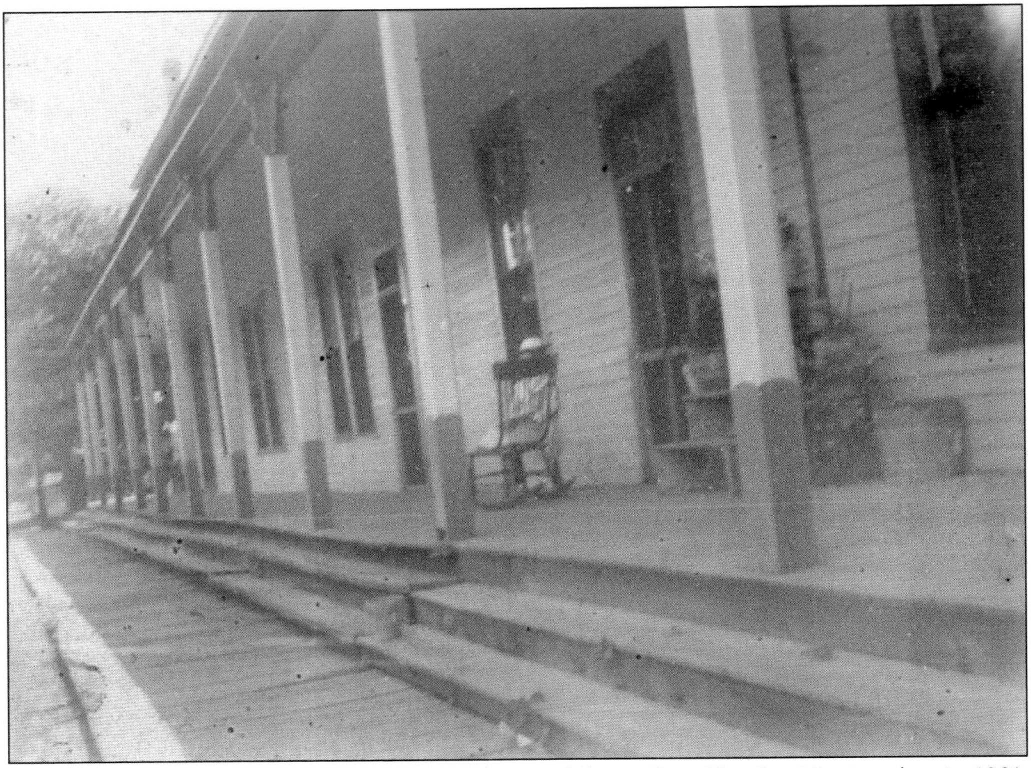

This is a close-up view of the front porch of the wood-frame Boas Hotel in Hoxie, taken in 1901. Originally built in 1883, the hotel was renovated and expanded by the time this photograph was taken. Early letterheads from the hotel boast of many modern amenities, such as charcoal-filtered rainwater for drinking, radiators, electric call bells, electric lights, and baths. The hotel also advertised a Frisco System dining hall. (JBW.)

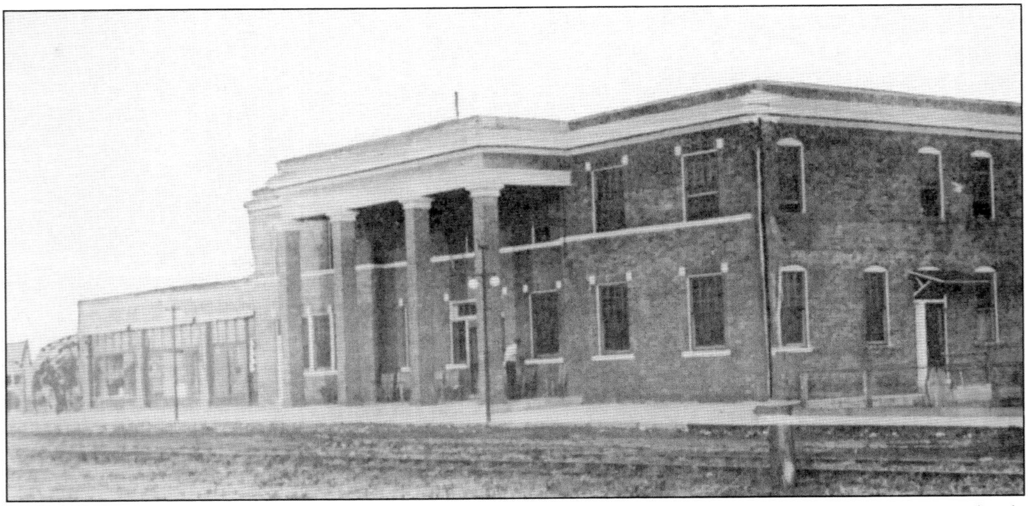

In 1913, the second Boas Hotel was constructed at the former location of the first. It was built by John S. Gibson and his wife, Annie Boas Gibson, daughter of Henry and Mary Boas. The Gibson home sat to the right of the hotel, connected by a covered walkway. The hotel and house were destroyed by fire in 1931. The house was rebuilt in the Tudor Revival style in 1935 and still stands today. (JBW.)

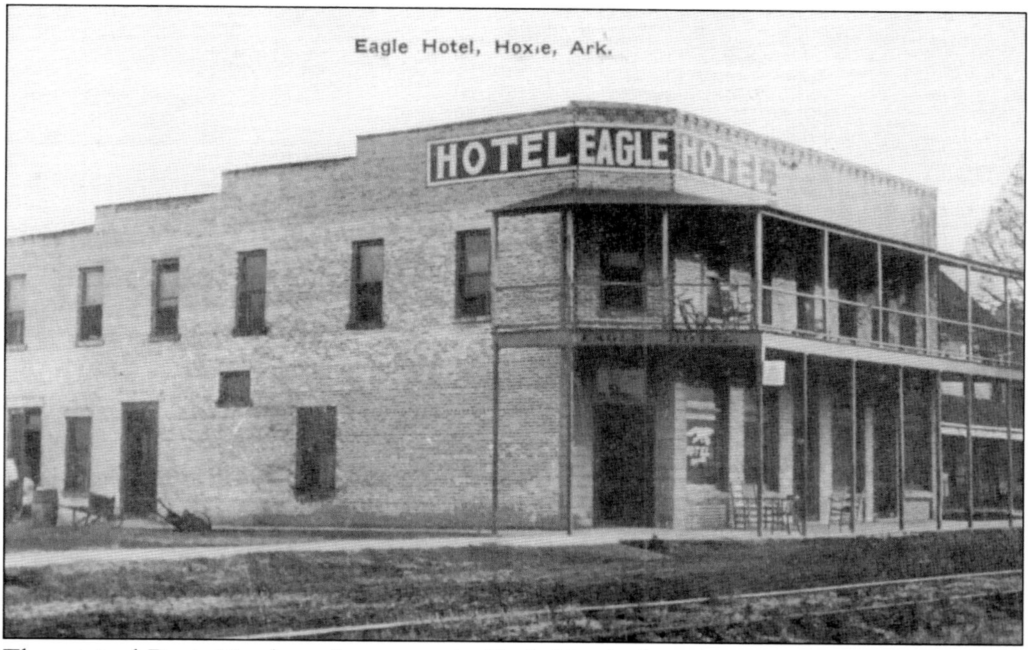

The original Davis Hotel was known as the Eagle Hotel when this picture was taken in 1921. Located on the corner of Texas and Annie Streets in Hoxie, the Hoxie and Walnut Ridge streetcar tracks are visible in front. By 1928, it had been completely leveled and replaced by a new gas station, with a hotel on the second floor. Today, this is the location of Budgie Little's service station. (JBW.)

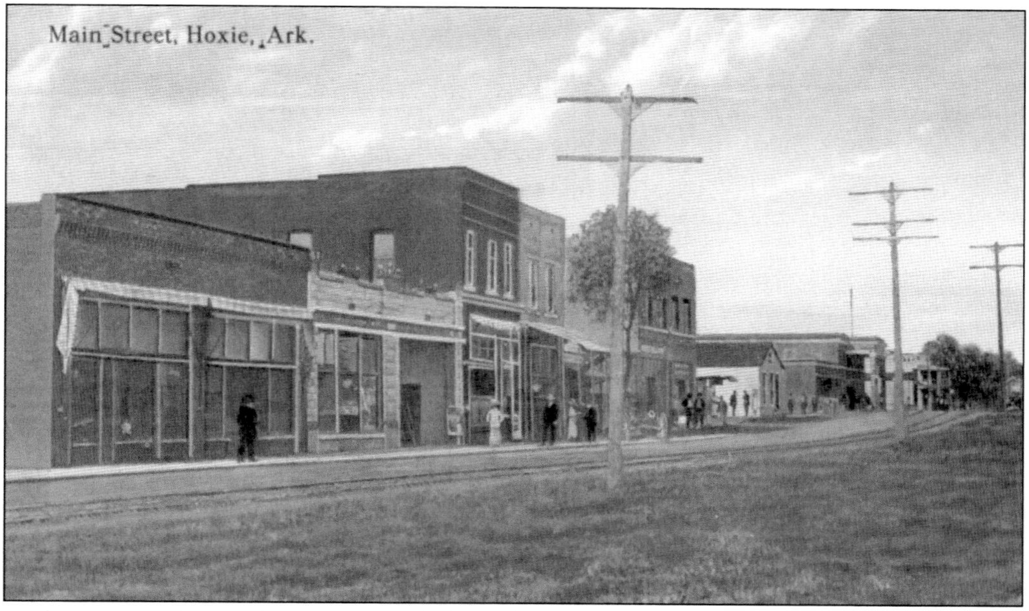

In this image taken in 1914, this stretch from Case to Annie Streets in Hoxie has many brick buildings constructed after the 1913 tornado. The lighter building, second from left, is the Triangle Theater. In later years, the theater moved left to the corner of Case Street. In the 1960s, the former theater became Sears Drug Store. In the distance, the old white post office is visible in the foreground of the Frisco tracks. The Boas Hotel and Eagle Hotel are beyond the tracks. (JBW.)

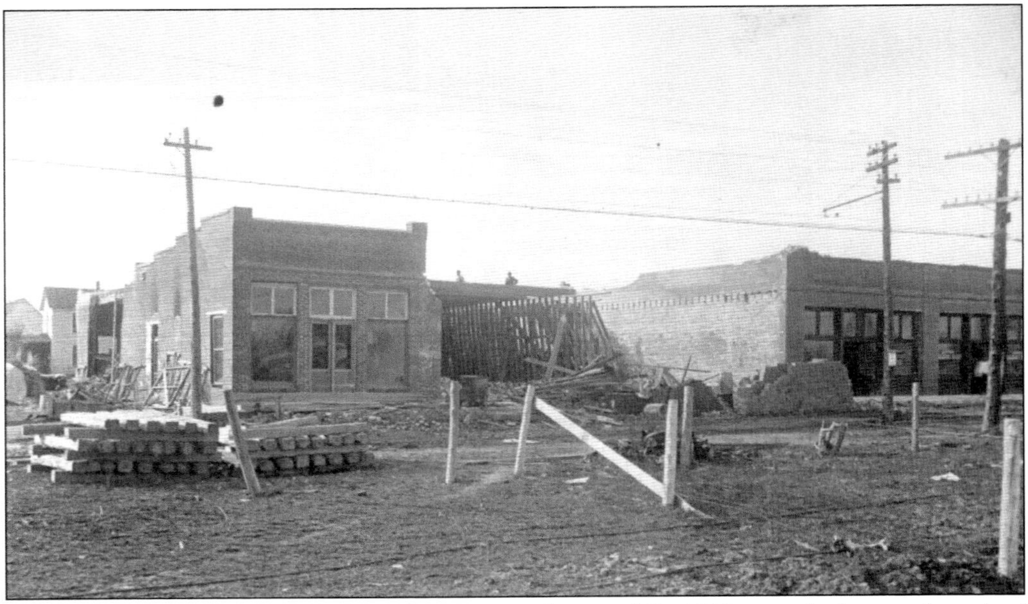

Hoxie was visited by two major tornadoes in its early years. The 1913 tornado destroyed much of the business district along Texas Street. Work began immediately to rebuild the growing town. The building on the far left is at the intersection of Texas and Case Streets, where workers are seen doing repairs. Today, Iberia Bank stands on this lot. The streetcar tracks are visible just in front of the buildings. (LD.)

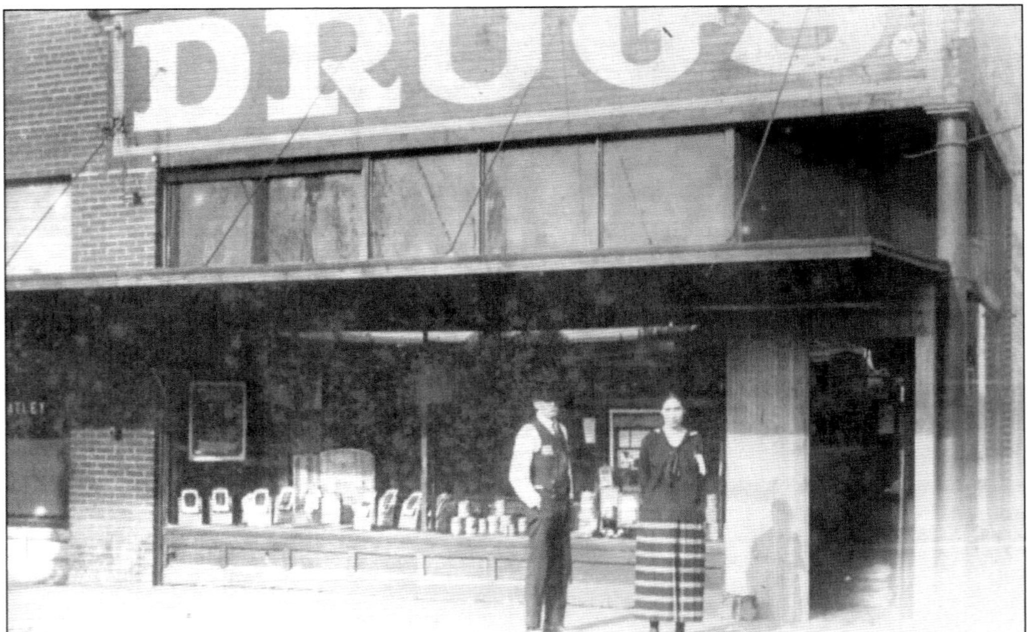

Seen here around 1920, Warner Drug Store of Hoxie, owned by Lucian R. Warner, was on the south side of the Frisco Railway line at the corner of Texas and Memphis Streets. Pictured are grocery store merchant James W. Abbott and Warner's sister Jennie Warner. Lucian Warner later moved across the Frisco tracks to the drugstore previously owned by Dr. John E. Pringle. Lastly, he bought Cooper Drugs on Main Street in Walnut Ridge. (JBW.)

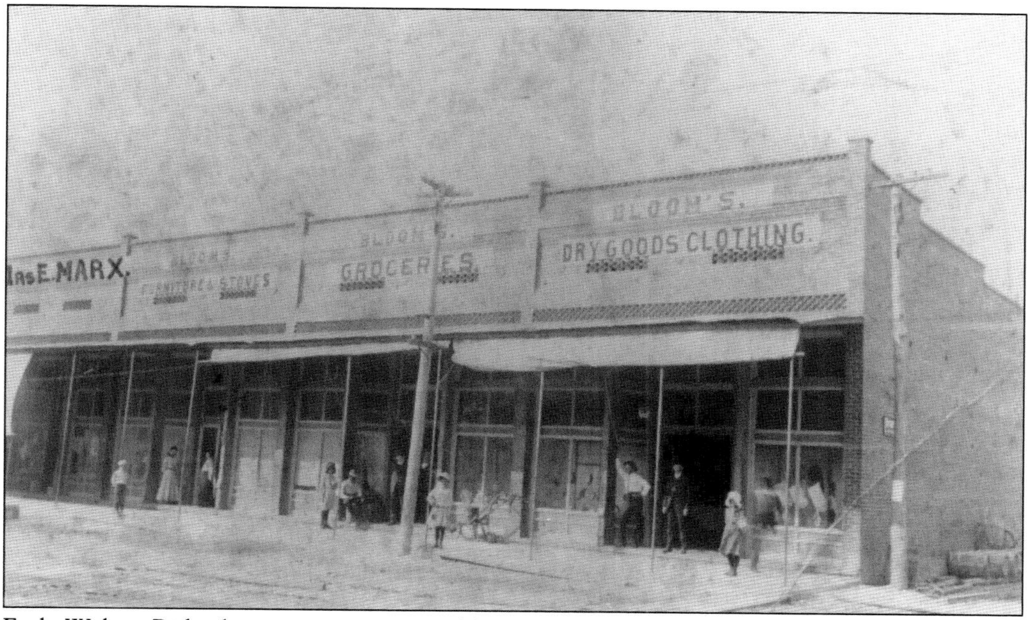

Early Walnut Ridge businesses were owned largely by men of Jewish descent, and many started as foot merchants. The building in this picture is but one example. Bloom's Department Store, started by brothers David, Dolph, and Charles Bloom, grew to be one of the largest department stores in northeast Arkansas by 1919. It burned to the ground in November 1930. These same lots were later the home of Van Atkins Department Store. (AHC.)

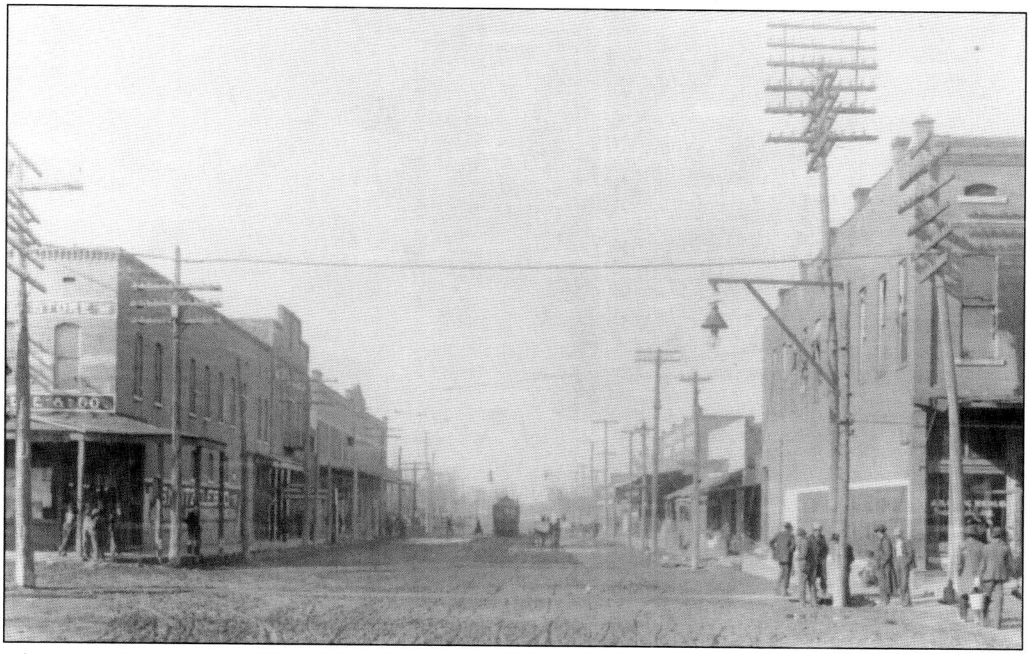

This view looks down West Main Street in Walnut Ridge, around 1914. Behind S.N. Pitzele Company (left), the old opera house, at the time of this photograph, houses Carroll and Carroll clothing store with a tailor shop in the rear. The Hotel Rhea is beyond it on the left, the drug sign from Mose Place is visible under the awning, and the streetcar is paused at Second Street to let off passengers. (AHC.)

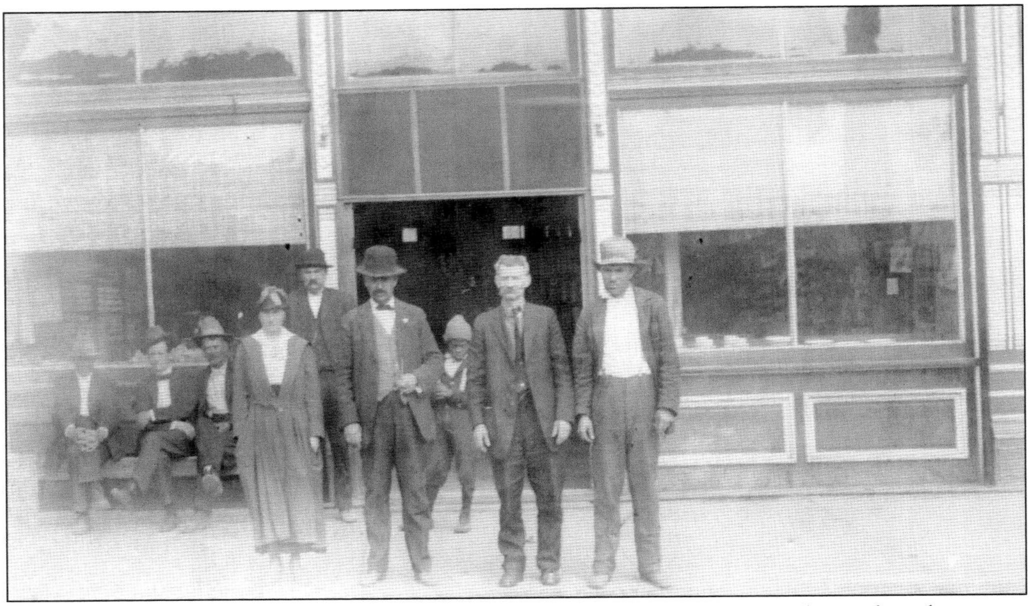

In the 1890s, the Peoples Store, with Followwill and Laser as proprietors, was located on the corner of West Main and Southwest Front Streets in Walnut Ridge. This partnership later dissolved, and James Walter "J.W." Followwill moved the Peoples Store to Northwest Front Street. Standing from left to right, in 1912, are Laura and George Teenor, Followwill, and Charles Hager. (JMS.)

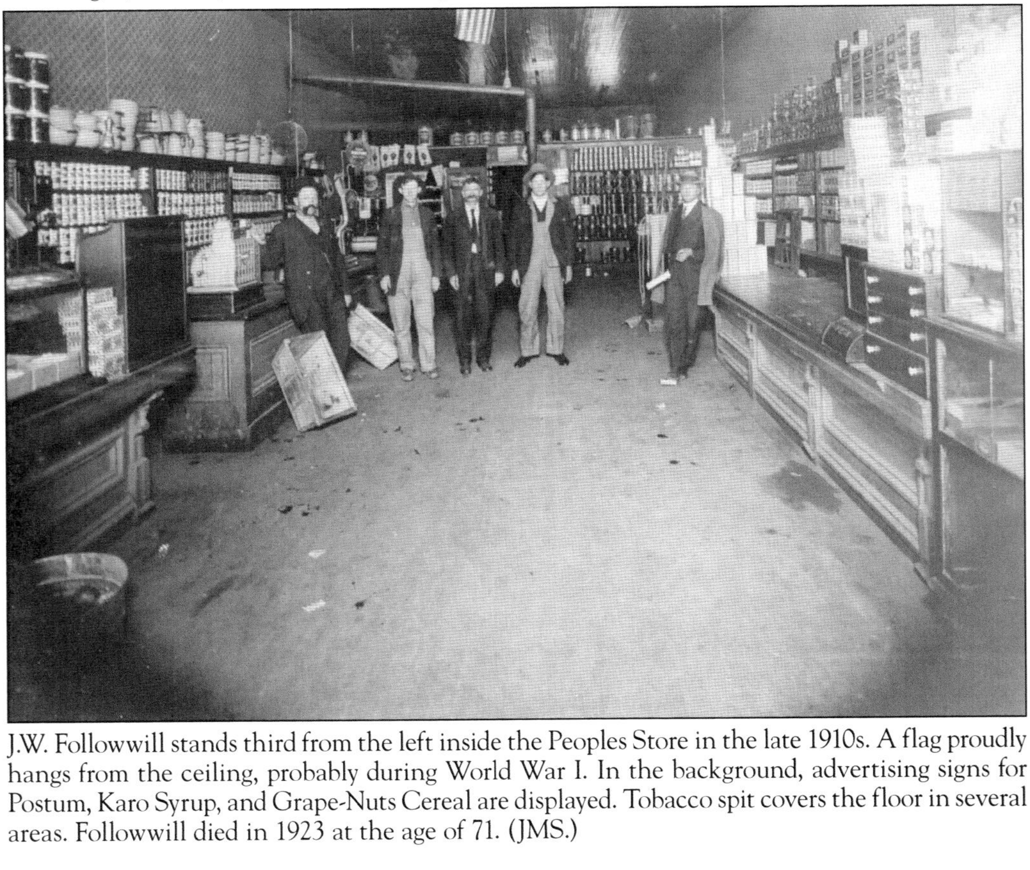

J.W. Followwill stands third from the left inside the Peoples Store in the late 1910s. A flag proudly hangs from the ceiling, probably during World War I. In the background, advertising signs for Postum, Karo Syrup, and Grape-Nuts Cereal are displayed. Tobacco spit covers the floor in several areas. Followwill died in 1923 at the age of 71. (JMS.)

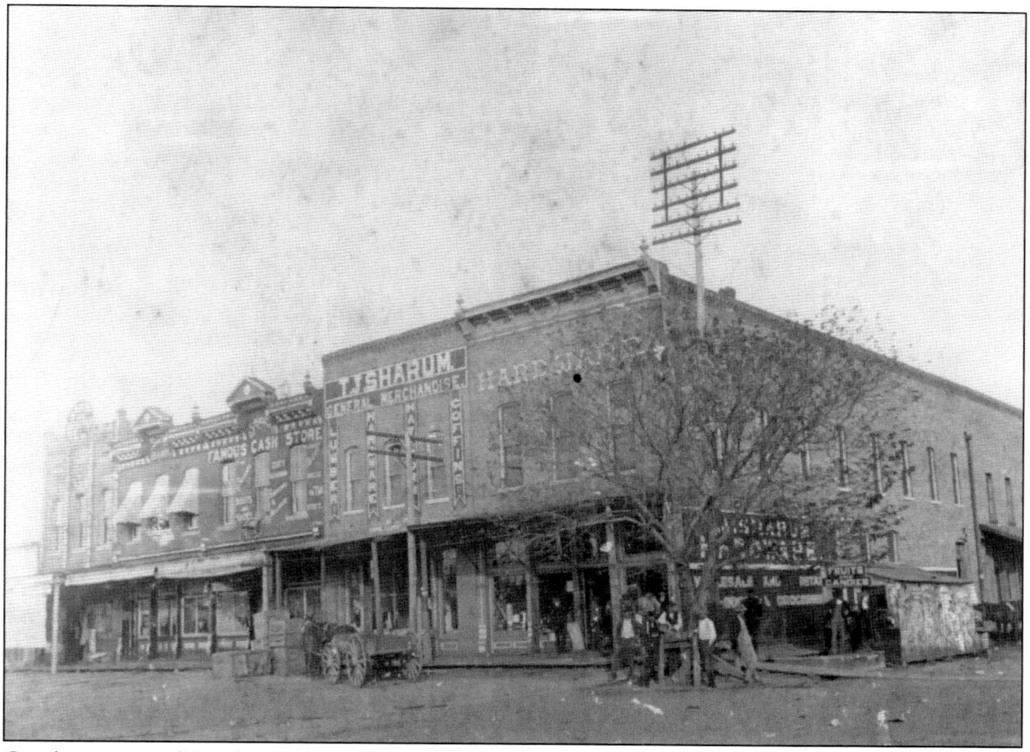

On the corner of Northeast Front and East Main Streets were the first commercial brick buildings erected in Walnut Ridge. From left to right are Herman Arndt Mercantile, built in 1893; the Lawrence County Bank and Riegler's Cash Store, both built in 1890; and T.J. Sharum General Merchandise and Hardware Stores, built by 1888. The leftmost building has been recently restored by Jon and Lesa Walter. (AHC.)

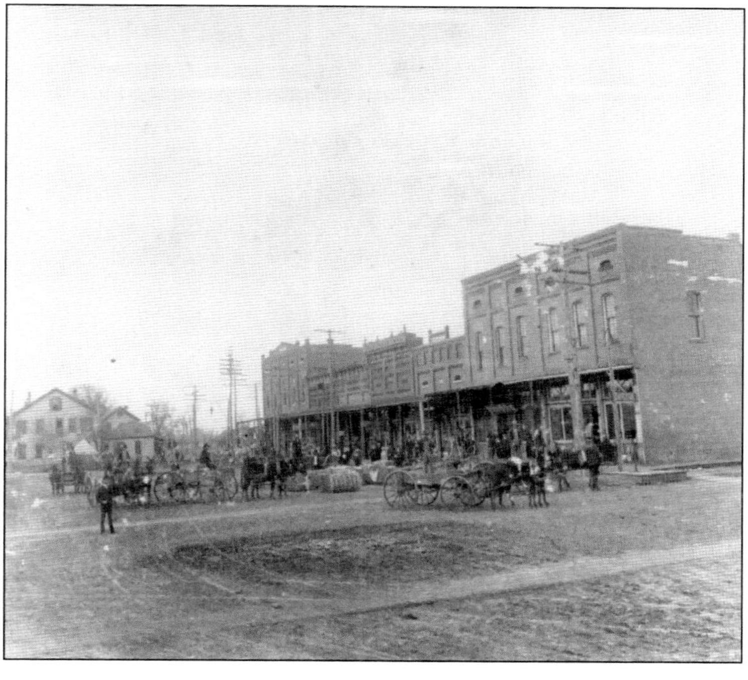

This cotton scene of Northwest Front Street in Walnut Ridge shows the old Iron Mountain hotel, built in 1877 by Henry and Mary Boas, on the far left of the picture. The new proprietor was Hattie Peters by this time, around 1904. The two-story hardware store on the far right was a shared meeting place for the Knights of Pythias and the Freemasons. (AHC.)

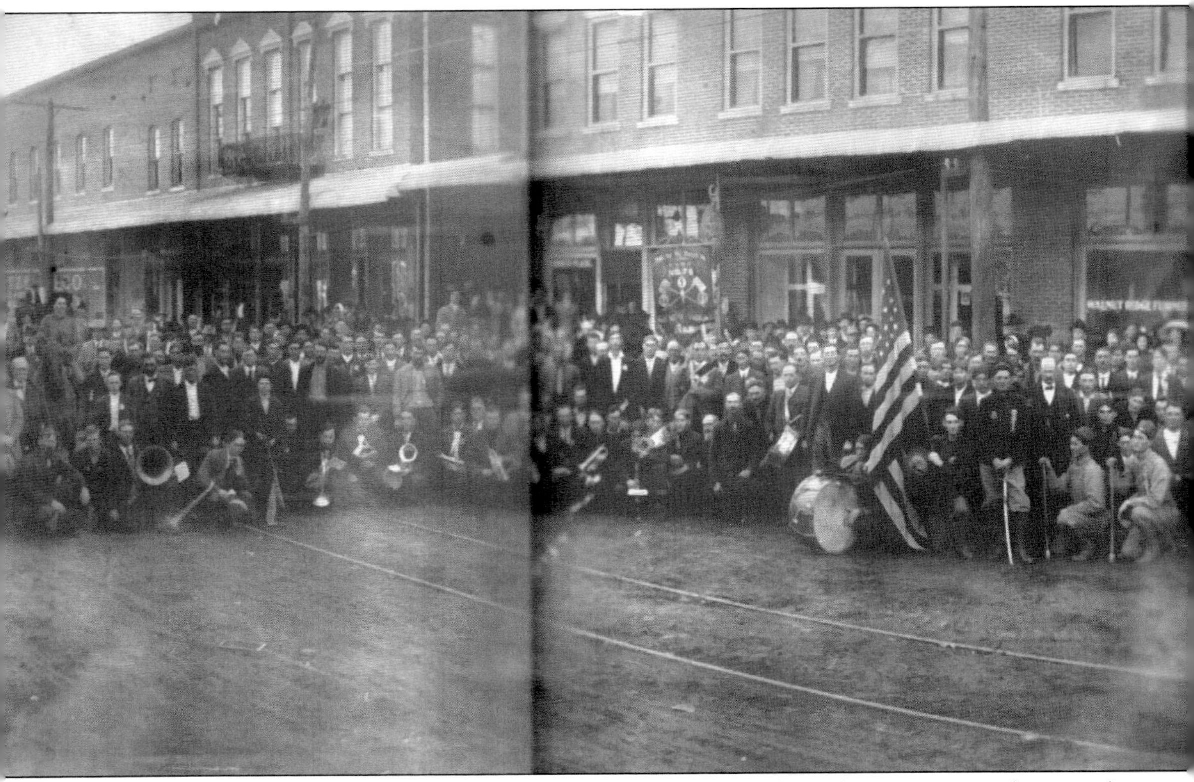

Something big must have happened in Walnut Ridge on this day. This panoramic photograph, three feet in length, shows the entire first block of West Main Street. The Black Rock Camp No. 75 Woodmen of the World line the streetcar tracks with their band, axmen, and goat mascot, along with other dignitaries in front of the Hotel Rhea around 1912. Buildings to the left of the

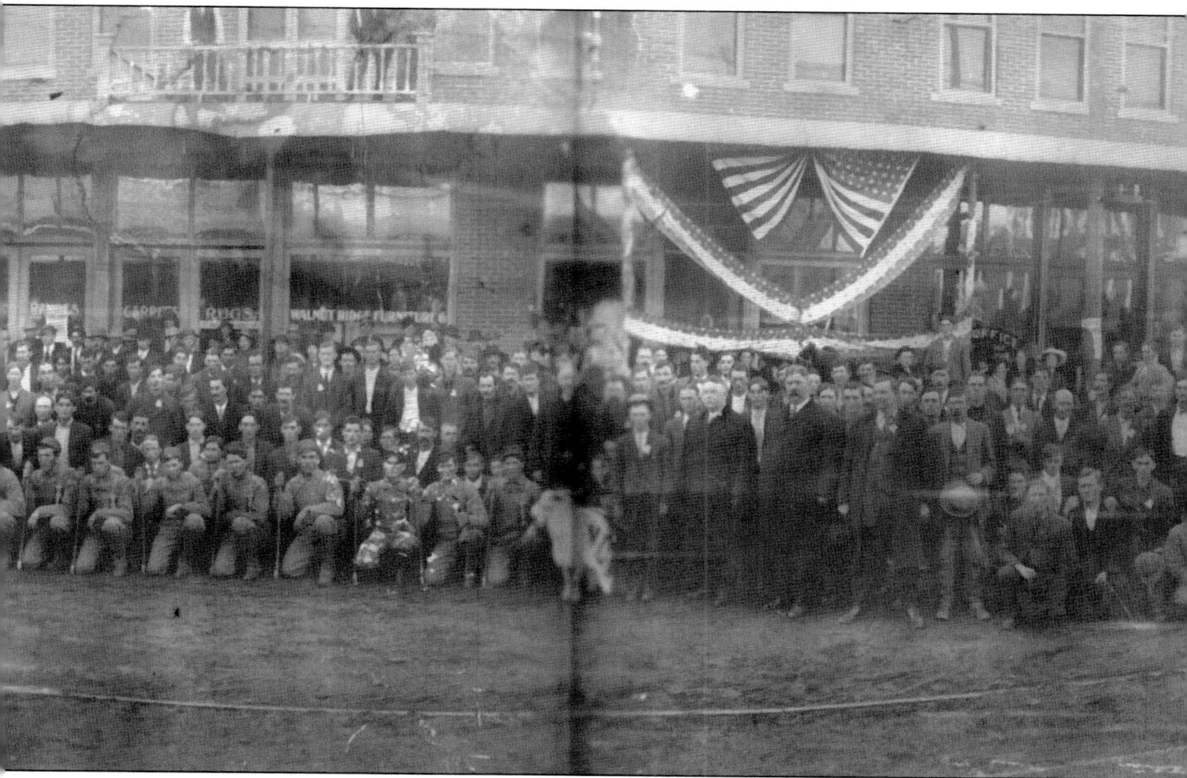

hotel are S.N. Pitzele and Company and the old opera house, which in 1912 housed a grocery store and clothing store. Businesses seen on the first floor of the Hotel Rhea are Mose Cooper's drugstore (Mose Place), a variety store, Walnut Ridge Furniture and Company, the post office, a barbershop, the hotel office, and A.A. Pope News Dealer. (LCCC.)

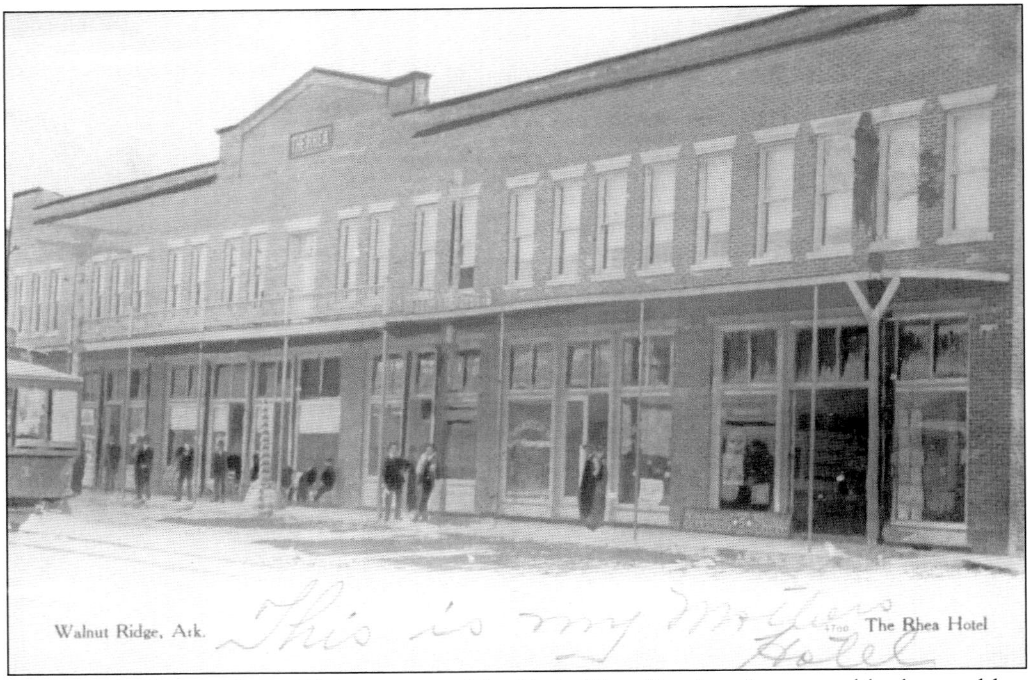

The Hotel Rhea, built in 1904, was owned by Lizzie Rhea Burel and managed by her and her husband, William C. Burel. According to newspaper advertisements at the time, "the Hotel Rhea had 64 sumptuously furnished rooms that were hardly adequate to supply the demand for accommodations at the time." It was destroyed by fire on November 15, 1914. The picture was written on by Lizzie's daughter Linnie Rhea, who died in 1910. (JCW.)

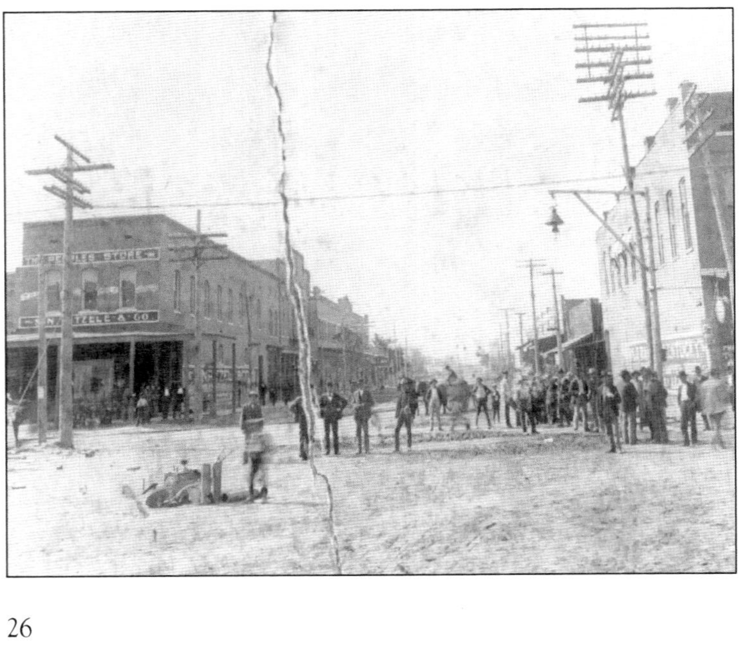

Early Walnut Ridge and Hoxie were littered with saloons until 1915, when the county became dry. This view, looking west along Main Street, shows one such saloon on the right, at the corner of Main and Northwest Front Streets. The side has a large mural advertising Kentucky whiskey. The Hotel Rhea, on the left in the distance, was built in 1904, the year this picture was taken. (AHC.)

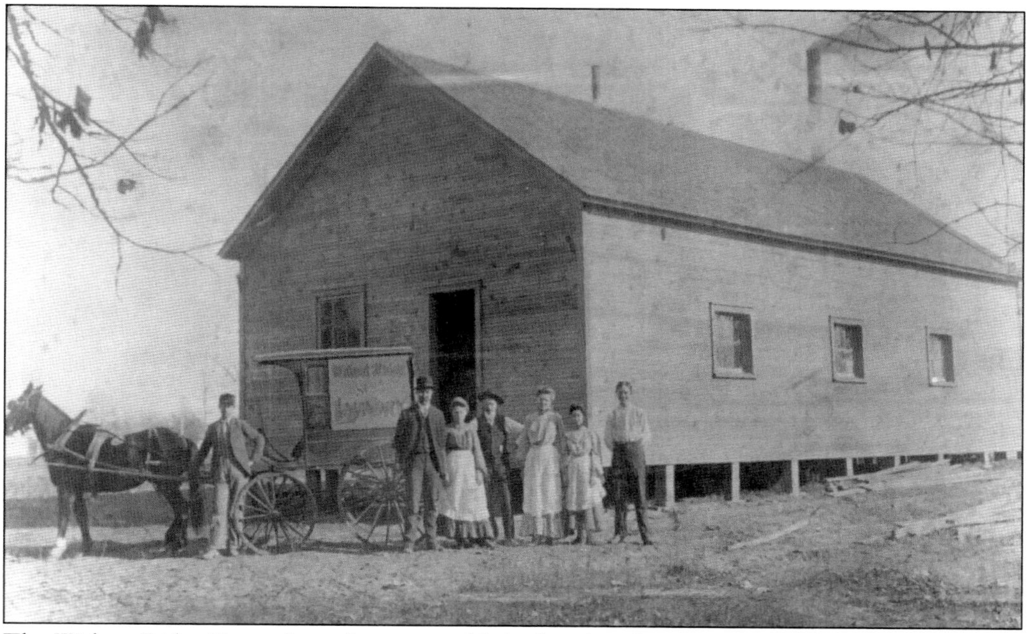

The Walnut Ridge Steam Laundry was established in October 1904. It was founded by partners W.E. Northern, a former lumberman from Virginia, and W.W. Moore, originally from Illinois. Both gentlemen moved to Walnut Ridge in the 1880s. The laundry, located at the corner of Southwest Front and Oak Streets, displays one of the first local phone numbers on the carriage—the single digit 6. (AHC.)

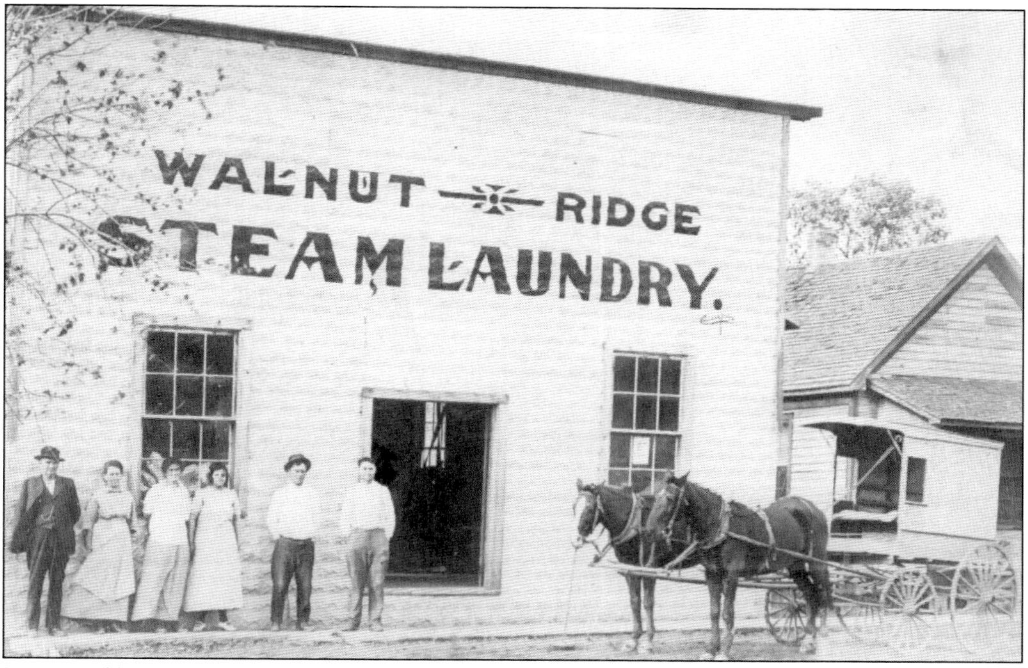

Destroyed by a tornado in 1913, the steam laundry was rebuilt in the same spot. The new laundry was framed with wood but clad in metal. It appears that the same carriage is being used but is now pulled by two horses. Like the previous building, it was powered by an underground steam pipe that connected across Oak Street to the Walnut Ridge Light, Power & Transit Company. (LJL.)

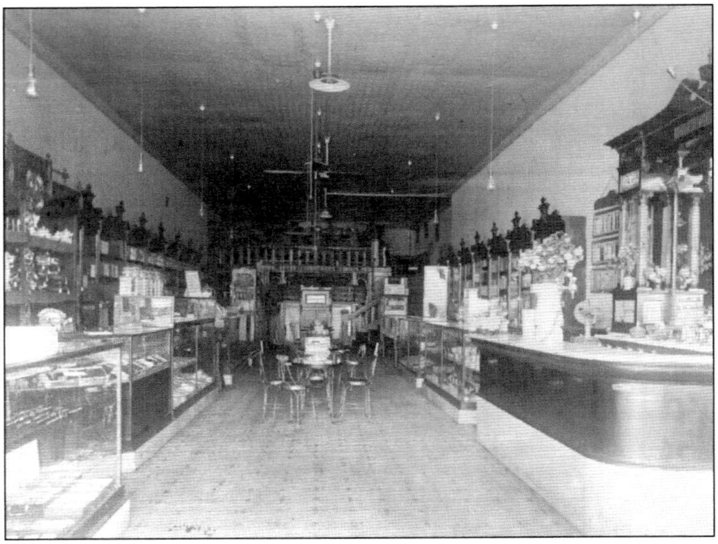

Pictured is the interior of the Cozy Corner Drug Store, owned by Bob Cooper. He opened the business in 1904 on the corner of Main and Northwest Front Streets. In 1915, he moved to the 200 block of West Main Street, next to the Lawrence County Bank and the post office. There, he opened Central Pharmacy, also known as Bob's Place. Cooper continued operation until his death in 1929. (BCAS.)

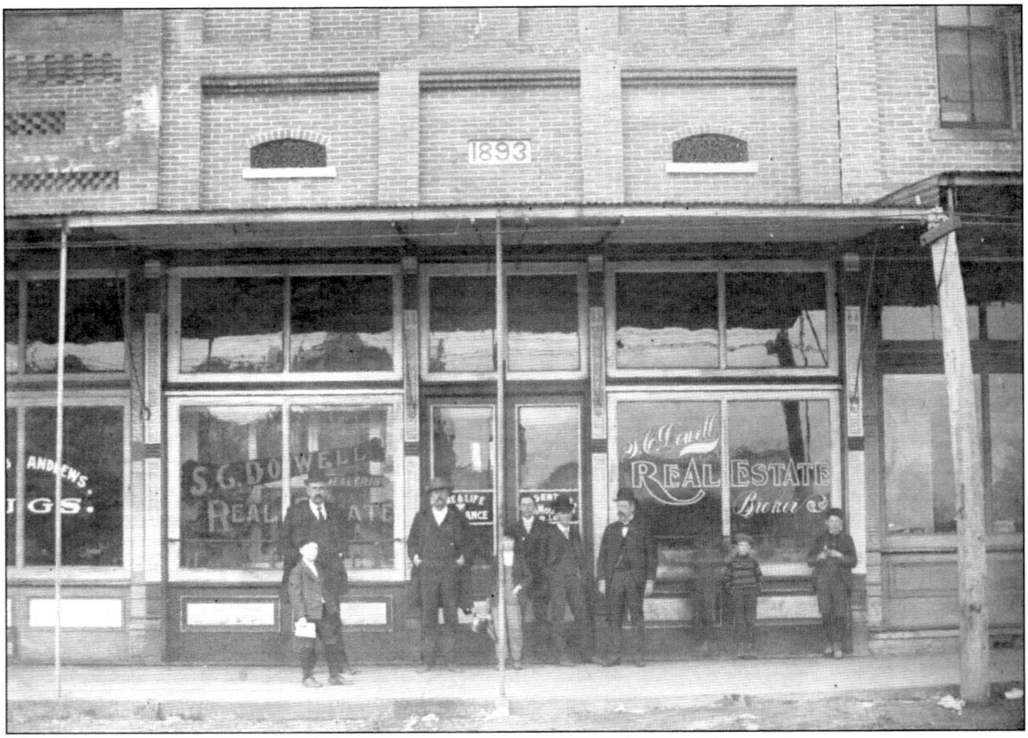

Swan C. Dowell (third from right) is shown standing in front of his real estate and insurance business on Northwest Front Street in Walnut Ridge. Sexton and Andrews drugstore is partially seen to the left. Dowell was a savvy businessman and held many other hats as president of Lawrence County Bank, president of the streetcar line, president of Running Water and Village Creek drainage commission, alderman, and mayor at one time. (BCAS.)

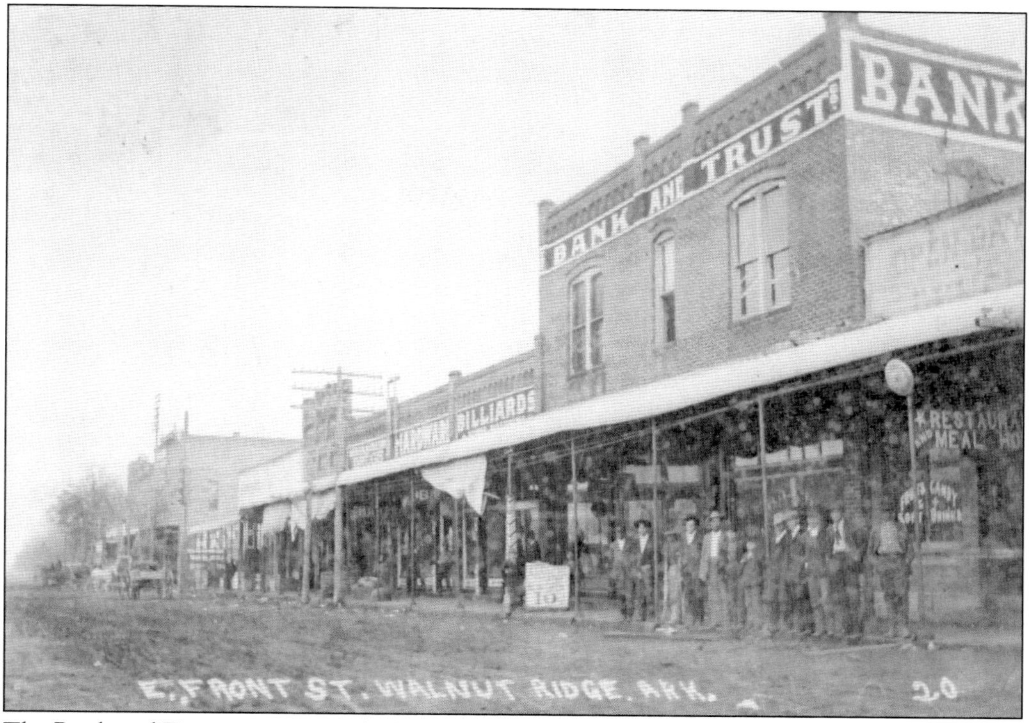

The Bank and Trust is prominently displayed in this photograph from around 1905 of Northeast Front Street in Walnut Ridge. To the immediate left of the bank are a billiard hall run by Harry Matthews, a hardware store, and a drugstore owned by Marvin M. Collier. A restaurant is on the right of the bank. A sign on the sidewalk advertises the new electric theater is open for 10¢. (JBW.)

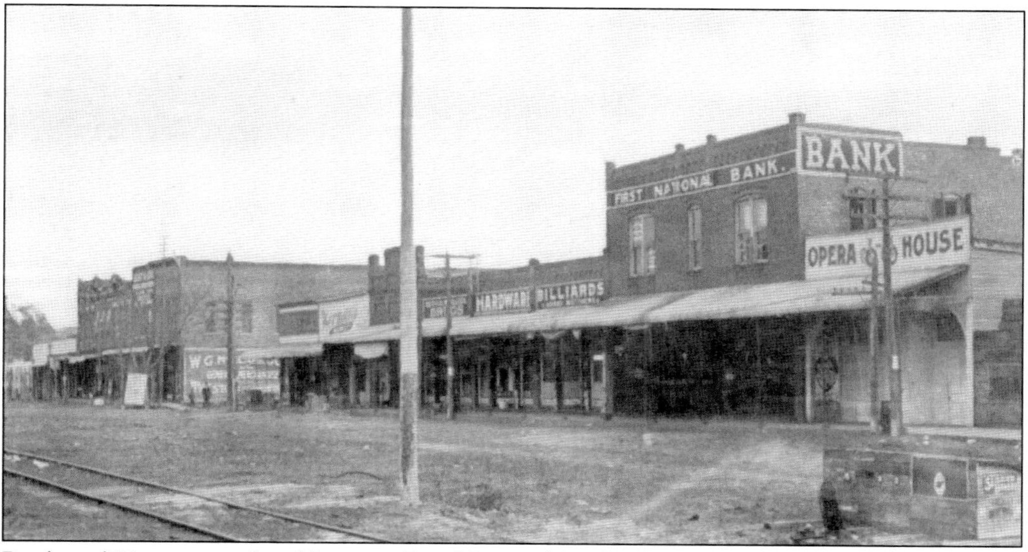

Bank and Trust merged and became First National Bank of Walnut Ridge in 1909. When this picture was taken in 1911, the restaurant on the right had been replaced by an opera house. Just past Collier Drug Store are a bakery, Herman's Meat Market, and a restaurant on the corner of Main Street. Across Main Street, W.G. McClamrock's general store is visible on the corner of Northeast Front Street. (JBW.)

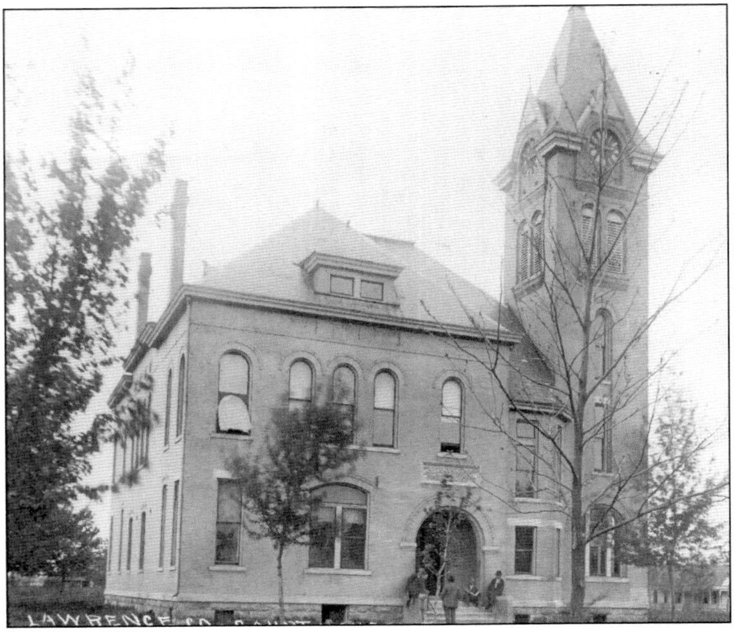

When the original courthouse on East Main Street burned in 1900, it gave an impetus for businessmen and county officials to construct a new one. This beautiful two-story courthouse with a clock tower was completed the same year. Before 1900, most businesses were along or east of the railroad tracks. With the new courthouse on the third block of West Main Street and the electric streetcar soon to follow, businesses migrated toward the courthouse. (JBW.)

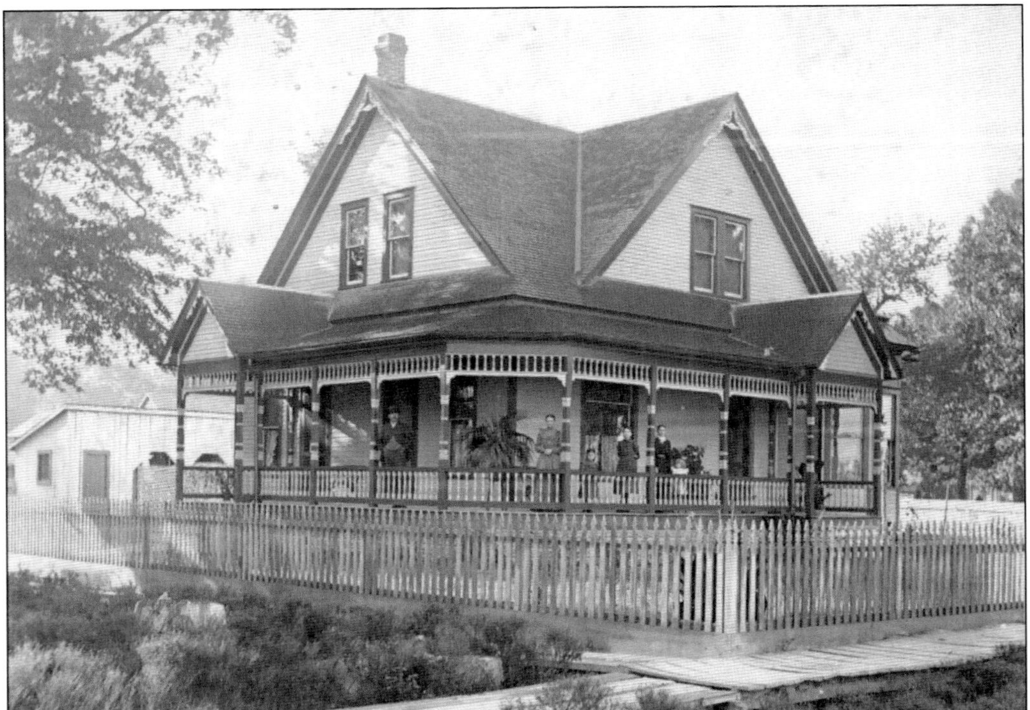

The fine home of Benjamin F. Graff was located on the 400 block of Southeast Front Street in Walnut Ridge. Graff and his brother, Fritz, arrived in Walnut Ridge from St. Louis, Missiouri, in 1877 with their parents. In 1888, they opened the very successful Graff Brothers Harness and Implements House, serving as agents for J.I. Case, Studebaker Wagon Company, Oliver Plow, John Deere Plow, and other well-known equipment companies. (BCAS.)

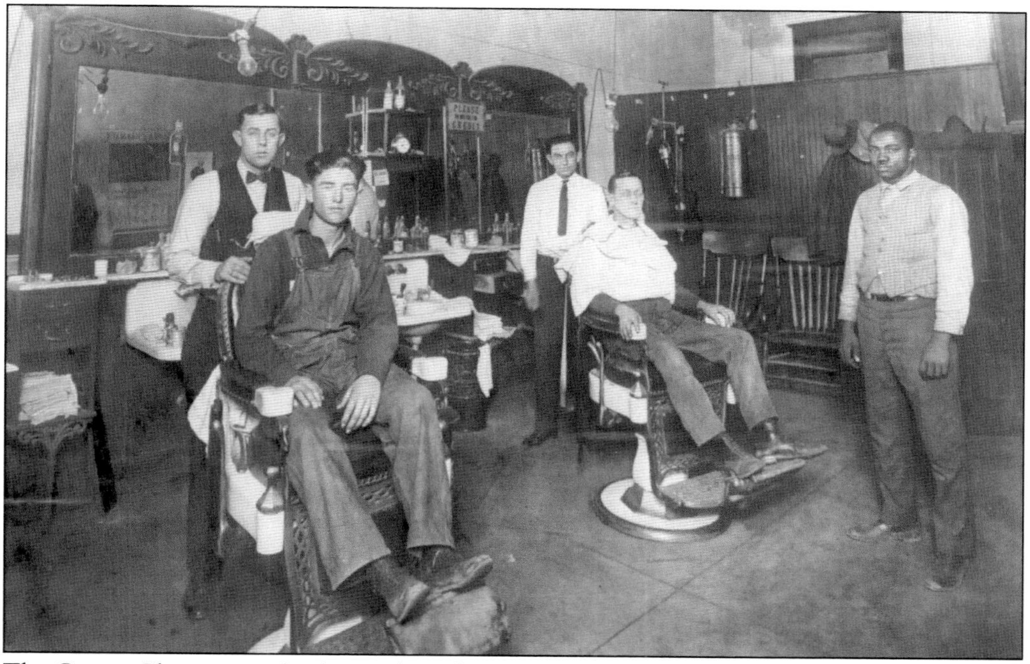

The Cooper Pharmacy calendar in the reflection of the mirror indicates this barbershop scene was taken during the month of January 1925 in Hoxie. The only identified person is Mose Weir, sitting in the right barber chair. Weir and his brother Clay were merchants in Hoxie. There were two barbershops on Texas Street—one near the Boas Hotel and the other just south of the Frisco tracks. (HW.)

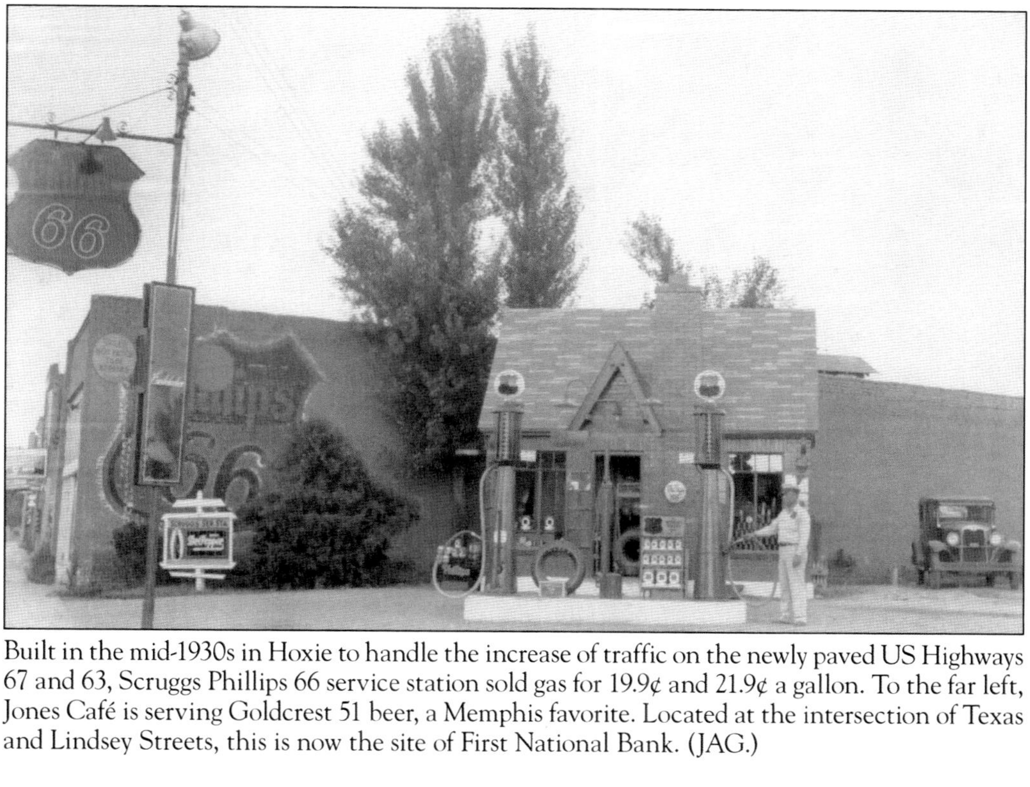

Built in the mid-1930s in Hoxie to handle the increase of traffic on the newly paved US Highways 67 and 63, Scruggs Phillips 66 service station sold gas for 19.9¢ and 21.9¢ a gallon. To the far left, Jones Café is serving Goldcrest 51 beer, a Memphis favorite. Located at the intersection of Texas and Lindsey Streets, this is now the site of First National Bank. (JAG.)

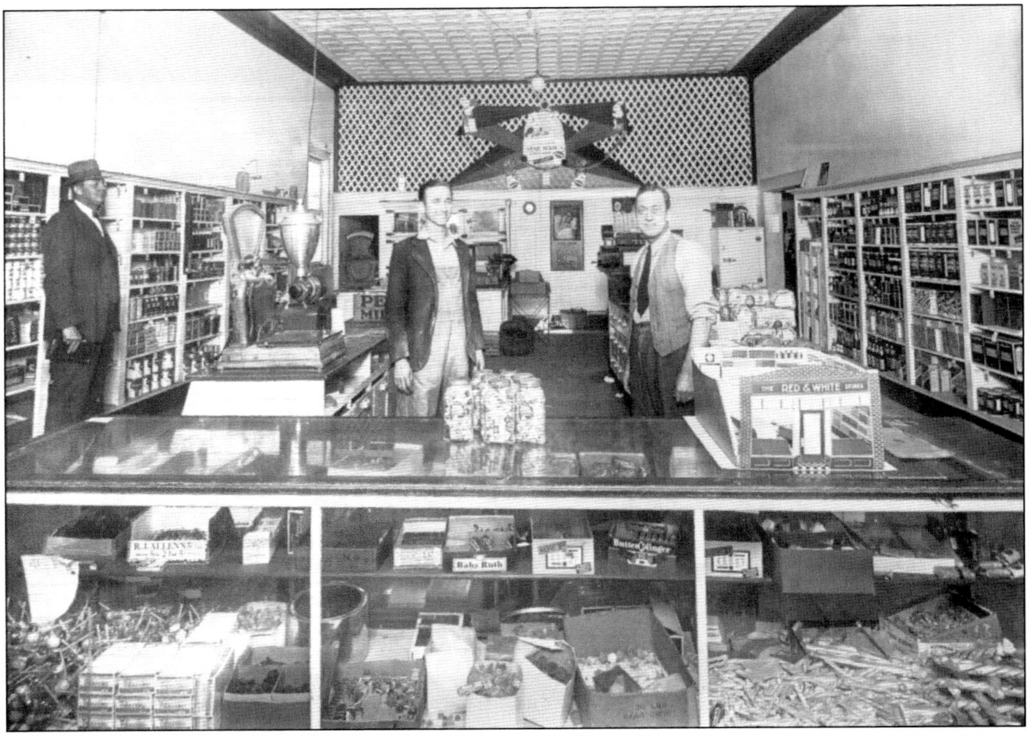

From left to right are a Mr. Dell, Cleo Weir, and Clay Weir, who are posing in Clay Weir's Mercantile-Grocery in Hoxie in 1932. Even though money was tight during the Great Depression, the store was well stocked. Five cents would buy a loaf of Colonial Bread, a Hershey's Almond Milk Chocolate Bar, or a box of cough drops. Butterfingers could be bought for a penny. (HW.)

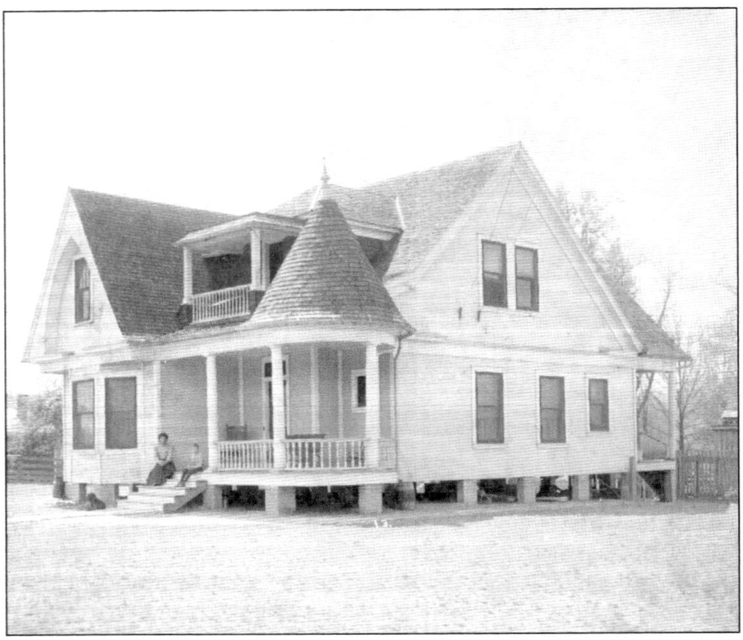

This is the home of Harry and Ida Boas, around 1907, on North Texas Street in Hoxie. Harry was the son of Henry and Mary Boas, founders of Hoxie. Harry and Ida had two sons, Harry Jr. and Jack. Jack married Ruby Land, and this was their home for many years. When the turret was demolished by a tornado, the home was remodeled and a carport added. Otherwise, this house has not changed in the last 100 years. (SB.)

These ladies are posed in front of the second Catholic church in Hoxie and the newly built Park Hotel sometime between 1921 and 1924. These buildings sat between Ruth and Jackson Streets on Northeast Second Street. The church was dedicated on May 15, 1914, after the previous one burned in 1913. It was torn down in 1924, and the third Catholic church was built further north between Towne and Cleveland Streets. (SB.)

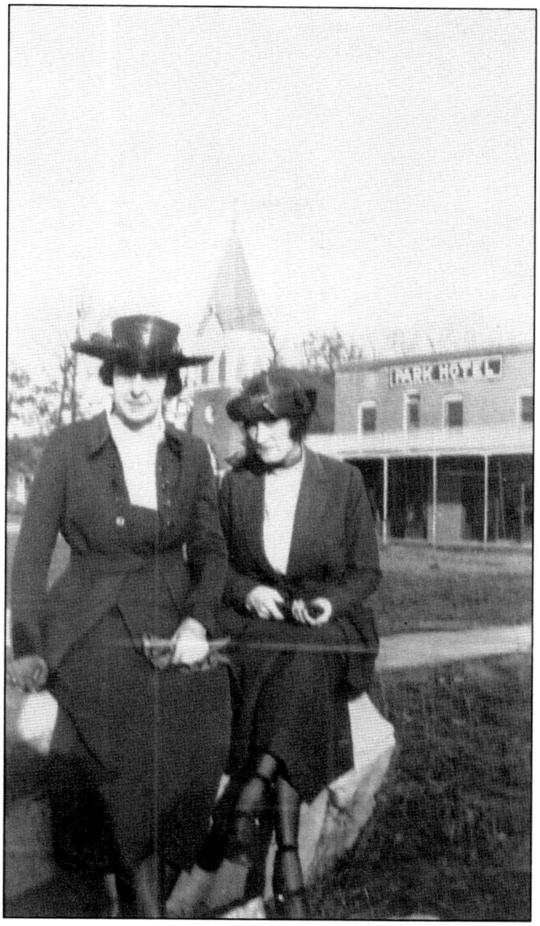

One of the last Jewish merchants in town was Sam Levit. Sam and Yetta Levit, born in Lithuania, came to Walnut Ridge in the 1920s. Their son Ervin was a star basketball player in school and later became a very successful lawyer in Memphis. The Sam Levit Store, on the corner of West Main and Southwest Second Streets, was recently restored by Fran Cavenaugh and is now the home of the Studio, an event center. (BCAS.)

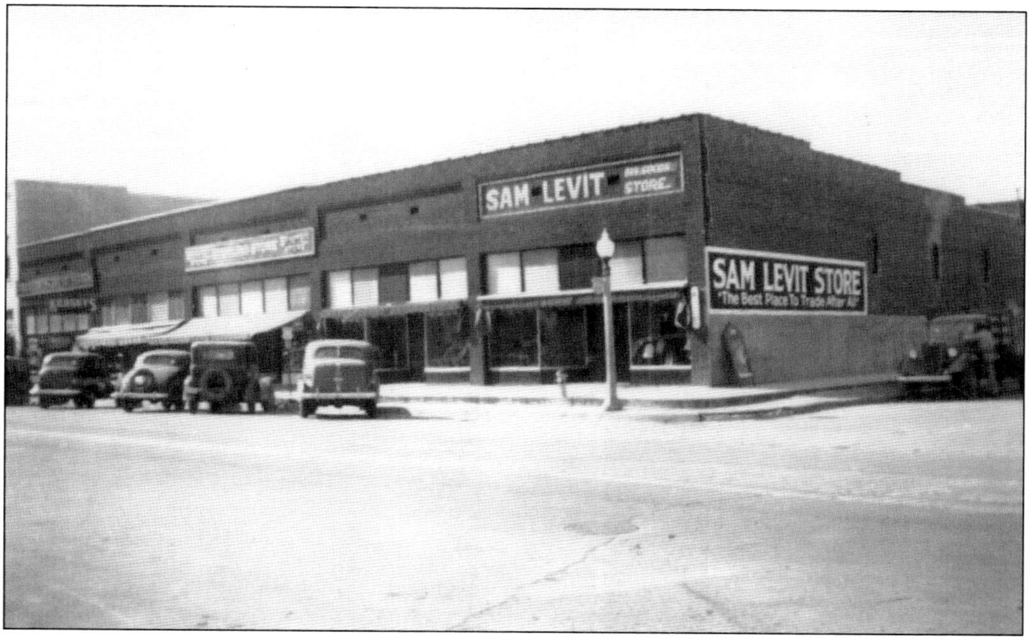

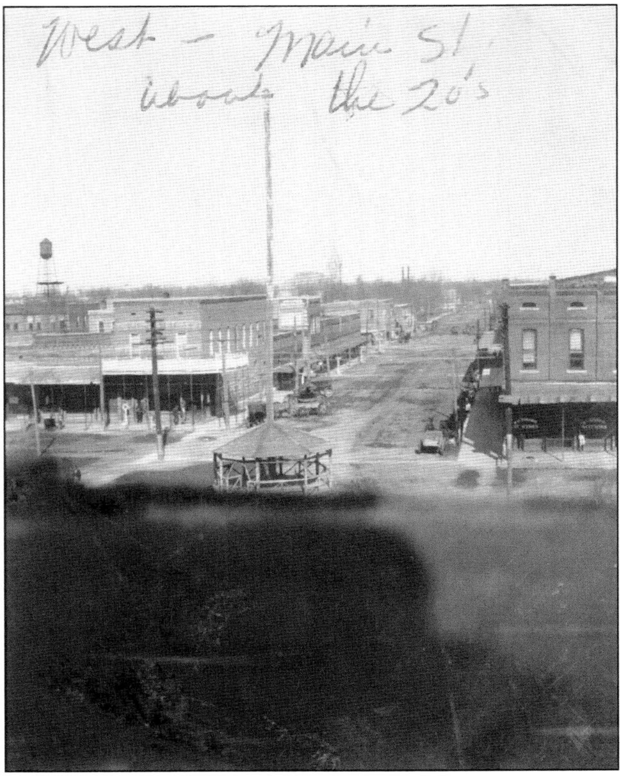

This 1921 view looks west down Main Street. A gazebo sits in the street at the intersection of Main and Front Streets. The Lane Hotel is marked on the far left, under the water tower. In the distant center is the 1900 courthouse with its clock tower. Two smokestacks from W.R. Lane's cotton gin are to its immediate right. (JCW.)

Lawrence County Bank, established in 1890, was the oldest bank in Walnut Ridge. In January 1922, it retained its name but merged with First National Bank of Walnut Ridge. A banner displayed on the front of the bank announces the merger in 1921. Located at the corner of West Main and Second Streets, this is now the location of First National Bank of Lawrence County. (JCW.)

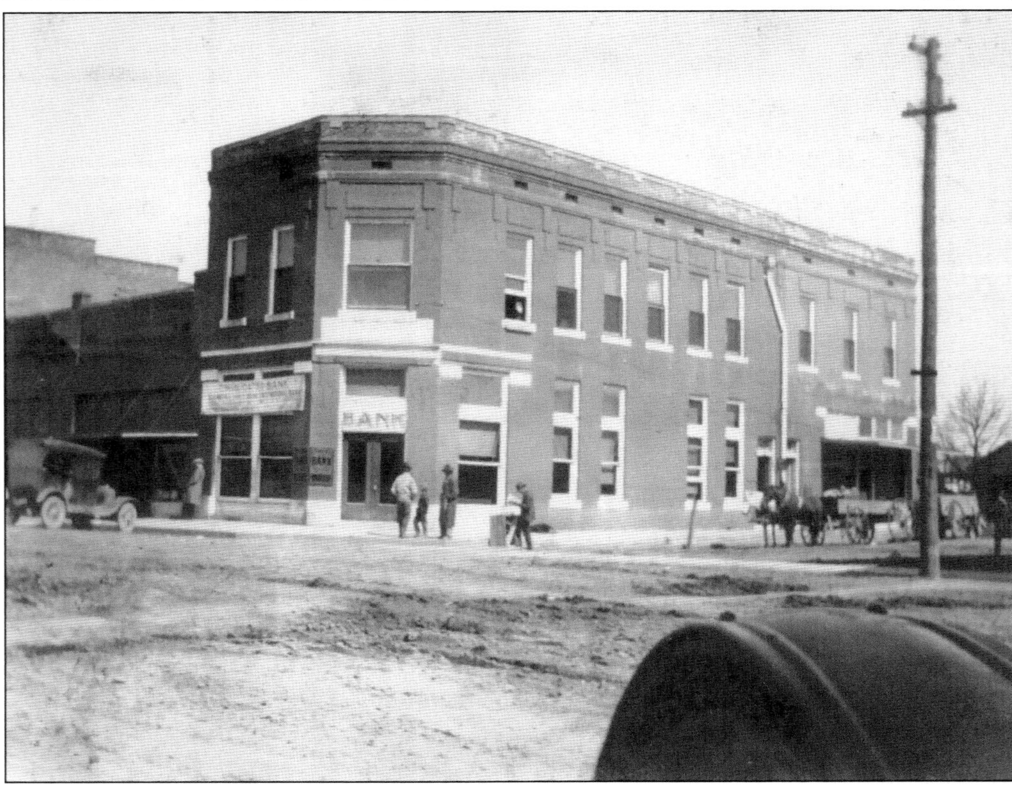

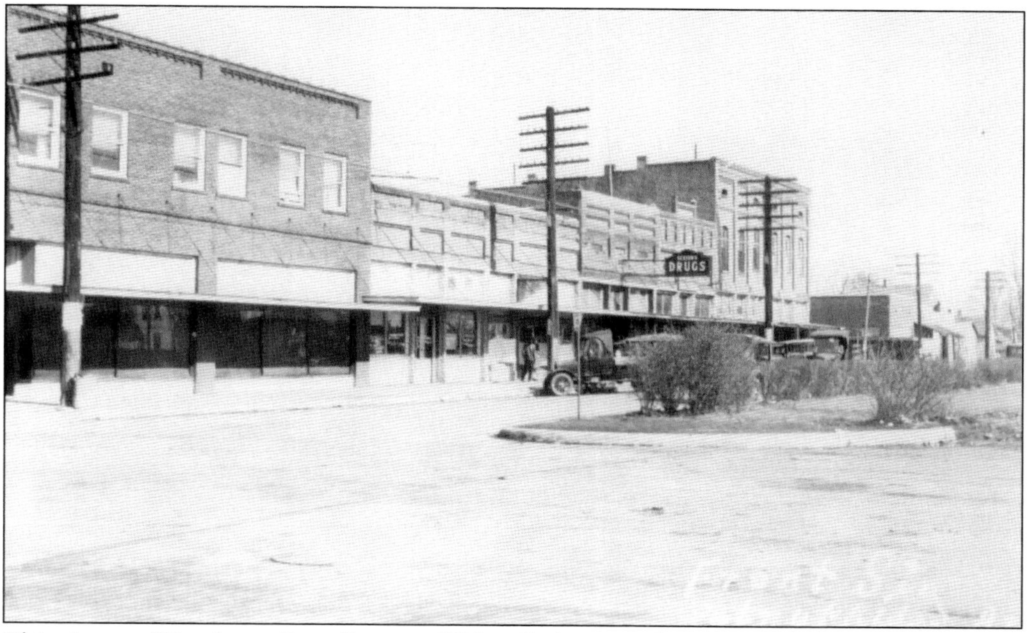

This picture of Northwest Front Street in Walnut Ridge was taken a few years later than the other one on this page. The scenes are nearly identical, with one exception. The two-story building on the far left in this picture is brand-new, and the other was destroyed by fire. The two-story building on the far corner is labeled Bickers Hardware. Sexton's and Dowell's buildings are now gone; the remaining are still standing and occupied today. (JMS.)

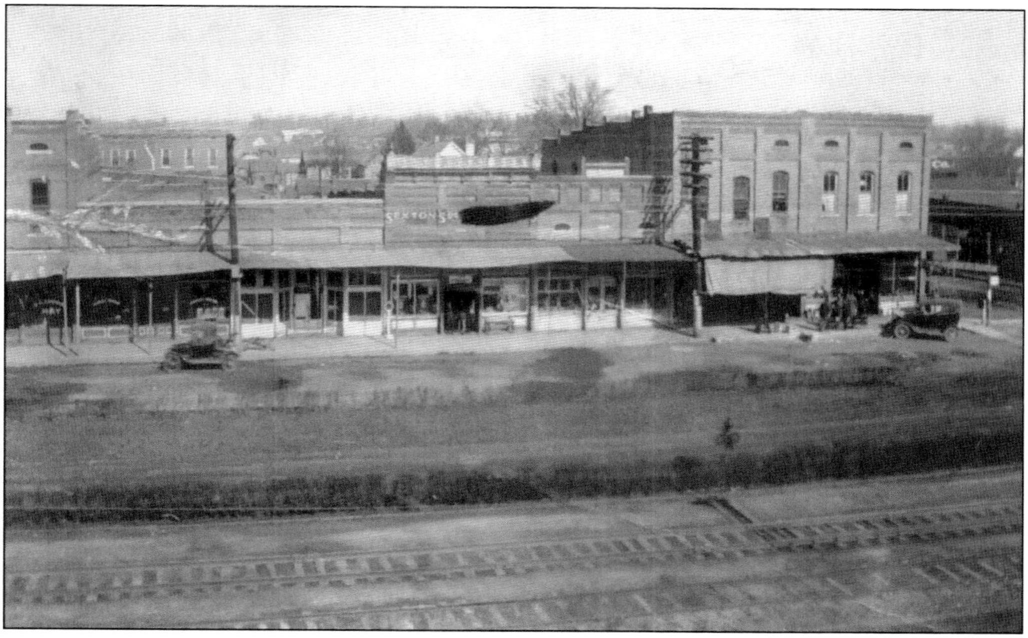

This view of Northwest Front Street in Walnut Ridge was taken in 1921. These buildings, stretching from Main to Walnut Streets, were all built in 1893 after a disastrous fire leveled this entire block. From left to right, businesses at the time are Eskridge Hay, Peoples Grocery, unidentified, Sexton's Drugs, Dowell Real Estate, and a hardware store. The two-story Lawrence County Bank can be seen behind this block toward the left. (JCW.)

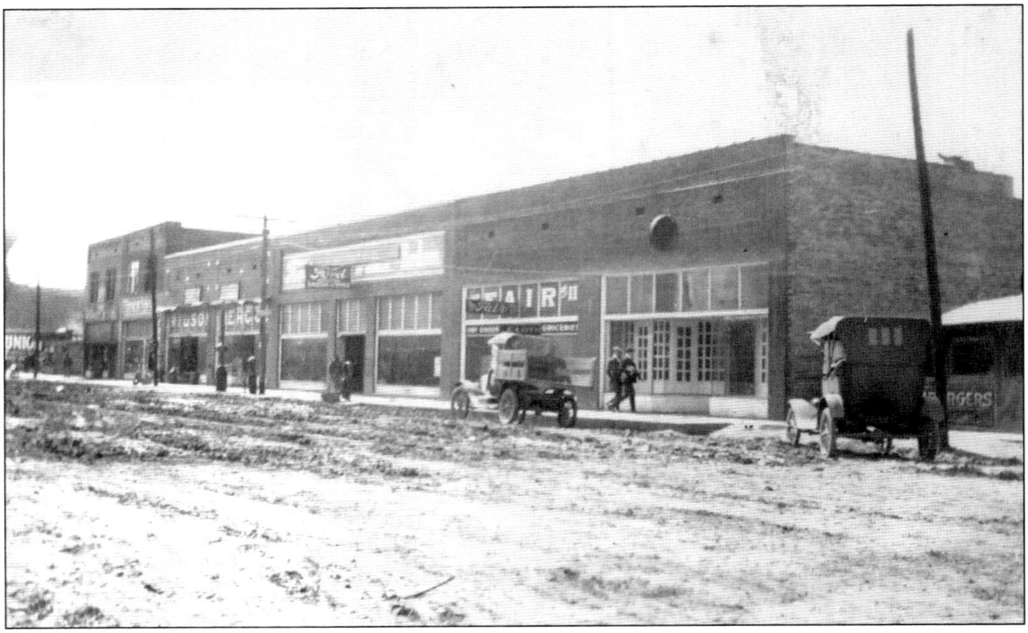

This 1921 photograph shows the south side of West Main Street between Second and Third Streets, flanked by two small hamburger stands. In the middle is an early home for a Ford Motor Company dealership, to its left is Wilson Mercantile, and to its right is Fair Dry Goods and Grocery. The rightmost building would later become a Kroger. (JCW.)

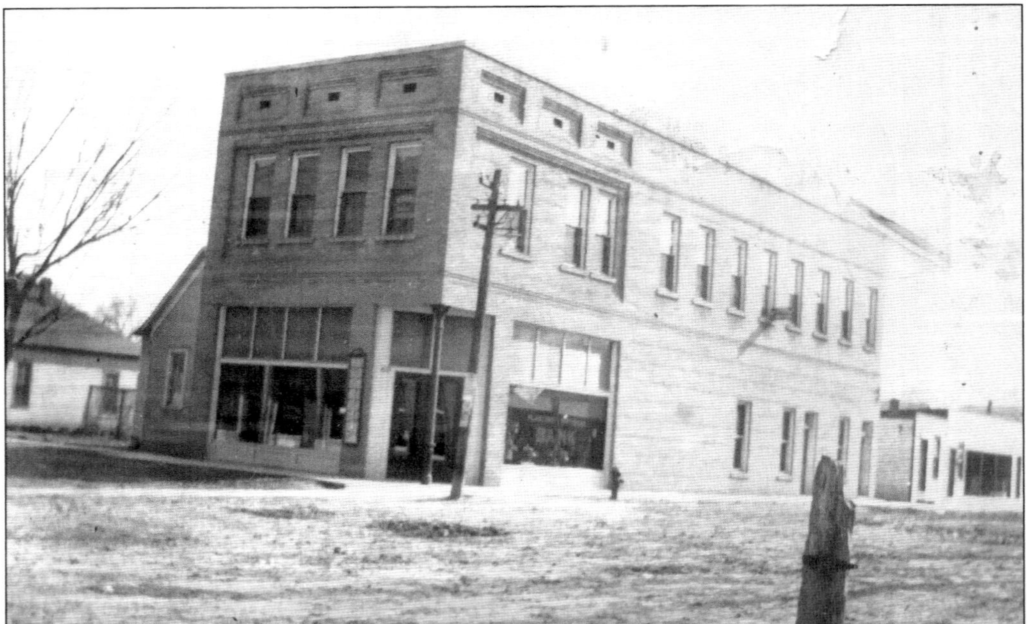

The Planters National Bank opened in Walnut Ridge in 1921, the same year this picture was taken. Located on the corner of Southwest Second and Elm Streets, it was only in business until 1930. The bank issued two different types of $5 national bank notes. Because of the bank's short existence, these notes are quite rare for collectors today. This building still stands but is abandoned as of November 2015. (JCW.)

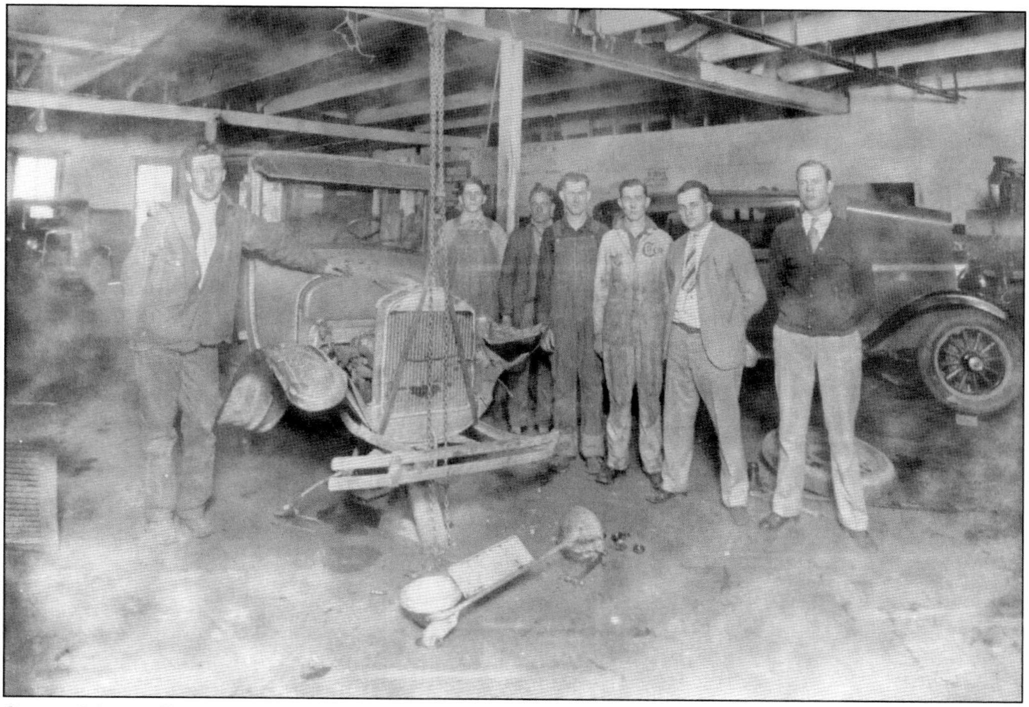

Snapp Motor Company was not the first Ford dealer in Walnut Ridge, but it has the longest history. Founded in 1932 by brothers Charles C. Snapp and Russell Snapp, it was in business for 66 years, finally sold to Don Cavenaugh in 1998. Pictured in the early 1930s are, from left to right, Everett Webb, Jake String, unidentified, Raymond Tolson, E.C. Tolson, Charles C. Snapp, and Ed Sharp. (AHC.)

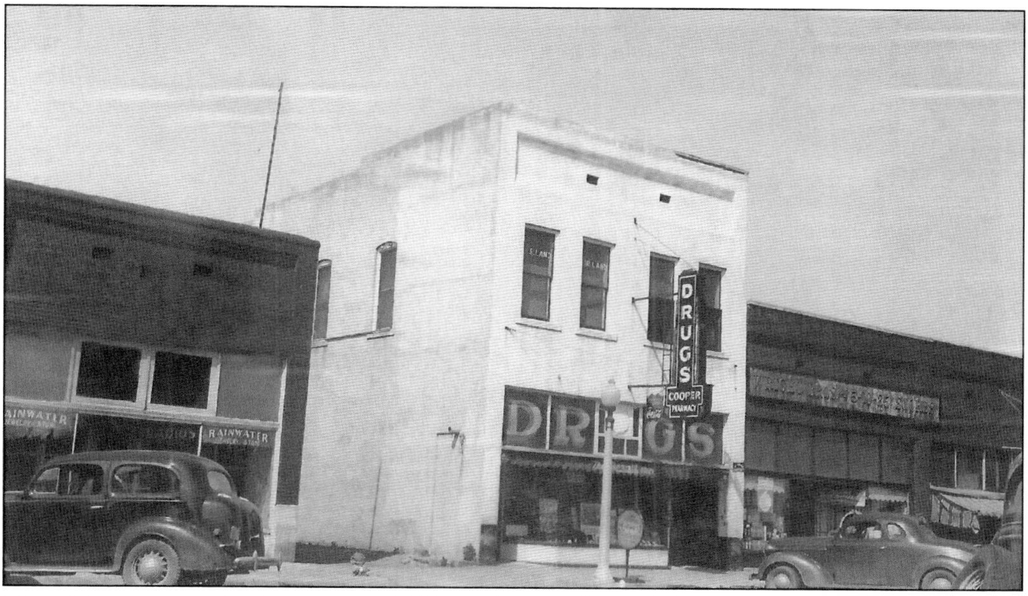

Mose Cooper started a drugstore in 1904 on the first floor of the Hotel Rhea. After fire leveled the hotel in 1914, Cooper rebuilt on the same lot. His son Rennard took over the business in 1930. Doctor Land's offices are on the second floor. To the left is an earlier location for Rainwater Jewelry Store. To the right is Wright Brothers Dime Store, which later became a Ben Franklin. (CS.)

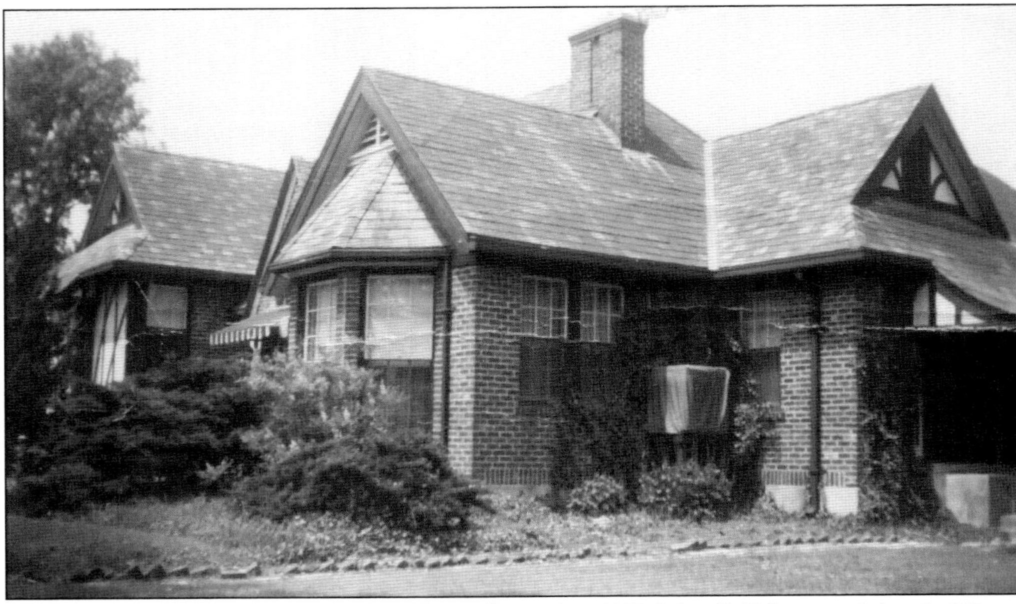

When the Boas Hotel and first Gibson home burned in 1931, John S. Gibson and Annie Gibson built this Tudor-style house in its place in 1935 in Hoxie. When Annie died in 1962, it was sold and turned into a truck stop. Later, Bama Fouts purchased it and helped return it to its former glory. Her daughter and son-in-law, Janene and Anthony Ashlock, are continuing the restoration. (JFA.)

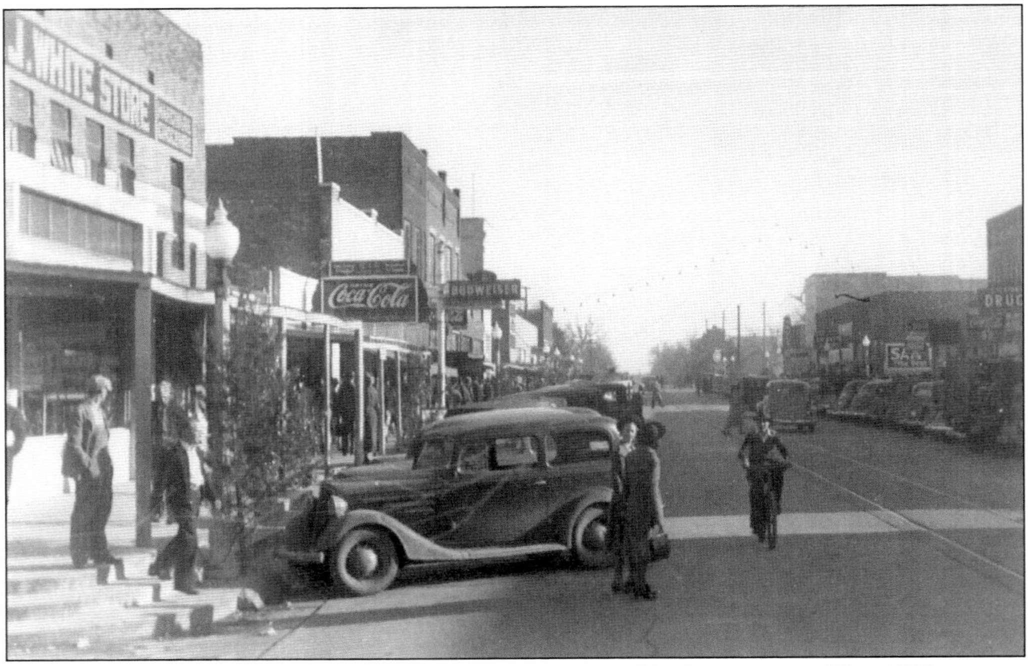

After Prohibition ended in 1933, Lawrence County was suddenly wet again. This 1930s picture of Main Street in Walnut Ridge shows a Budweiser sign midway down the left side. In 1943, the county voted to ban alcohol again; this time it lasted until present. T.J. White Furniture (left) occupied the old Swan Theater building after it burned around 1930. About 1940, it was reopened as the Sharum Theater. (AHC.)

Two

Later Years, 1940s to 1980s

Photographs from the 1870s to 1890s in Walnut Ridge and Hoxie are extremely rare. Most of the pictures in chapter 1 are from 1900 to the early 1920s. Likewise, images from the mid-1920s to 1930s are almost nonexistent; understandably there were more important things to spend money on during the Depression. The combined population of both towns dropped 15 percent almost overnight and stayed at that level until after World War II.

Things changed in the 1940s. Empty storefronts, caused by the Depression, were suddenly leased for office space to support the Army airfield in Walnut Ridge. Restaurants, stores, gas stations, and other merchants were busy once again, infused with the additional 4,000 people assigned to the base.

Things did not slow down after the end of the war. The airfield was given to the City of Walnut Ridge, which then gave part to Southern Baptist College (now Williams Baptist College); the remaining area was converted into an industrial park. Jobs were suddenly available within a few miles of Hoxie and Walnut Ridge. Both town economies were boosted, and the population started increasing rapidly again. From 1940 to 1980, the combined population doubled.

Highways 63, 67, and 412 all intersected at Walnut Ridge and Hoxie. Highway 67 brought anyone traveling from St. Louis to Hot Springs right through the middle of both business districts. Several tourist courts, motels, hotels, restaurants, and gas stations opened to cater to the increased automobile traffic.

One-car families became two-car families, and with inexpensive gasoline, teenagers would borrow one of their parents' automobiles on the weekends. It became popular to "cruise" the streets, continuously circling the Polar Freeze restaurant in Walnut Ridge and then driving to Hoxie and circling the Green Lantern restaurant and other hot spots, like the bowling alley in Walnut Ridge.

Times were simpler then. Children played outside more and literally had the run of the town on their bicycles from dawn until dusk. Trips to town on the weekends were anticipated—moms shopping at the grocery and department stores, dads outside catching up on the news, and children spending time at the dime stores and soda fountains.

By the 1980s, the stores on Main Street were suffering, replaced by larger supercenters and the ease of traveling to nearby Jonesboro for shopping. A whole block of Hoxie's main business district was leveled in 1982. Both towns are starting to reinvent themselves today, finding a niche to bring businesses back to downtown.

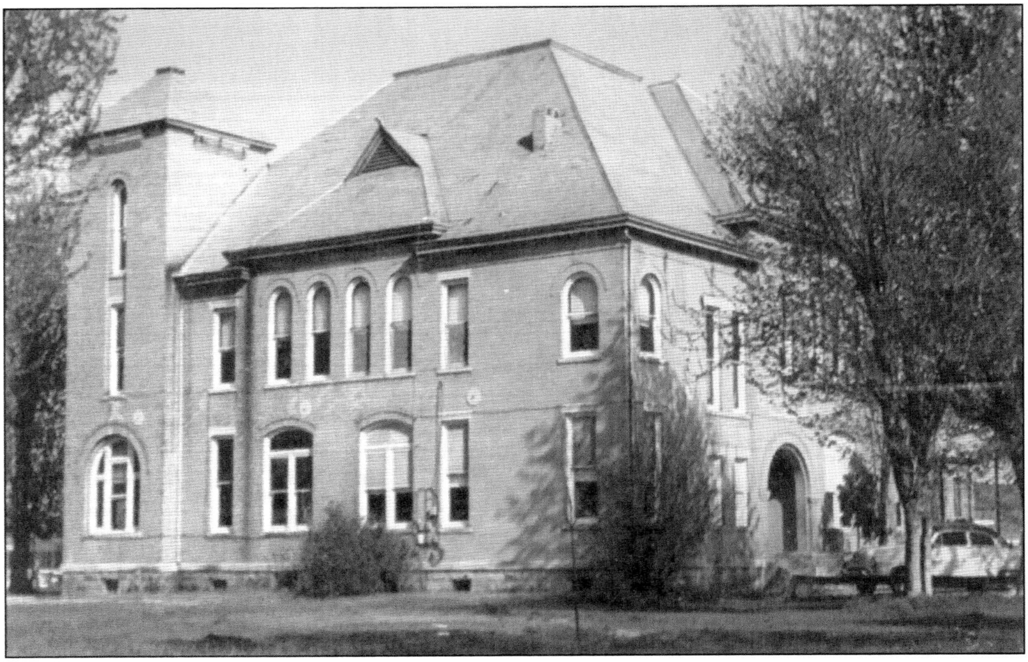

The second of three courthouses in Walnut Ridge was a two-story, tan-brick building with a five-story clock tower, built in 1900. The only execution in Walnut Ridge's history occurred on January 31, 1913, when Dock Driver was hanged from a scaffold in the attic of the courthouse for killing Marshal J.P. Biggers. By 1960, the top two floors of the clock tower had been removed. This building was replaced with the current courthouse in 1965. (JBW.)

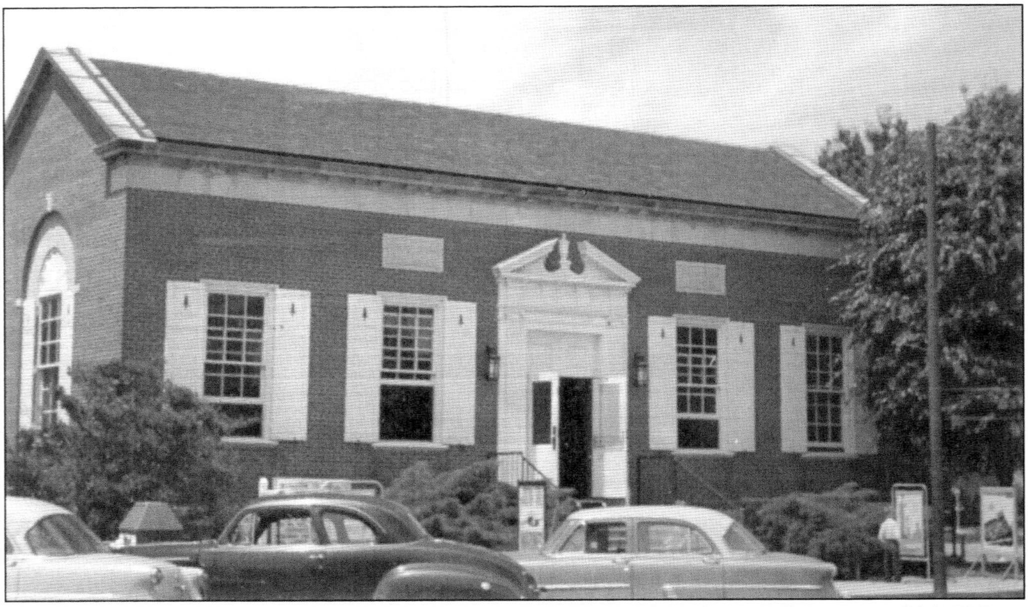

Walnut Ridge's first post office was granted in 1870. Located in the area known as Old Walnut Ridge, it moved in 1874 when the current town was platted. After occupying several locations, including the Hotel Rhea, it moved to this redbrick Colonial Revival structure, built at the corner of West Main and Third Streets in 1935. In 1977, this became the home of the *Times Dispatch* newspaper. It is listed in the National Register of Historic Places (JBW.)

When Warner's Drug Store moved from Hoxie to Walnut Ridge in 1950, Danny P. Sears opened Sears Sundries in Hoxie, selling items such as beauty aids, newspapers, magazines, soft drinks, and Yarnell's Ice Cream. Pauline, his wife, ran a beauty shop in the back of the store. Here, Danny kneels in front with his son Dan in the summer of 1956. Young Dan later became a well-known Mid-South radio DJ. Danny's oldest son, Gary, is a pharmacist in Walnut Ridge. (DS.)

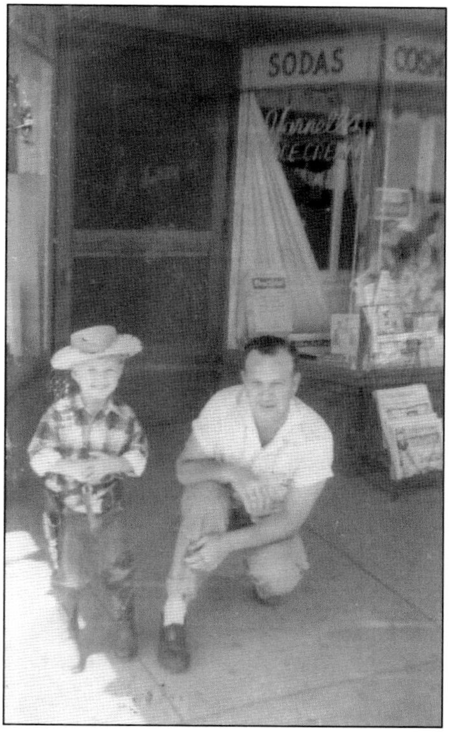

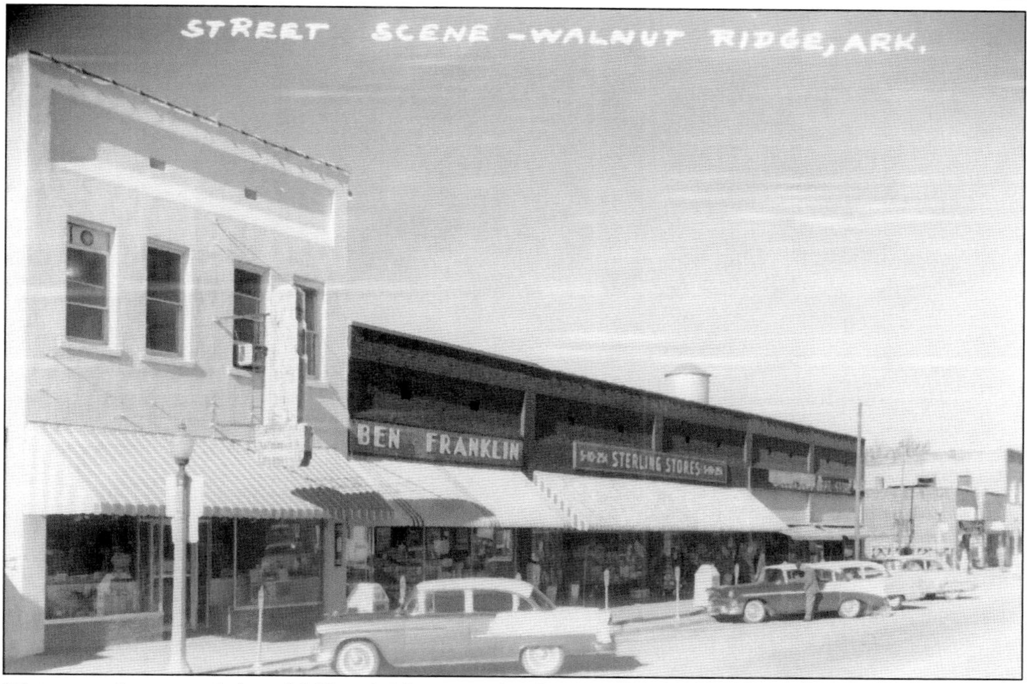

This was the site of the old Hotel Rhea until it burned to the ground in 1914. The leftmost two-story building was rebuilt by Mose Cooper as Cooper Drugs. In this late 1950s scene, it is Lucian Warner's drugstore, later becoming Going's Drug Store. The other storefronts shown were constructed later in stages. From left to right are Ben Franklin, Sterling Stores, and Wilcoxson's Department Store. (JBW.)

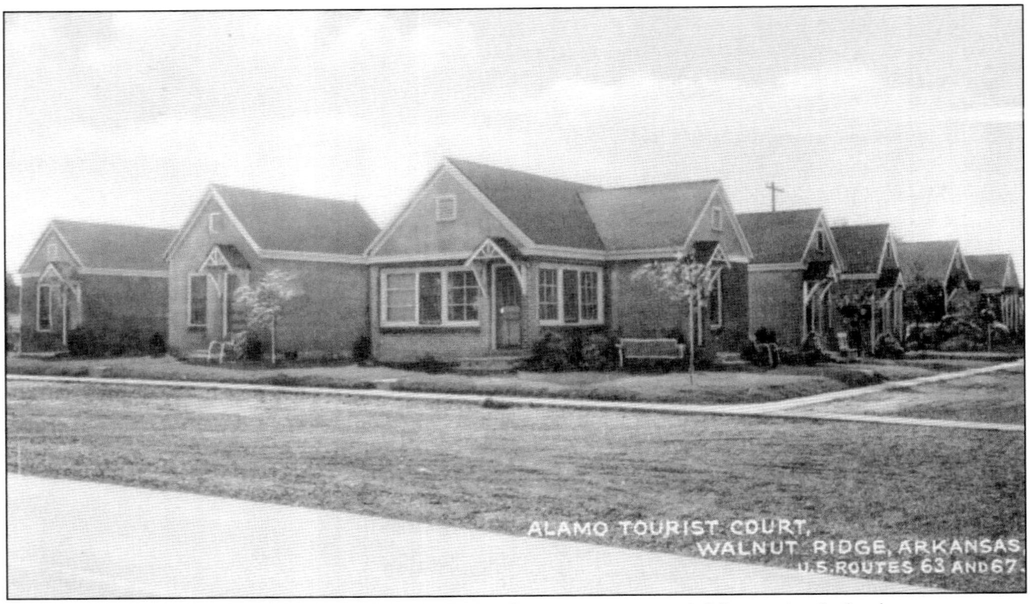

Located in Walnut Ridge, the Alamo Tourist Courts were available as single-bedroom or two-bedroom cottages in the 1940s. Recognized as one of the premier stops halfway between St. Louis and Hot Springs, the cottages were replaced in the 1960s with a newer generation of buildings and joined the Best Western motel chain. Unusual for this time period, the Alamo had a segregated area for African Americans. (JBW.)

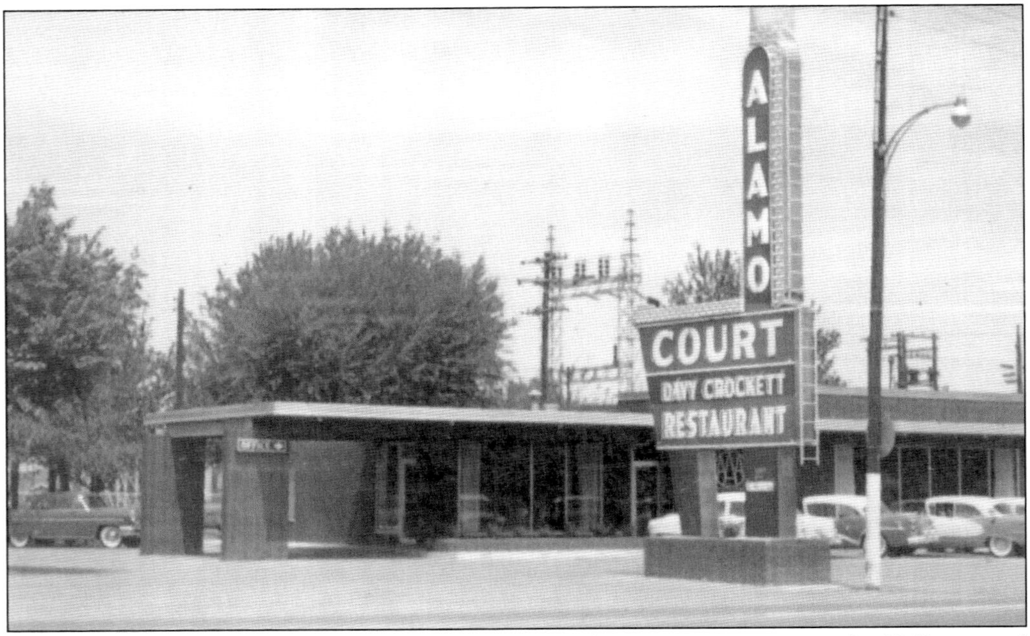

The Davy Crockett restaurant joined the remodeled Alamo Tourist Courts in the 1960s, named when the Walt Disney miniseries starring Fess Parker was popular. It was not uncommon to serve 150 meals a night at the fine dining establishment, which offered lobster tails and butchered its steaks on-site. The motel and restaurant maintained 22 different billboards around Arkansas and southern Missouri. The neon sign was removed in 1980. The buildings all remain but are used for different purposes. (JBW.)

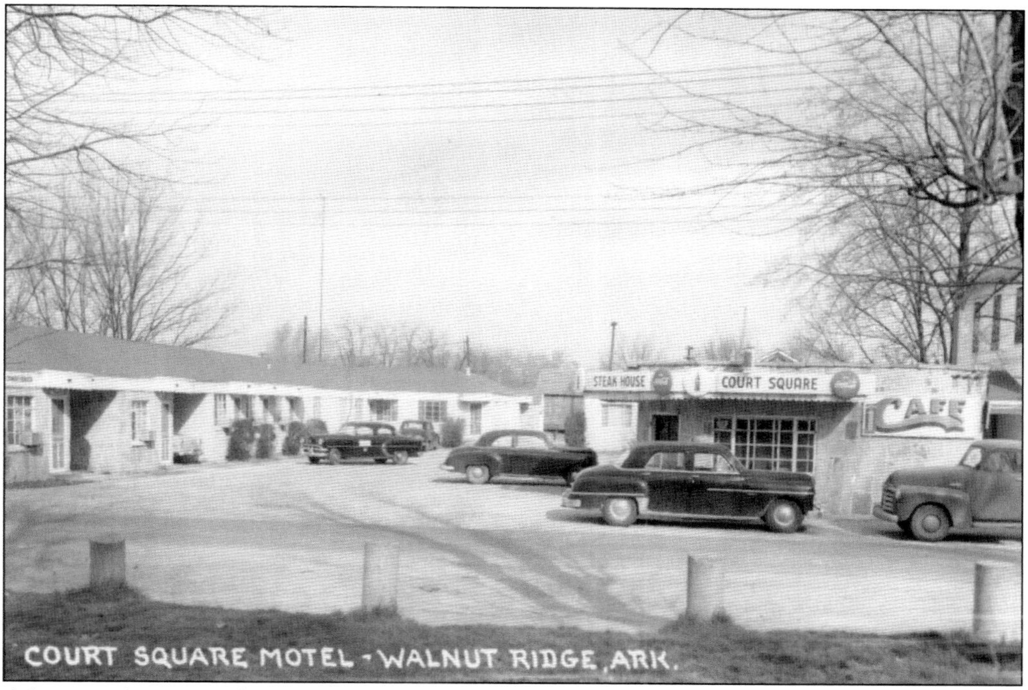

After spending several years in California, Wilsey and Hazel Brewer returned to Walnut Ridge and opened the Court Square Motel around 1950. Hazel was the daughter of W.R. and Duffie Lane and sister of Goldie Lane. The U-shaped motel was between the Brewer home and the Higginbotham Funeral Home (previously the W.R. Lane home), facing the courthouse. It was later converted into apartments. (BCAS.)

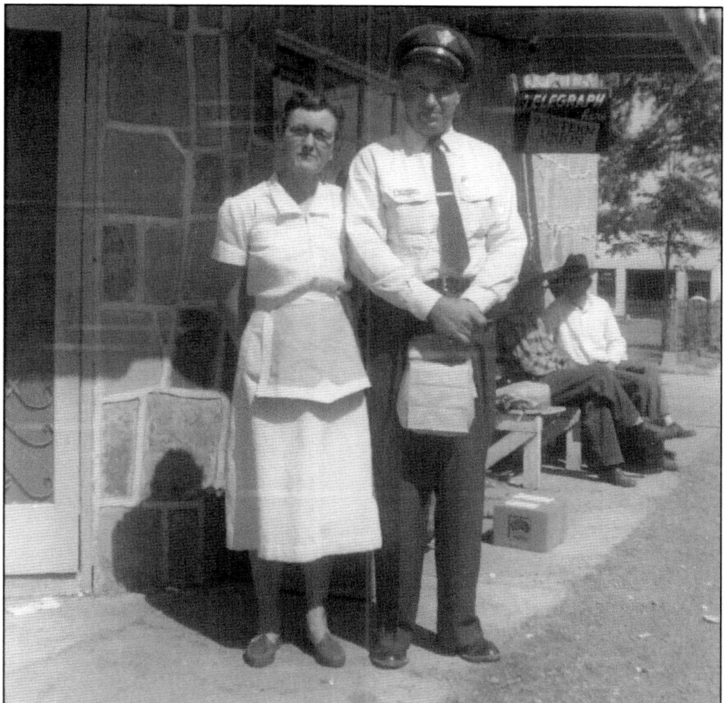

Charlie Mae Kincade Johnson, a waitress at the Court Square Café, stands in front with a bus driver around 1955. The café also served as the home office for the 69 Cab Company, a bus stop, and a Western Union telegraph service. The motel was removed in the 1960s to increase parking for the Higginbotham Funeral Home. The former café has a white brick facade today and was incorporated into the back of the funeral home. (SJD.)

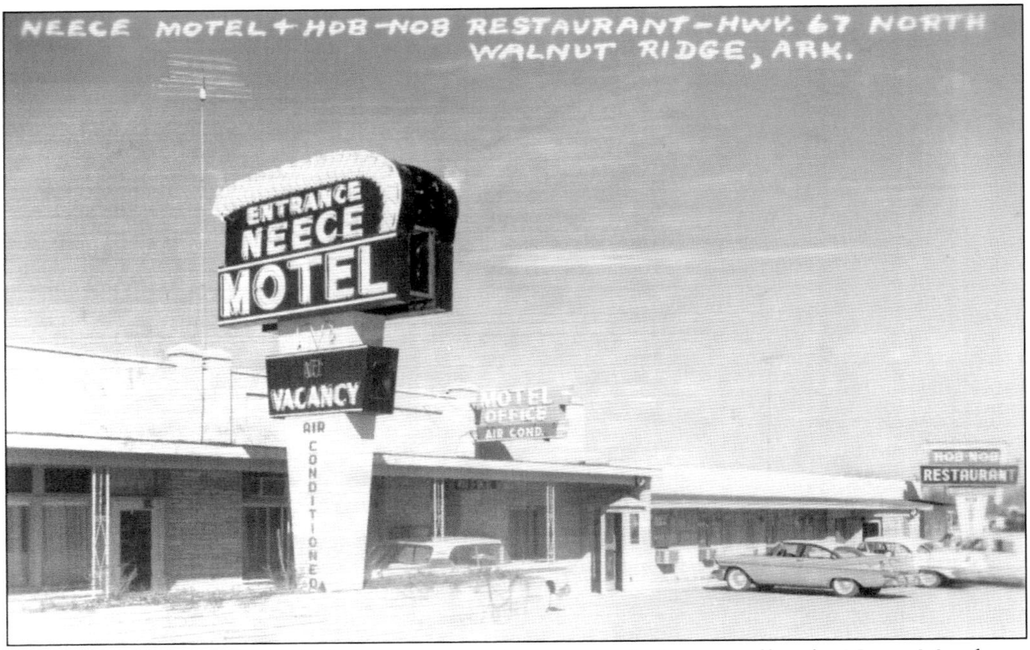

Built in the 1940s by Melville Neece to serve the growing highway traffic, the Neece Motel was located at the northern edge of Walnut Ridge on US Highway 67. It had an adjoining café and service station. The café later became the Hob Nob restaurant and was a local favorite for years until burning in 2008. Besides Neece, Ed and Gladys Summers, and then Bob and Bobbie White, were also longtime proprietors. (JBW.)

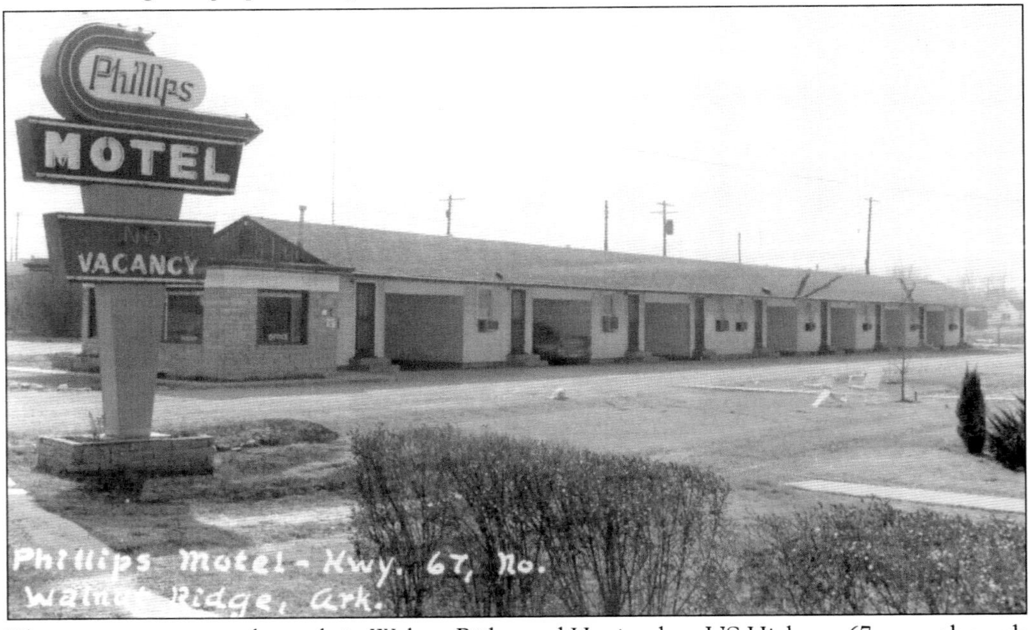

There were many travel motels in Walnut Ridge and Hoxie when US Highway 67 came through the middle of both towns. Built in the early 1950s by G.H. Phillips, the Phillips Motel of Walnut Ridge is still in operation today, complete with the neon sign. Originally, each small room had an adjacent covered carport. In later years, the carports were eliminated and the spaces used to expand the size of the rooms. (JBW.)

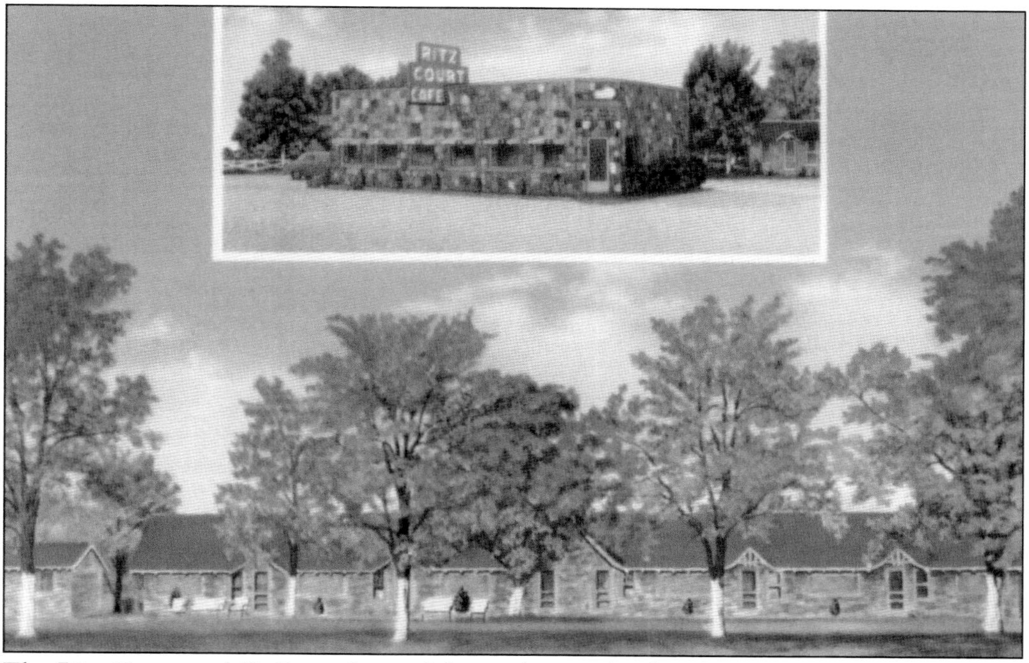

The Ritz Court and Café was located five miles north of Walnut Ridge at the Lawrence-Randolph County Line on US Highway 67. It served the traveling public with fine food and accommodations at reasonable rates and was recommended by the American Travel Association (ATA). Managed by Ralph Clark when this photograph was taken in the 1950s, the Ritz has been gone for years. (JBW.)

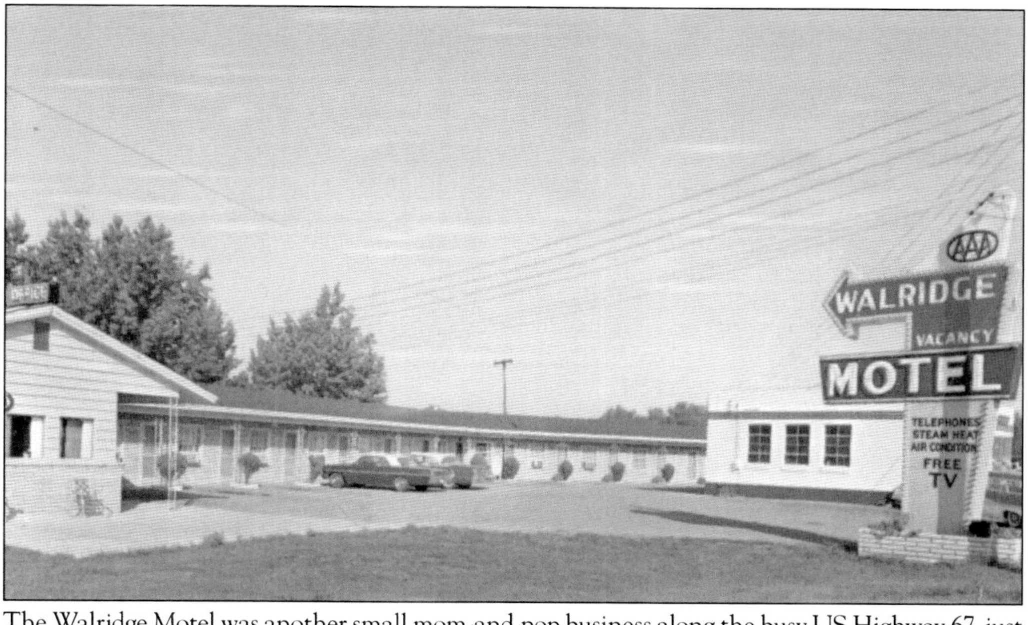

The Walridge Motel was another small mom-and-pop business along the busy US Highway 67, just south of Village Creek in Walnut Ridge. It was opened around 1955, with a Gulf service station out front. The service station, run by Jewel Mitchell in the 1950s, is partially hidden behind the motel sign on the right. A restaurant was added later. Barton's Lumber Company now occupies this location. (JBW.)

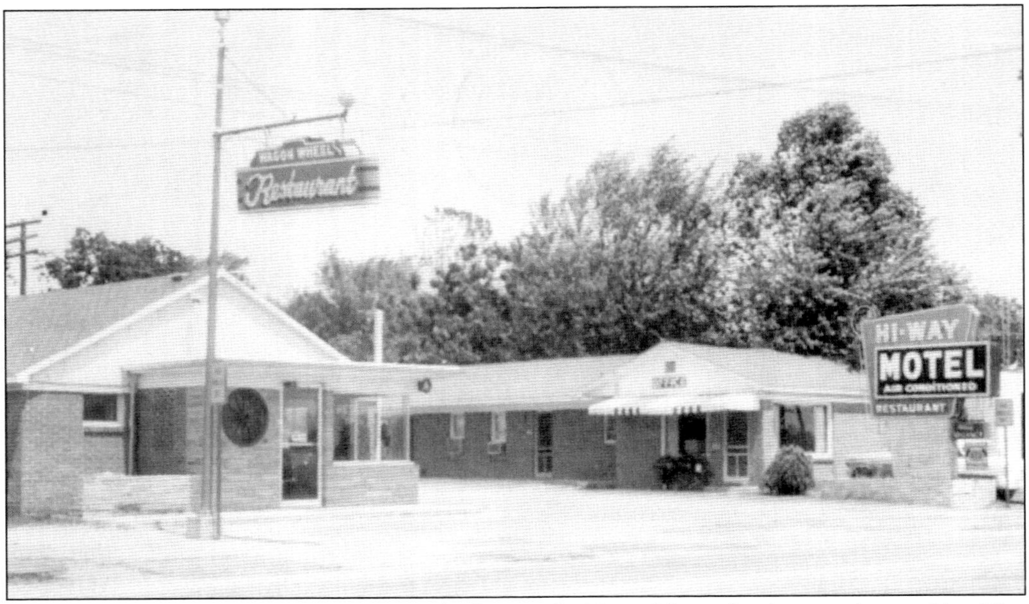

The Hi-Way Motel and Café was established around 1954 in Hoxie for the traveling public. The 16-unit modern motel, with air-conditioned rooms, was operated by the Calvin Rychtarik family. By the time of this picture, the café's front facade had added an embedded wagon wheel, and the name had been changed, accordingly, to Wagon Wheel. The restaurant closed several years ago, but the motel is now known as the Ole Hickory. (JBW.)

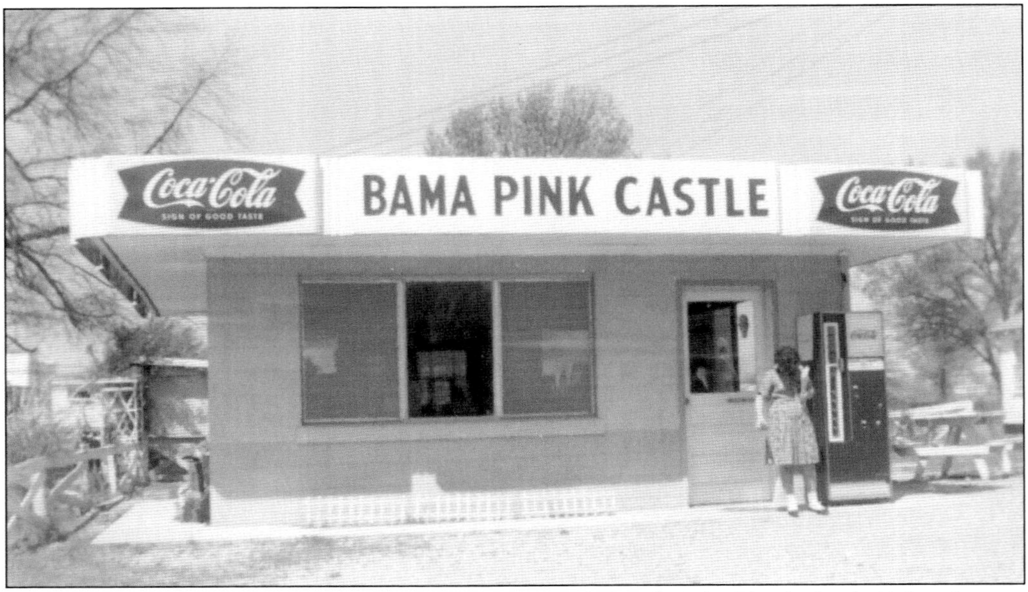

Janene Fouts stands in front of her mother's Bama Pink Castle. The Fout's Circle F Gas Station is visible at left in the distance. Bama Fouts built the Pink Castle in 1961, and it served Hoxie students until the late 1970s. Situated next to the school campus, the pink block building served fast-food items at reasonable prices. It was recently removed to create gym parking for the Hoxie Mustangs. (JFA.)

This 1974 view of First National Bank was taken just before it was torn down to make room for a new three-story bank. It was built in 1913 by the Lawrence County Bank, which did not survive the Depression and closed for liquidation in 1931. Two years later, First National Bank of Black Rock moved to Walnut Ridge and changed its name to First National Bank of Lawrence County. (FNB.)

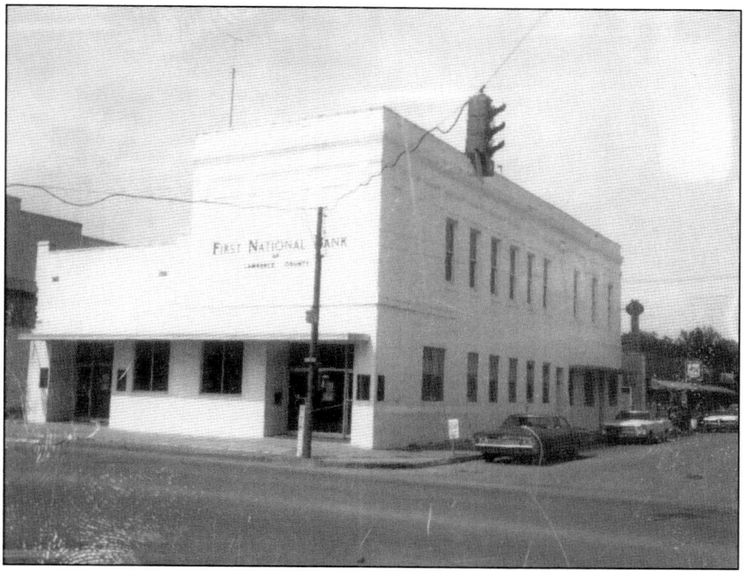

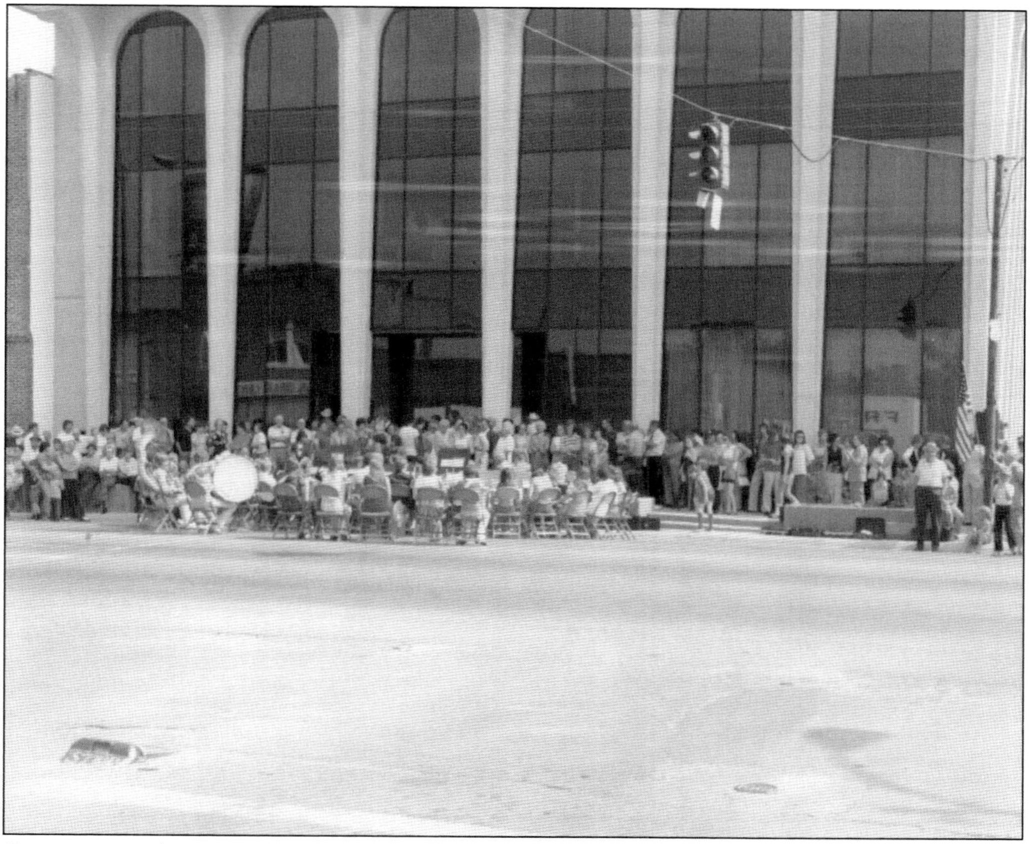

Construction began in June 1974, and on Labor Day 1975 First National Bank of Lawrence County held a grand opening for the public. A crowd, estimated at 6,500, toured the new three-story modern structure. Some of the highlights of the day were musical entertainment by the Walnut Ridge High School Band, an hourly drawing for prizes, and a $500 savings account as an end-of-the-day grand prize. (FNB.)

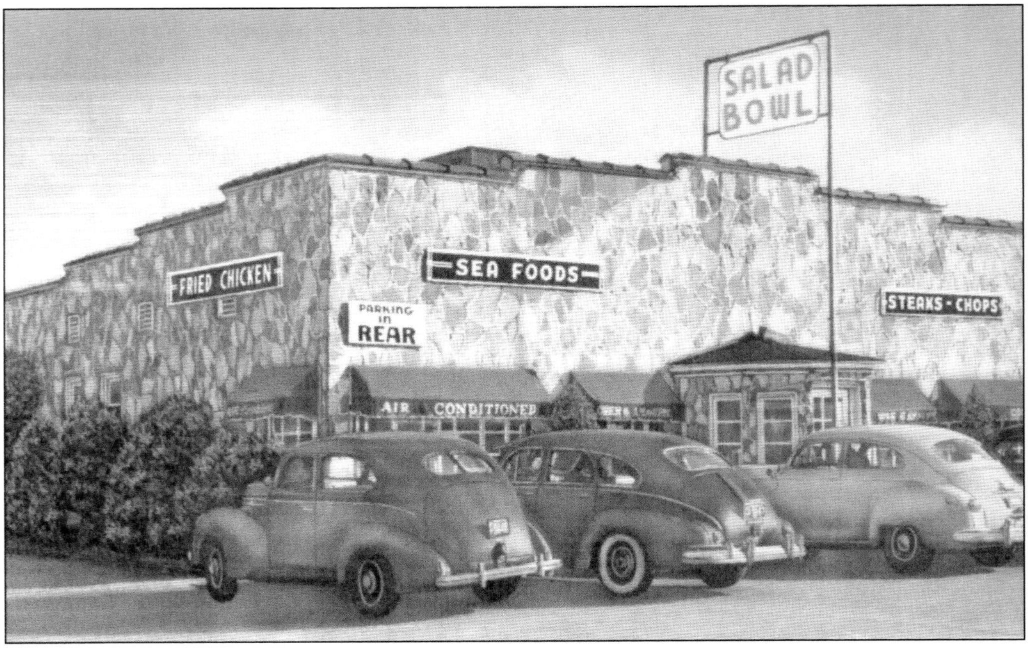

Byron and Bess Sullivan opened the Salad Bowl restaurant in Walnut Ridge in 1946. It quickly became popular throughout the South and was known for its excellent food, fine dining, and white tablecloths. For 200 miles north and south of Walnut Ridge on Highway 67, billboards announced to drivers how many minutes until they reached the Salad Bowl and could quench their appetites. (JBW.)

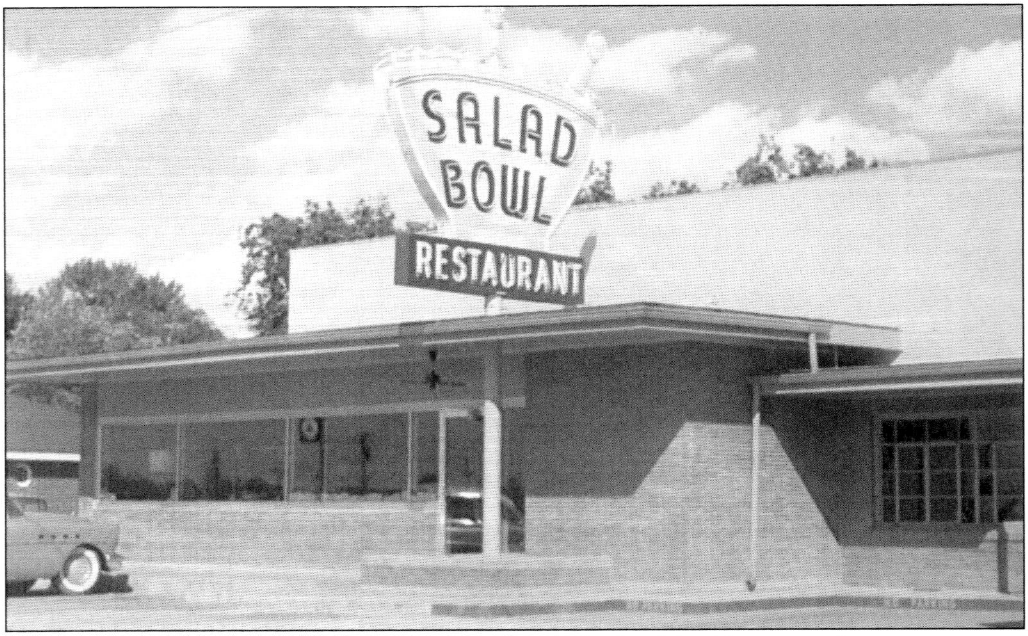

By the 1950s, the stone Salad Bowl was replaced with this brick building, near the intersection of old Highway 67 and Poplar Street. The Salad Bowl offered an extensive à la carte menu (including live Maine lobster) and a gift shop, featuring unique items such as Blenko glass, Red Wing pottery, and wingback earrings. (JBW.)

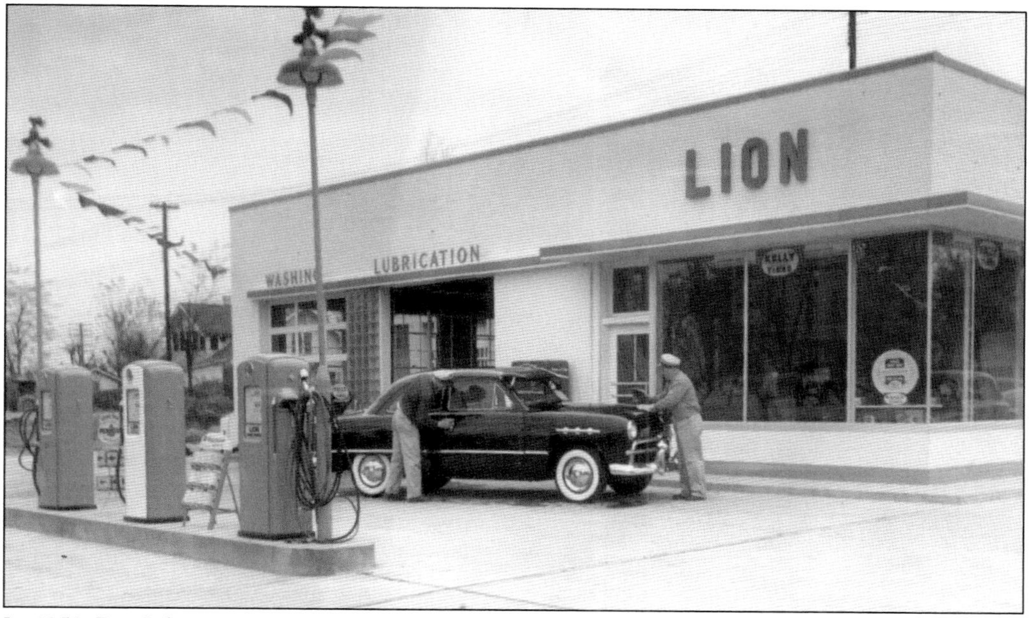

In 1950, Roy Johnson opened this full-service Lion station on West Main Street across from the courthouse. Earlier, he owned a Lion station at the intersection of Southwest Front and Elm Streets, which later became a parking lot for Piggly Wiggly. Before Johnson built here, this site was home to the B B Cab Company and an automobile repair shop. Walnut Ridge City Hall occupies this location now. (JJ.)

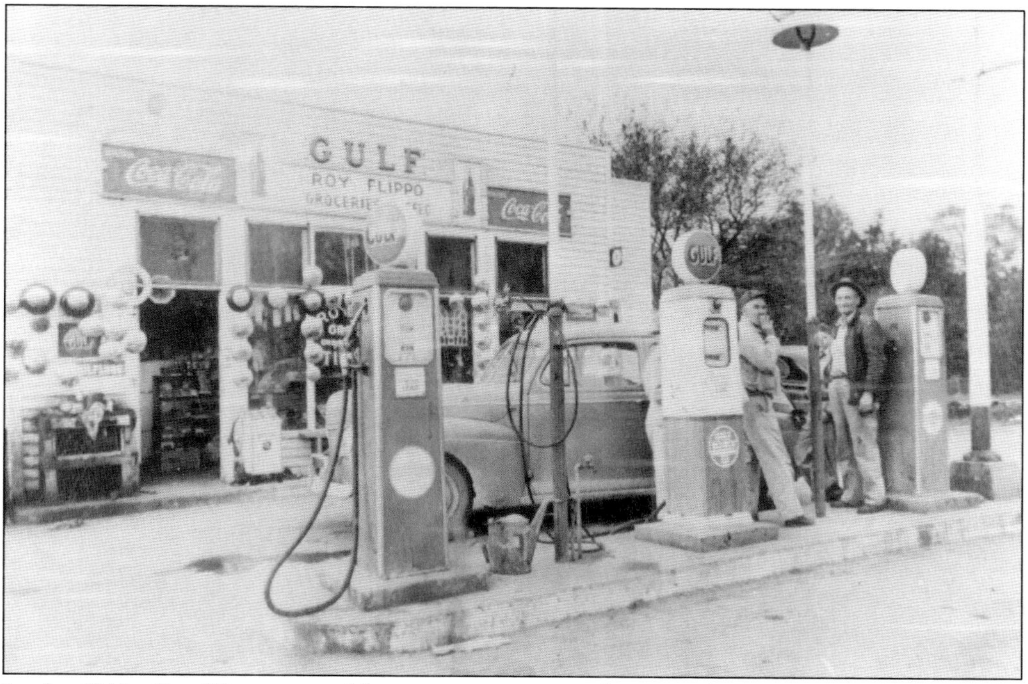

In the 1940s, Roy Flippo moved his service station and grocery business at Texas and Cotter Streets to a new location at Texas and Edgar Streets in Hoxie. Flippo (right) talks with a customer as his son Jerry fills the car with Gulf Premium No-Nox gasoline in this photograph from around 1950. Due to health issues, Flippo closed his business in 1961. (DF.)

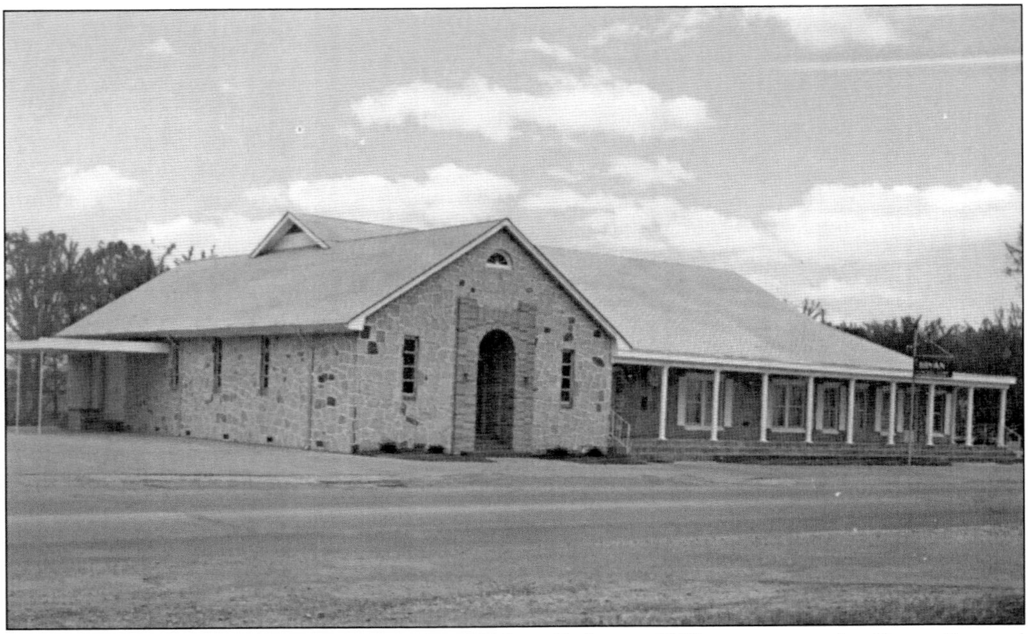

William C. and Sue Belle Bryan moved to Walnut Ridge in 1935 to manage the Gregg Funeral Home. Desiring to own their own business, they purchased the Johnson Funeral Home on Northeast Front Street in 1943. In 1948, the Bryans moved to Hoxie and opened Bryan Funeral Home. Still in the same location, the business is under the direction of the fourth generation of the founding family. (JBW.)

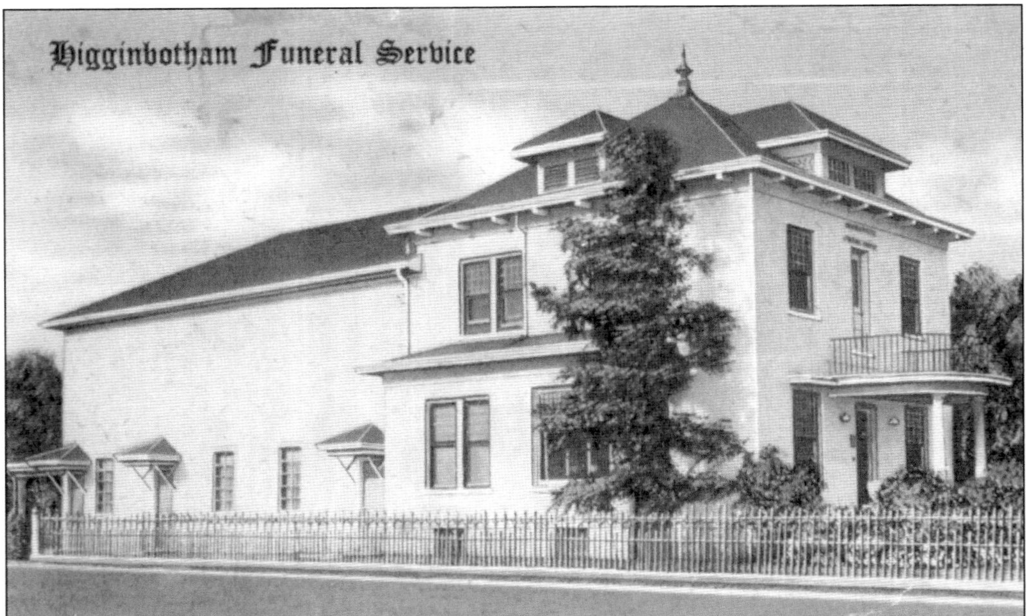

Higginbotham Funeral Home started in western Lawrence County in the late 1800s, expanding to Walnut Ridge in 1933. In December 1949, an open house was hosted in its new location, the newly remodeled home of W.R. Lane on the corner of West Main and Fourth Streets. The business sold and was moved out by 2012. The majestic home, built in 1908, is empty now and needs a new owner and restoration. (JBW.)

Major-league pitcher Johnny Sain retired from the Yankees and opened an automobile agency in Walnut Ridge in 1953. The dealership, seen at top, was located on the corner of Southwest Front and Main Streets. Sain got back into baseball in 1959 as a respected pitching coach for the Kansas City Athletics, New York Yankees, Minnesota Twins, Detroit Tigers, Chicago White Sox, and Atlanta Braves. (JBW.)

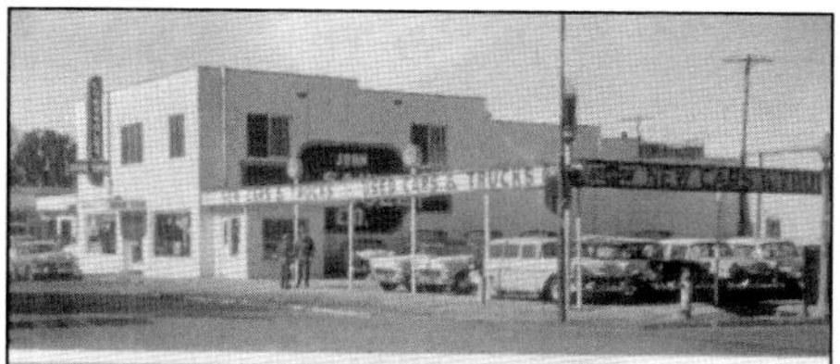

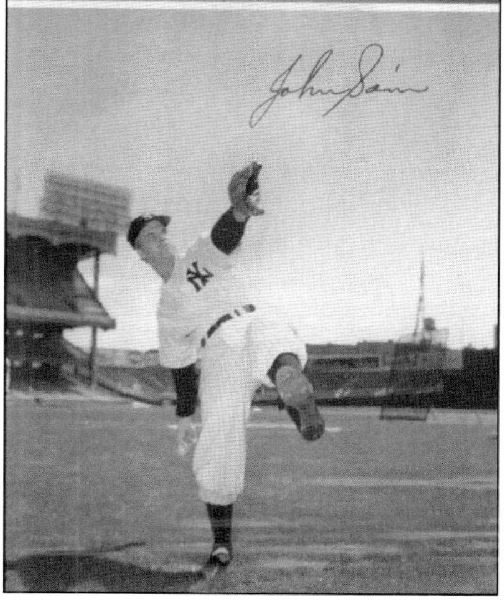

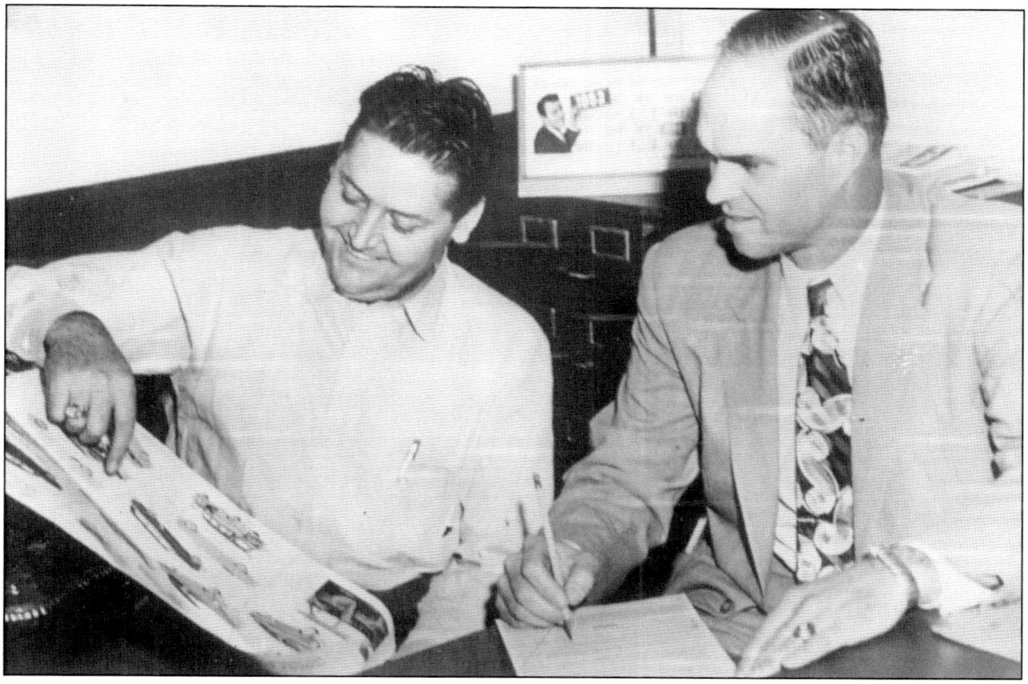

John Sain is shown here talking with Alvin Wilcoxson (left), who was his first sales prospect. Sain had the distinction of being the last pitcher to face Babe Ruth and the first pitcher to face Jackie Robinson. From 1946 to 1950, Sain and his fellow Boston Braves (now Atlanta Braves) pitcher Warren Spahn were known for the popular catchphrase, "Spahn and Sain and pray for rain." Sain and his wife, Doris, raised four children in Walnut Ridge. (JBW.)

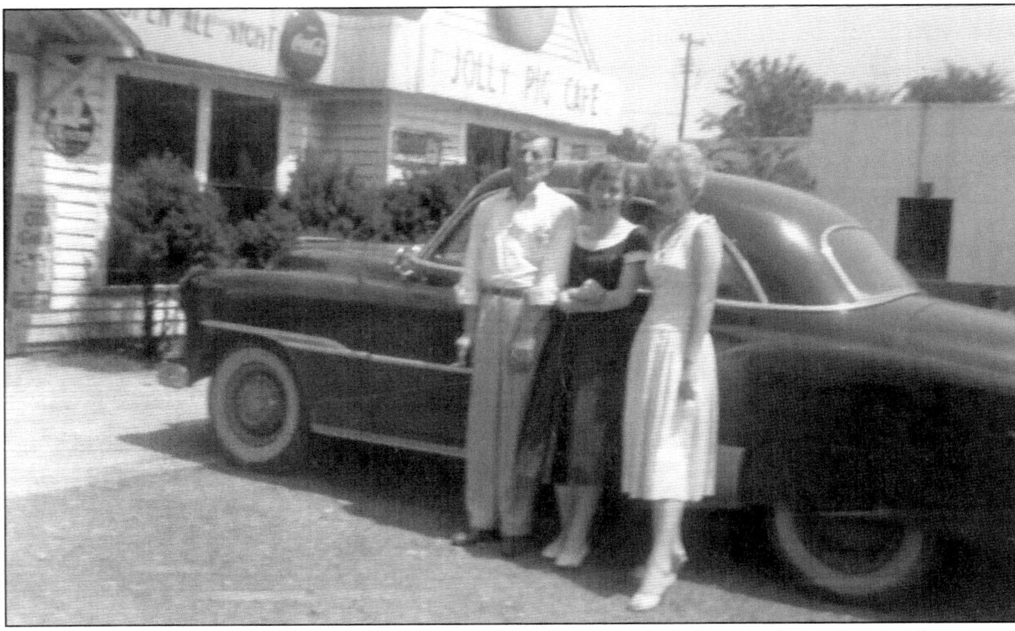

From the 1930s to the 1960s, the Jolly Pig Café was one of Walnut Ridge's favorite hangouts. Located on the corner of West Free and Southwest Front Streets, the Jolly Pig served customers 24 hours a day and also operated as a bus stop. Pictured from left to right are Charles Hembrey, his niece Lucille Williams, and an unidentified friend in the 1950s. The Jolly Pig was replaced in the 1960s with the Big Star grocery store. (THJ.)

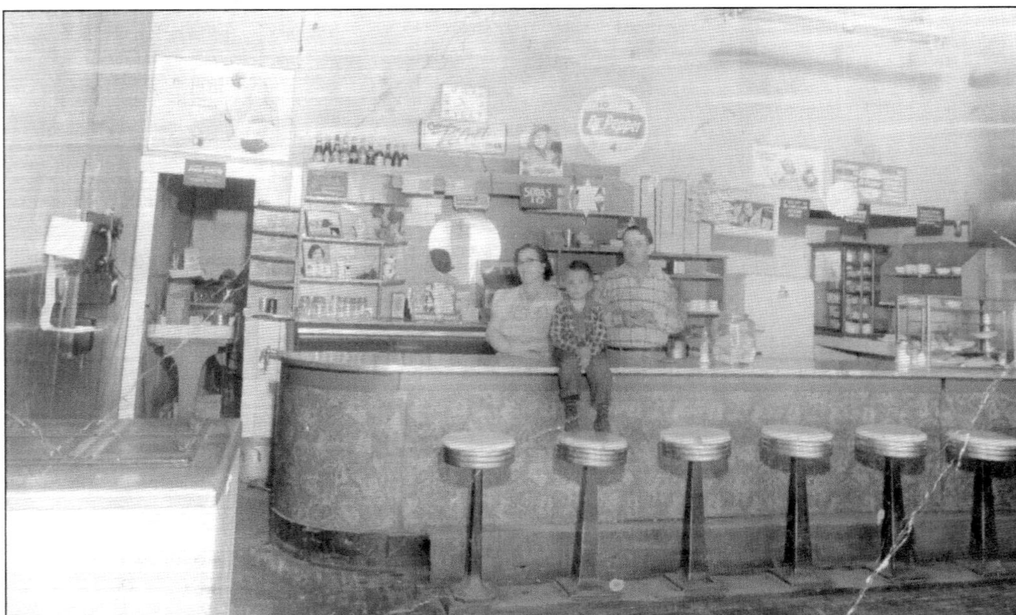

The original Warner's Drug Store in Hoxie, at the corner of Texas and Memphis Streets, was home to a series of restaurants and cafés after Lucian Warner moved his business across the tracks in the early 1900s. By the 1950s, it was known as the Corner Café. Managers Helen and Childers Crossno, with their grandson Gene Crossno, pose inside around 1958. Available sodas (priced at 10¢ each) are displayed in the background. (HRS.)

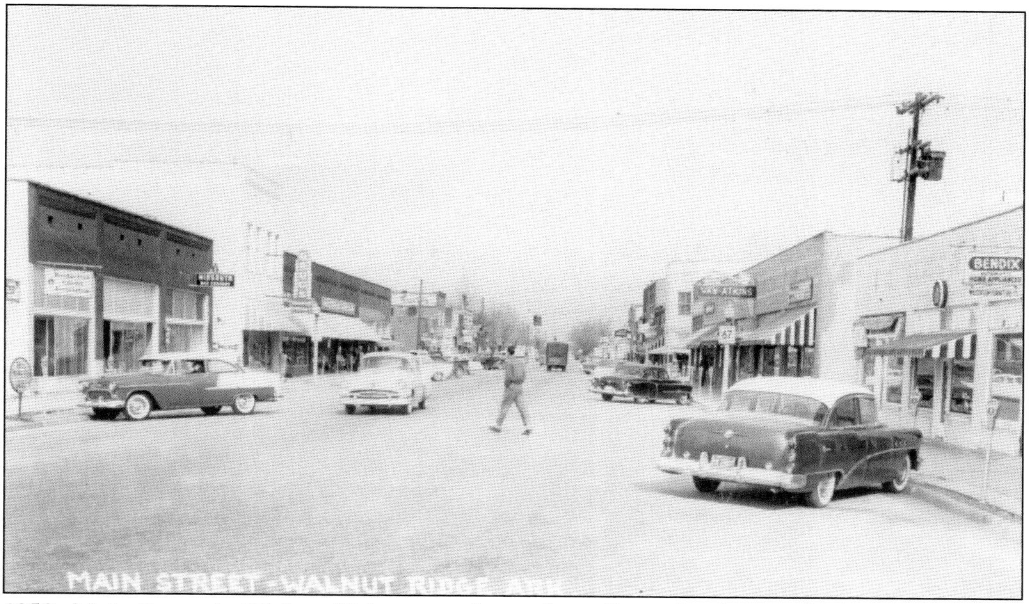

1950s Main Street in Walnut Ridge was a busy place. From the front right heading west are Wilcoxson's Furniture Company, Dunham's Jewelry Store, and an unmarked storefront that later became Melody Music Mart. Those three storefronts were recently leveled to make a parking lot. Beyond the alley are Western Auto, Van Atkins Department Store, the *Times Dispatch* newspaper office, Family Shoe Store, and Moore's Feed Store, where Buster Secoy sold newspapers on the corner. (JBW.)

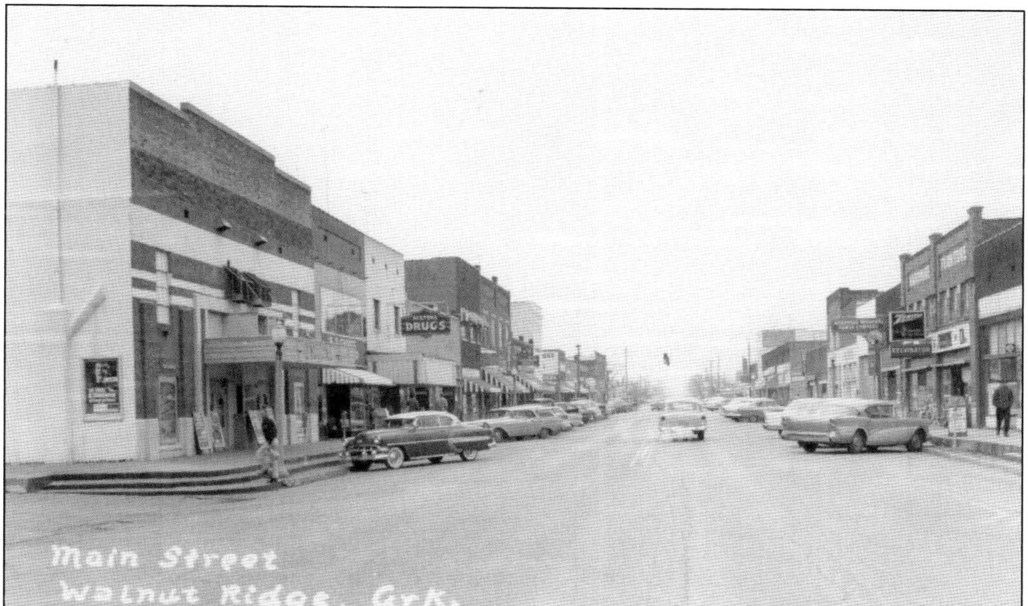

The Sharum Theater, far left, was showing *The Curse of Frankenstein* on this day in 1957. Built as the Swan Theater in 1924 by Swan C. Dowell, it was the nicest cinema in northeast Arkansas until it partially burned around 1930. J.J. Sharum restored it to its former glory about 1940. A longtime feud was settled inside the theater in October 1955, when Marvin Hurst shot and killed Bolden Thrasher. (JBW.)

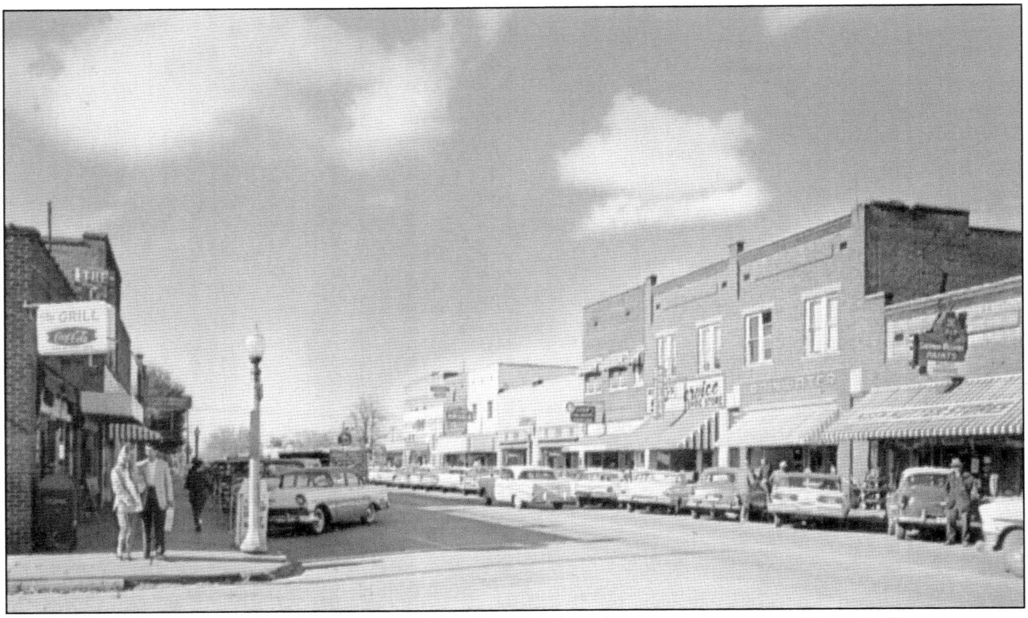

Walnut Ridge's Main Street in 1961 still had angled parking with meters. The Grill restaurant, on the near left, was a popular café with tabletop jukeboxes. Maloy Hardware, on the near right, was later purchased by First National Bank, becoming the spot for its three-story building today. To the left of Maloy's are Rainwater Jewelry Store, Robert's Shoe Store, Robb's Children's Center, Sloan's Department Store, Sexton's Drugs, Western Auto, and the Sharum Theater. (JBW.)

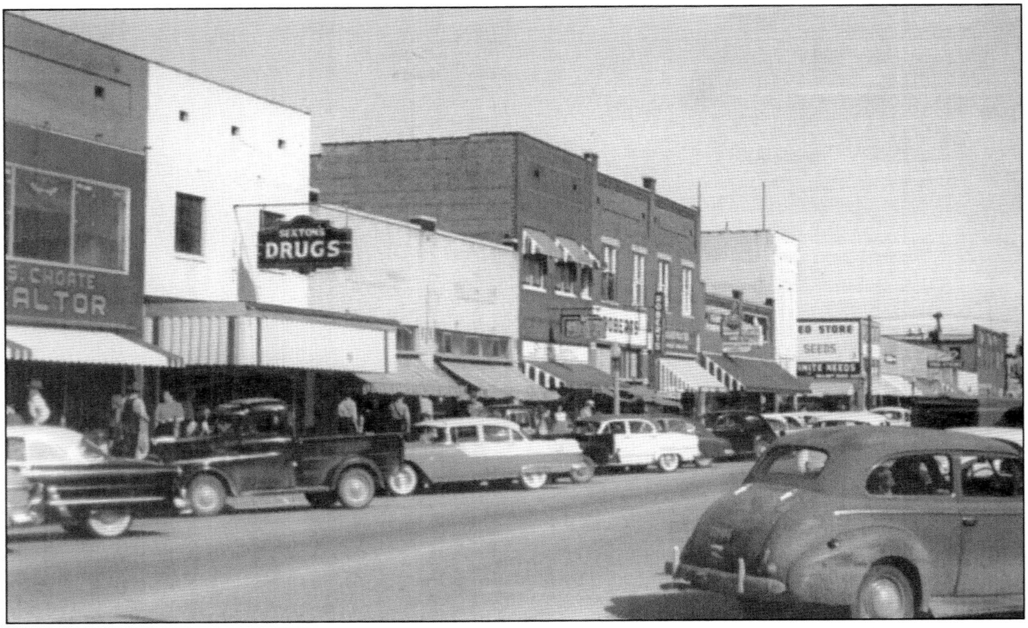

By 1955, the streetcar tracks on West Main in Walnut Ridge had been paved over. In this picture, with a view looking east, the first building visible to the left is R.S. Choate Real Estate, which later became Western Auto. To its right is Sexton's drugstore, which is still located in the same spot today. Sexton's, established in 1886 on Northwest Front Street, is the oldest continuously running business in Walnut Ridge. (JBW.)

The view in this photograph looks east on Main Street in Walnut Ridge in the mid-1950s. The post office building, near right, became the home of the *Times Dispatch* newspaper in 1977. The buildings to its left are a Kroger grocery, R.D. Burrow Hardware and Furniture, Arkansas Missouri Power Company, Citizens National Bank, Tom's Superette, Floyd's Barbershop, and the Grill. The streetlight at the corner of Main and Third Streets is no longer there. (JBW.)

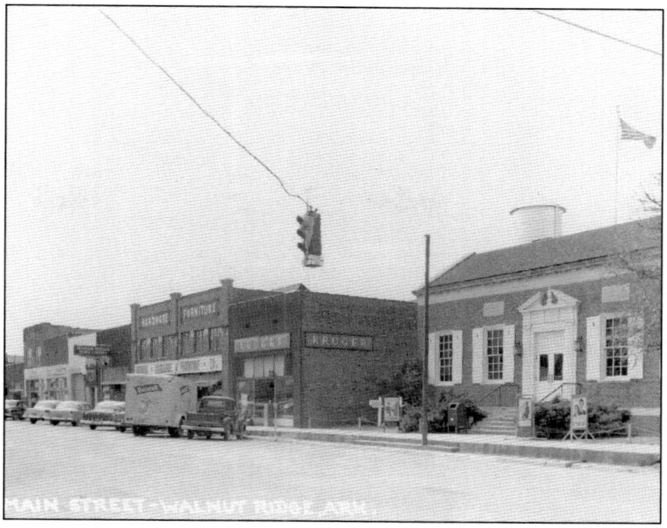

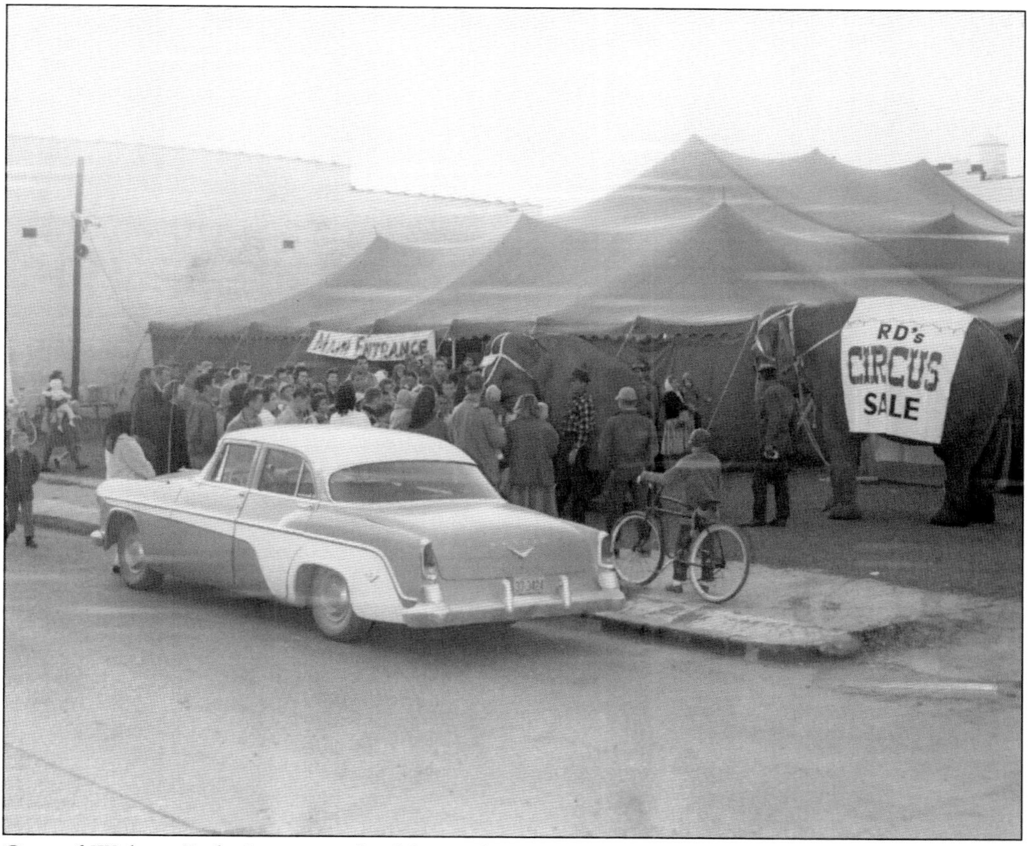

One of Walnut Ridge's most colorful merchants was R.D. Burrow. He protested the use of parking meters in the city by cutting down the ones in front of his store. He was known for many sales gimmicks, such as his continual "going out of business" sales. Burrow's circus sale in 1961 featured live radio broadcasts over KRLW, elephant rides, and a large tent full of merchandise for purchase. (CA.)

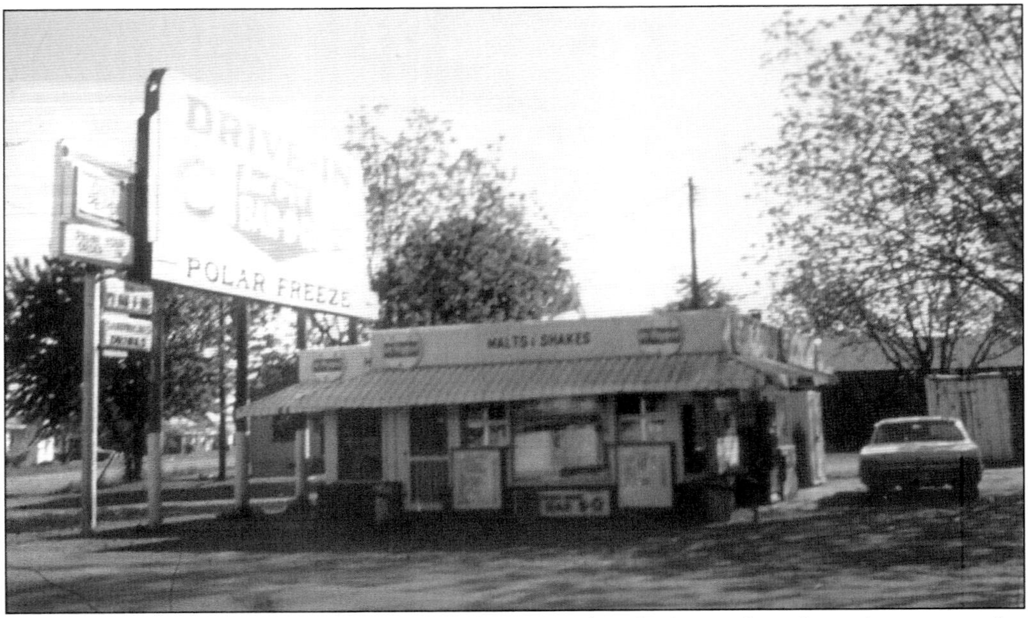

The Polar Freeze in Walnut Ridge, with its famous real pit barbecue, has always been a popular spot for teenagers and adults alike. Started by Herman Hood, it was bought by Thurlo and Ruth Davis, and then sold to Jack Allison and his mother, Polly, in 1958. Jack and Velma Allison are still running the landmark business today. The current building, constructed in 1969, replaced the original building, shown here. (KAY.)

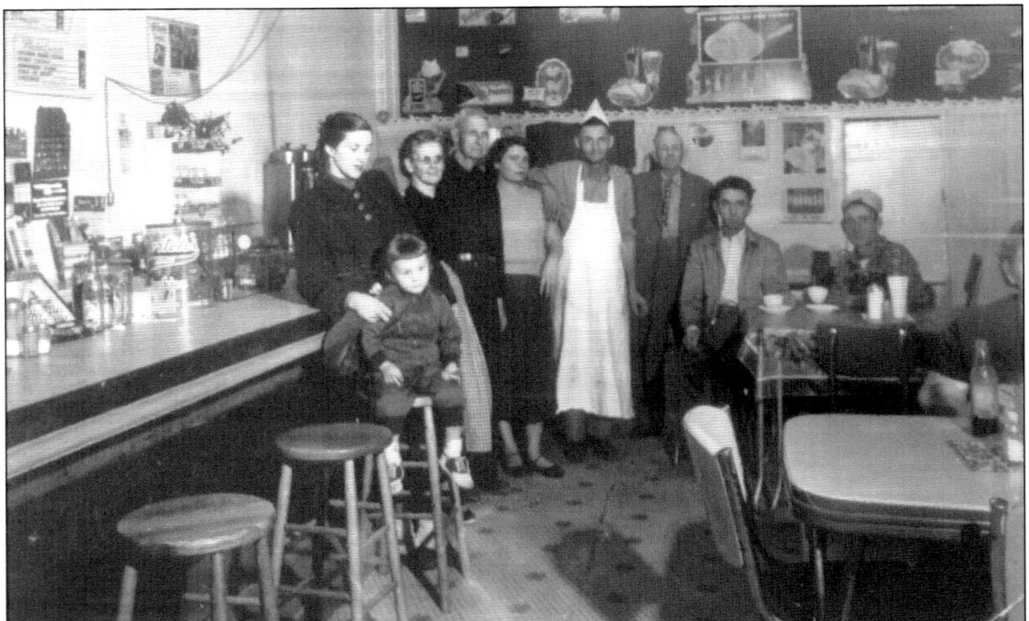

Two doors south from the Corner Café in Hoxie was the two-story City Hotel with the City Café on the first floor, both owned by Dave and Ethel Allison in the 1950s. Earlier, the café was owned by Leon Hubbs and named the Victory Café during World War II. Mozelle Wilson Spades and her two-year-old daughter, Becky Spades (Wood), are on the far left. Owners Dave Allison and Ethel Arnett Allison are third and fourth from left. The other four people are unidentified. (GSM.)

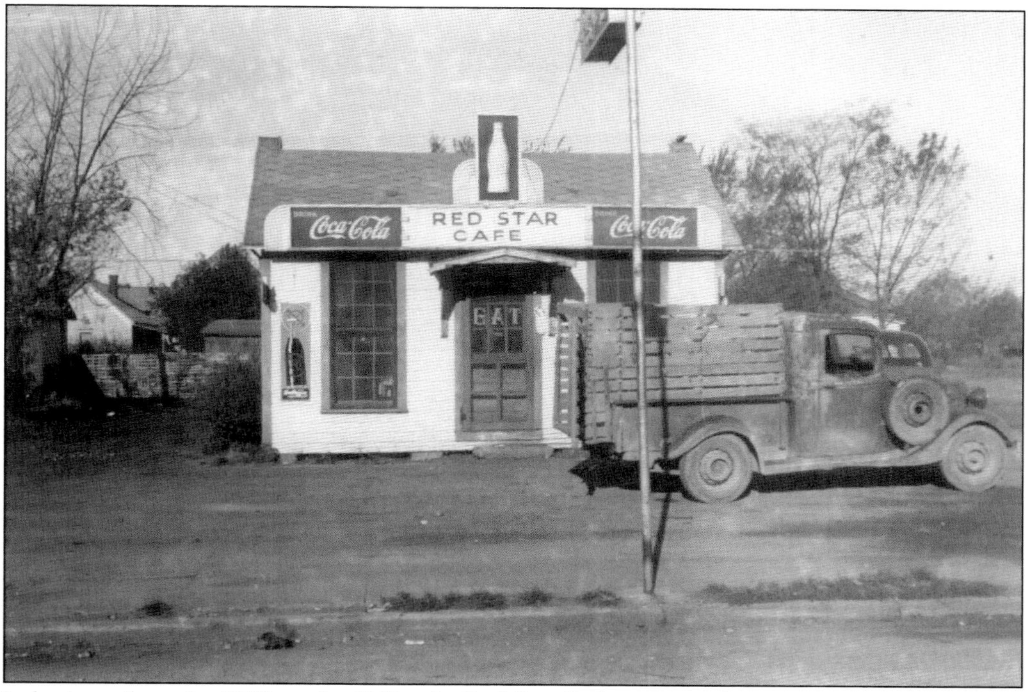

In business from the 1930s to the 1960s, the Red Star Café was one of Hoxie's most popular eating establishments. Boas Gibson owned the café and the Red Star Service Station, which were side by side on the corner of Highway 67 and Lindsey Street. He leased both to several different people. The Red Star Café was razed to make way for a Delta station, operated by Kenneth Quarry. (NJS.)

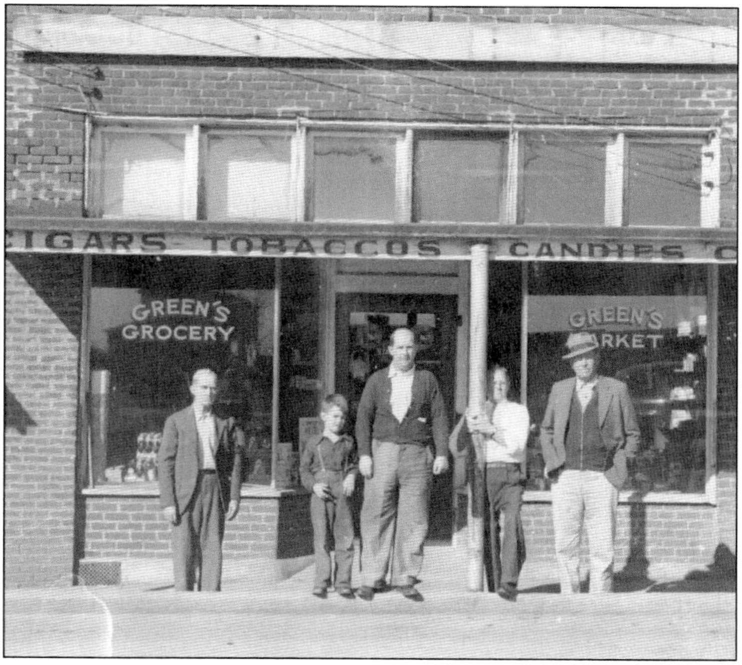

A.B. Green started Green's Grocery in the 1920s, serving Hoxie residents with quality items until the 1960s. Located in the middle of the main business block, between Case and Memphis Streets, the Hoxie Masonic Lodge met upstairs. Standing in front in 1949, from left to right, are A.B. Green, Jim Green, Herbert Green, Edward Rice, and Jim Steed. This entire block was demolished in 1982 to make room for the Hoxie Plaza. (JG.)

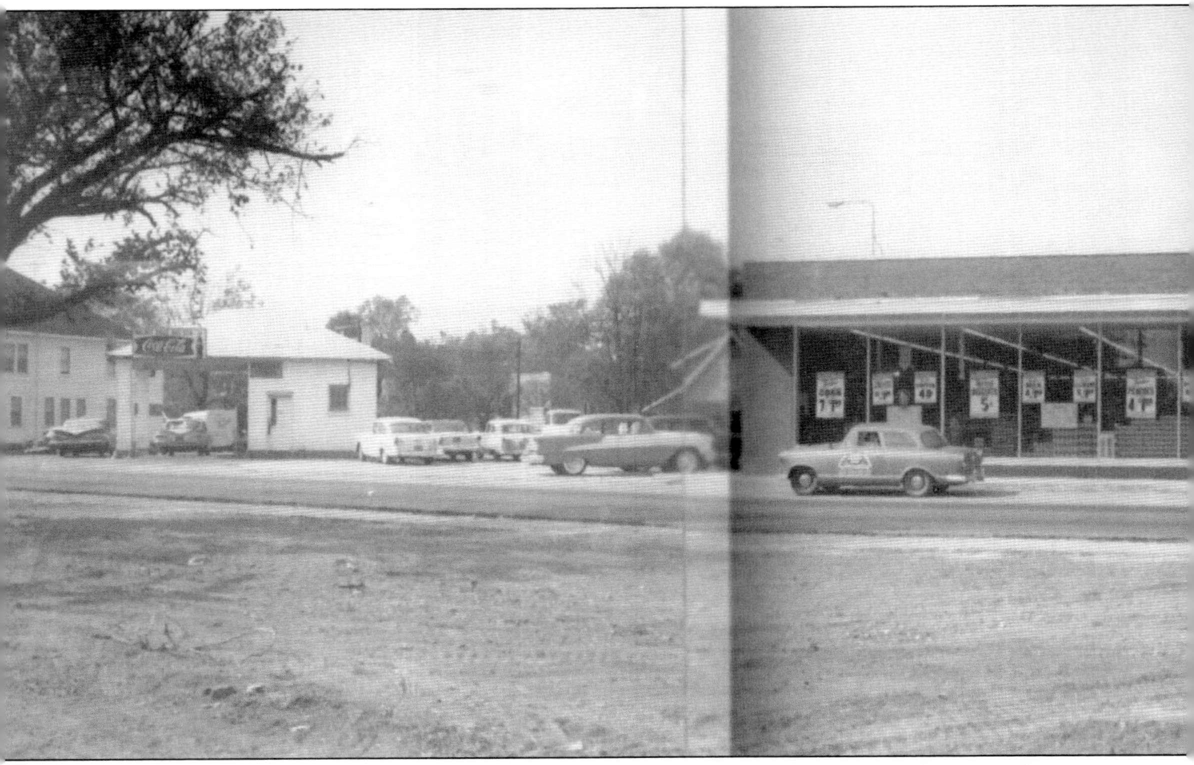

On May 7, 1927, when the Piggly Wiggly grocery store in Walnut Ridge had its grand opening, 1,676 people registered as visitors. Formerly located at the corner of Southwest Second and Elm Streets, it moved across from the depot at Southwest Front and Elm Streets in the 1950s. Business was so good at the new location that the store was doubled in size just a few years later. Early owners Leo and Dorothy Davis bought the business in the 1940s and passed the reins to their

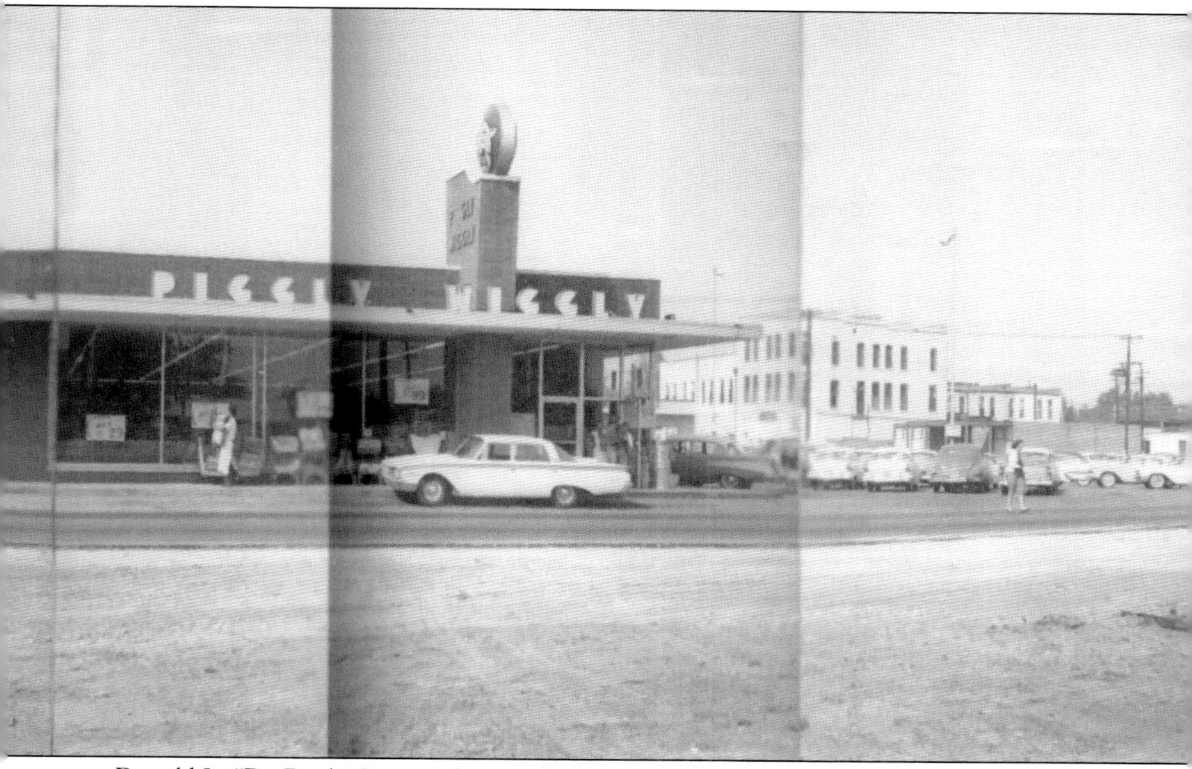

son, Donald L. "De Duck" Davis, who ran the store until his death in 1980. During the time of this picture, shortly after the expansion, this Piggly Wiggly was the largest grocery store in Arkansas for a few short months, until a larger one was built in Little Rock. An early bus stop is visible to the left of the store, with a two-story boardinghouse to its left, now the location of First Baptist Church. (DD.)

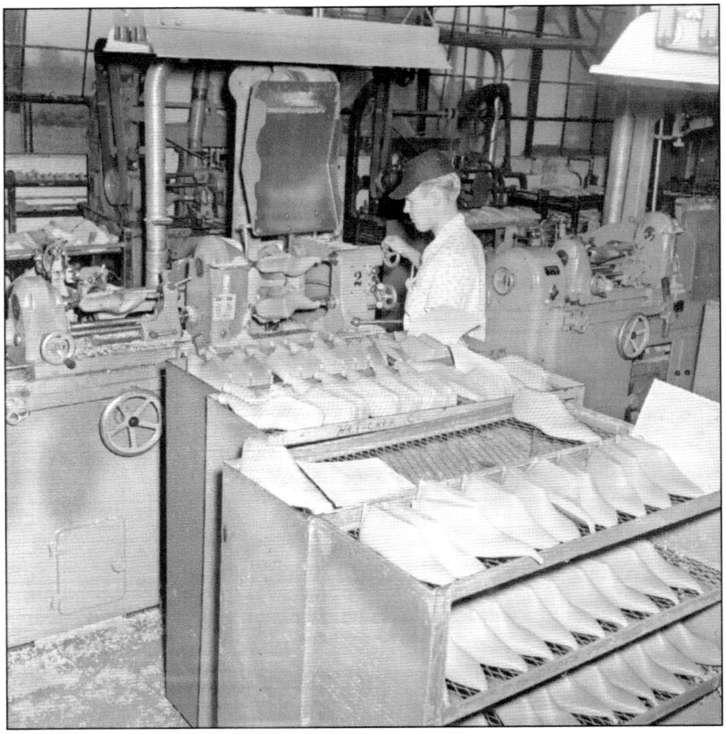

Jones & Vining shoe last factory in Walnut Ridge is the only remaining factory in the United States that still produces lasts. When formed in 1959, it was known as the Vulcan Corporation. Cloyce Richey operates a factory machine in this 1960s photograph. Originally made from maple wood, lasts today are made from the same plastics used to produce bowling balls. (AHC.)

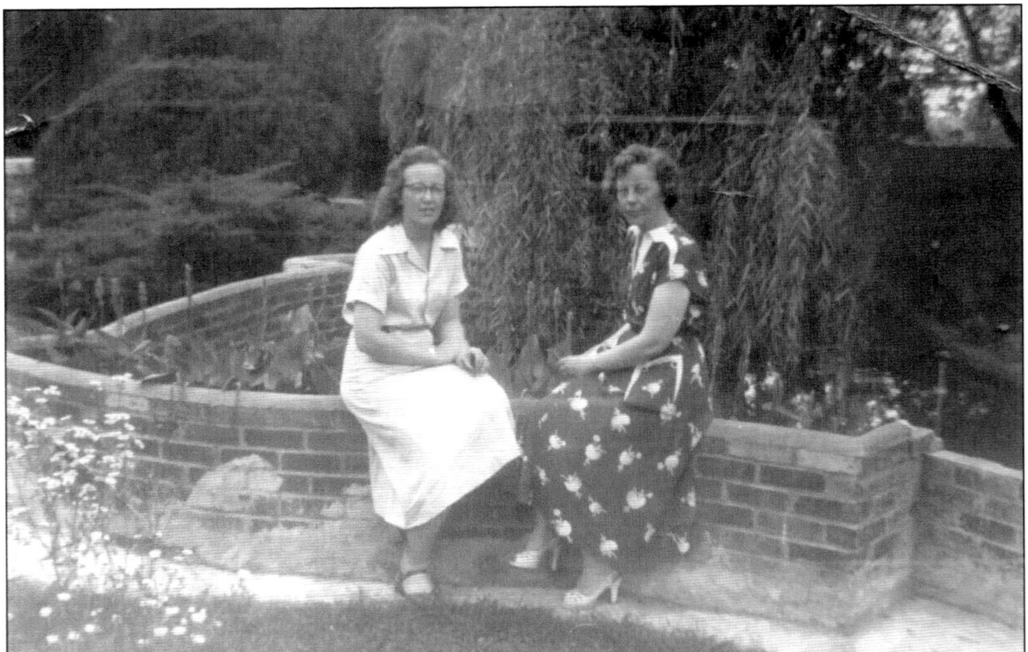

The John S. and Annie Boas Gibson home in Hoxie, located at the corner of Texas and Annie Streets, was built in 1935 after their original home burned with the Boas Hotel. It is remembered by many for its beautifully manicured lawn, complete with an English garden next to Turkey Creek. Pauline Sears (left) and her sister Mildred Leathers pose in the mid-1950s at the koi pond. (DS.)

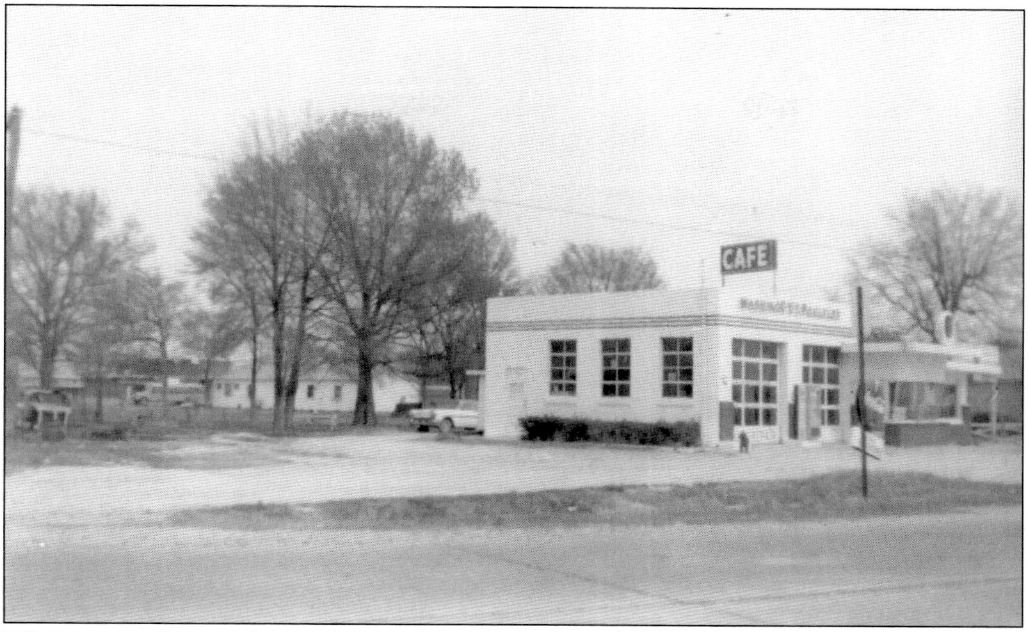

While not performing his regular construction worker job, C.E. Fouts would spend every spare minute building the Circle "F" Gulf Service Station and Café. Completed in 1956, it was located on Highway 63, adjacent to and just south of the Hoxie School campus. While Fouts attended to the service station side, his wife, Bama, operated the café. It became a popular spot for teenagers to eat lunch. (JFA.)

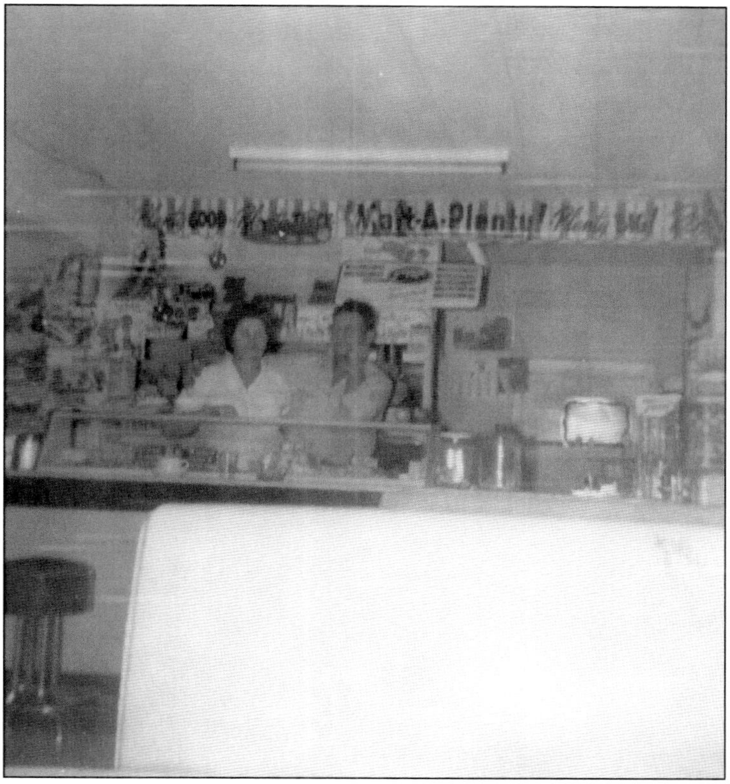

C.E. and Bama Fouts stand behind their counter in the Circle "F" Café in the 1950s. One of the many fast-food items served was Harry Burt's Malt-a-Plenty, a malted milk shake so thick a customer could eat it with a fork, made from low-fat powdered milk. Business was so good with the nearby school students that the Fouts decided to build the Pink Castle a little closer to campus in 1961. (JFA.)

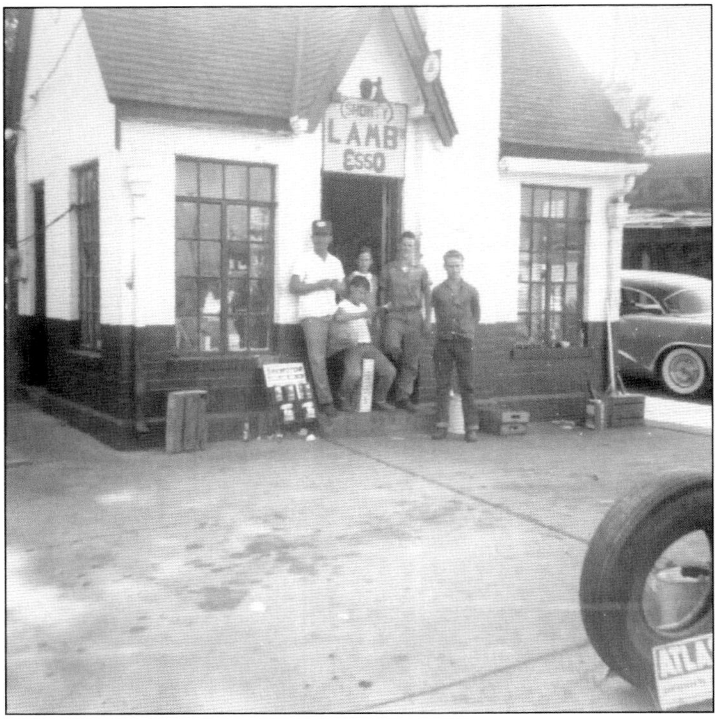

In the 1930s, this was Scruggs Phillips 66. At the time of this October 1960 photograph, Shorty Lamb owned the small, iconic station at the busy intersection of Texas and Lindsey Streets in Hoxie. From left to right, Shorty stands in the doorway with his children—Earl, Betty Jo, Floyd Charles, and Boyd. Later a location for Bud Whitmire's barbershop, the building was demolished in 2001 to make way for a branch of First National Bank of Lawrence County. (BL.)

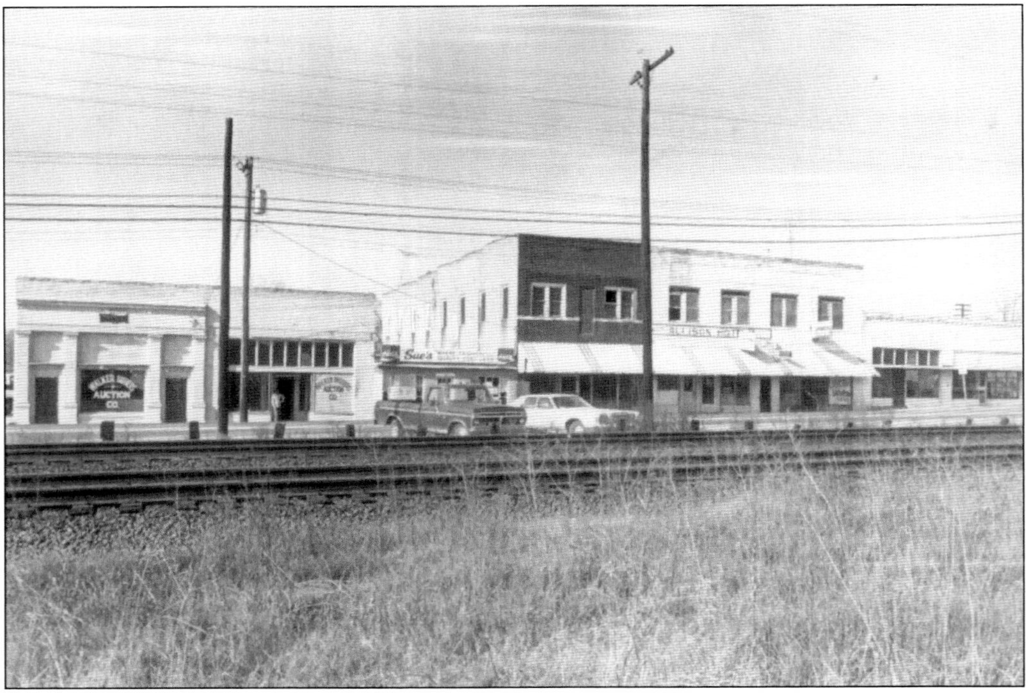

The original business district for Hoxie was between Case and Memphis Streets, along Highway 67. Most of these buildings were constructed or reconstructed after the 1913 tornado and survived the 1927 tornado, but none survived the wrecking ball of January 1982. According to an article written by Lucian Warner at the time of this photograph, this block was the most expensive commercial real estate in the county in the 1920s. (HCH.)

Three

Transportation

Transportation is an important part of the history of Walnut Ridge and Hoxie. Without the railroad, neither town would exist. Many think that the Iron Mountain Railroad was the first to lay tracks through this area, but in fact, the Cairo & Fulton Railroad had that honor. In 1872, the Cairo & Fulton announced its plan, and by 1873, the timetable showed Walnut Ridge as a stop between Moark and Texarkana. The St. Louis, Iron Mountain & Southern Railway, commonly known as the Iron Mountain, first ran through Walnut Ridge and the area that would become Hoxie on April 30, 1874, after its merger with the Cairo & Fulton. This is now the Union Pacific Railroad.

The second railroad came through Hoxie in 1883. On March 6, 1883, the St. Louis–San Francisco Railway, commonly known as the Frisco, made plans to build a railroad from Springfield, Missouri, to Memphis, Tennessee. By October 20, 1883, the entire 279-mile line from Springfield through Hoxie to Bridge Junction, Arkansas, was completed. This is now the BNSF Railway.

Completed in 1896, the third railroad ran from Hoxie through Walnut Ridge to Pocahontas. Known as the Hoxie, Pocahontas & Northern Railway, it eventually merged with the Frisco and reached from Hoxie to St. Louis, competing with the Iron Mountain route. The former route of this railway is now a paved walking and biking trail, linking Hoxie and Walnut Ridge.

A mule car line, linking the two towns along the east side of the Iron Mountain Railroad, was incorporated on June 25, 1889, with 19 shareholders. In 1904, the mule car was replaced with an electric streetcar that ran on the opposite side of the Iron Mountain Railroad, from the roundhouse in Hoxie to the Frisco depot on West Main Street in Walnut Ridge. The streetcar was discontinued in the late 1920s.

After the streetcar, Hoxie and Walnut Ridge were full of taxis. They would line up five and six deep at the Hoxie depot, 24 hours a day, seven days a week. There was also a bus driven by John Stewart that ran from Hoxie to Walnut Ridge every hour for 12 hours a day for a 10¢ fare.

Until the 1910s, horses and buggies were the favored means of travel for the public. By the mid-1920s, the dirt streets were full of automobiles, but in the 1930s, streets began to be paved.

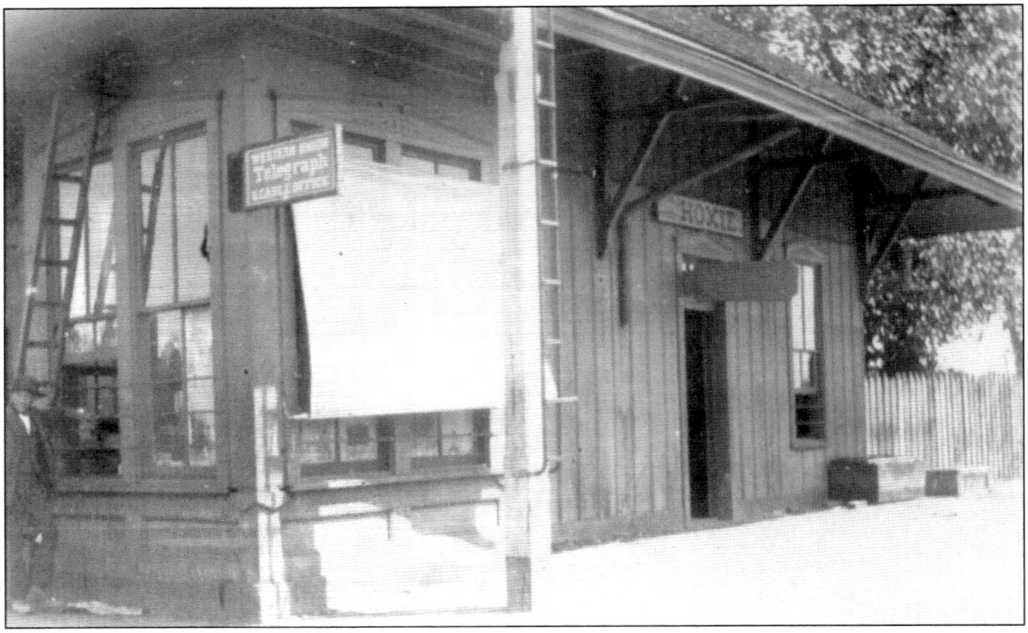

There have been three depots in a particular location on the southeast corner of the railroad crossing at Hoxie. Dated 1901, this is the only known photograph of the first one. Placed in operation shortly after the Frisco came through in 1883, it was replaced in 1906 with the heavily photographed Union Station. A Western Union telegraph and cable office sign is visible on the corner. (JBW.)

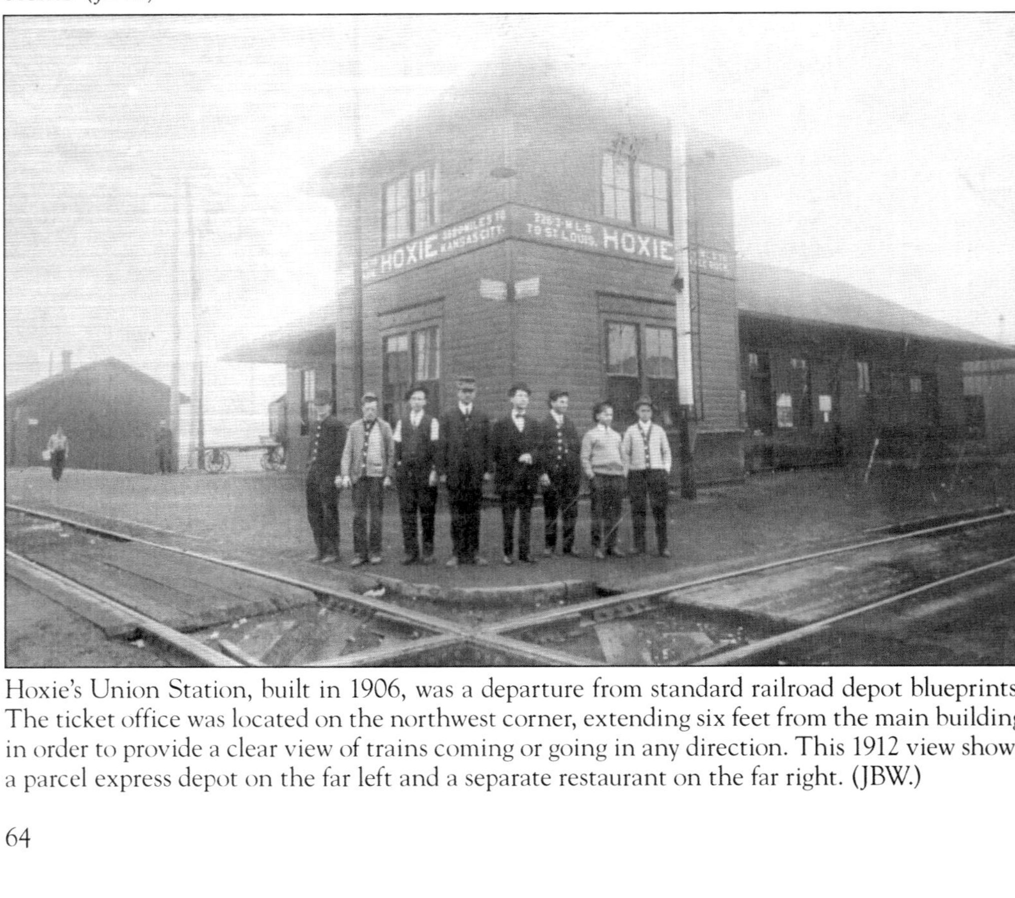

Hoxie's Union Station, built in 1906, was a departure from standard railroad depot blueprints. The ticket office was located on the northwest corner, extending six feet from the main building in order to provide a clear view of trains coming or going in any direction. This 1912 view shows a parcel express depot on the far left and a separate restaurant on the far right. (JBW.)

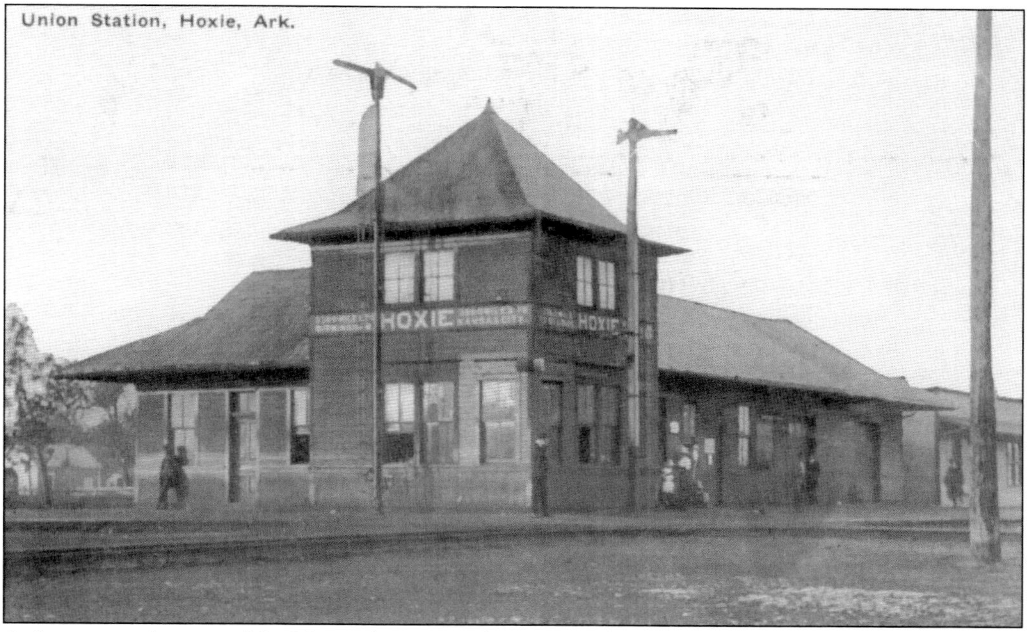

A distinctive feature of the Hoxie depot was the crossroads sign. On the north side, it listed 336.9 miles to Birmingham and 398 miles to Kansas City. On the west side, it displayed 226.3 miles to St. Louis and 119.3 miles to Little Rock. The two-story office divided the African American waiting room on the left from the larger waiting room, baggage room, and covered brick platform on the right. (JBW.)

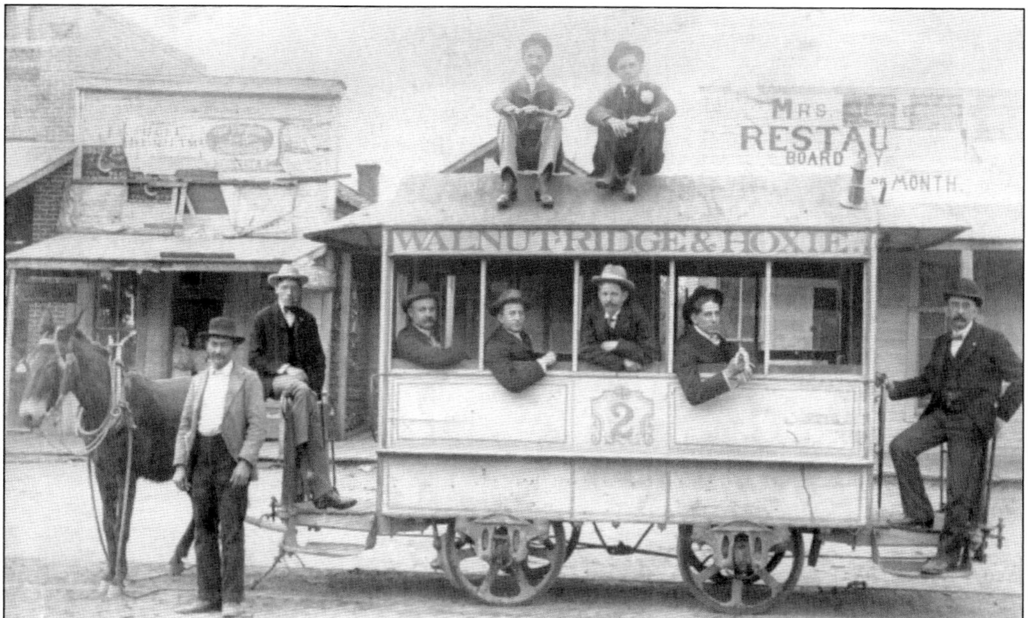

The Walnut Ridge and Hoxie Street Car Line was incorporated on June 25, 1889. By 1904, when the electric streetcar was put into service, the Mule Car Line dropped its rate to a penny to compete. "Old Jack" the mule put in 14 years of service. The man with the banana is W.K. Surridge, who later obtained the rank of brigadier general in the Arkansas National Guard, serving as the adjutant general. (JMS.)

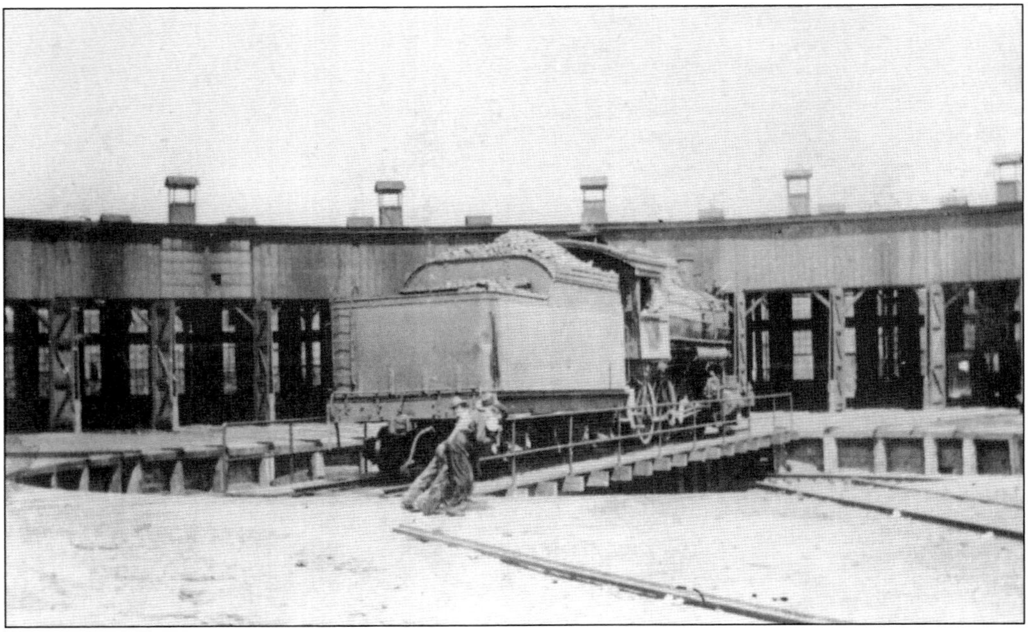

An economic boom in Hoxie began in 1901 when the Iron Mountain Railroad built a roundhouse, a huge semicircular structure used for servicing locomotives. A turntable directed trains into each stall of the roundhouse. When first installed, the turntable was operated manually. After the Walnut Ridge and Hoxie Light, Power & Transit Company was installed in 1904, the turntable was powered by electricity. (RB.)

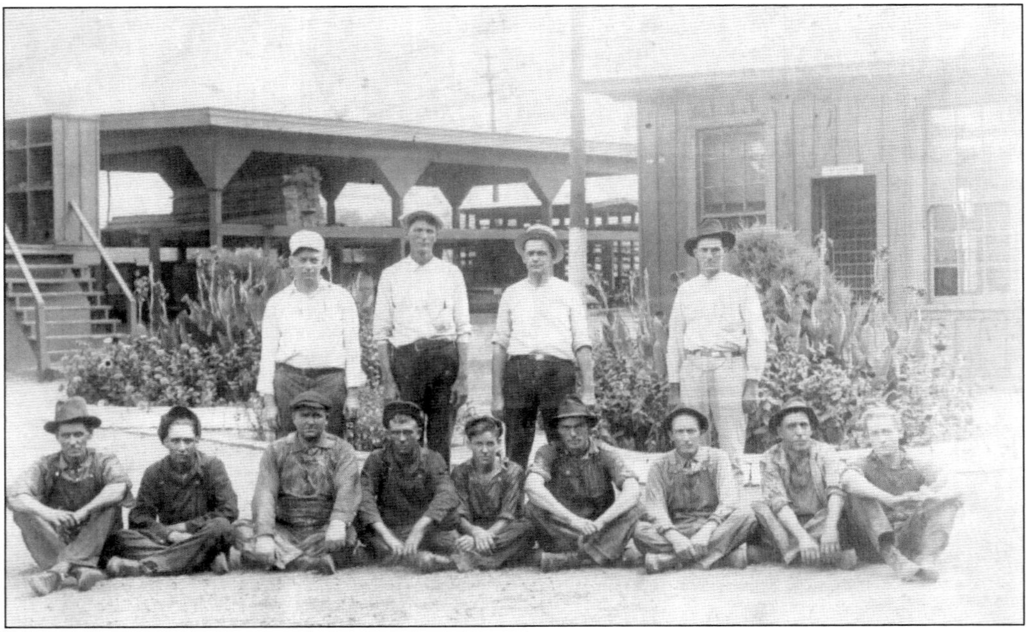

This 1926 image shows railroad workers at the roundhouse in Hoxie. Pictured are, from left to right, (front row) John Anderson, Earl Burnett, Tom Smith, unidentified, Vance Broadway, H.O. Blankenship, J. Pierce, Gilly Chapel, and unidentified; (back row) Arch Talfirt, roundhouse foreman; O.E. Burnett, car shop foreman; a Mr. Marshel, roundhouse foreman; and an unidentified taxi driver. (RO.)

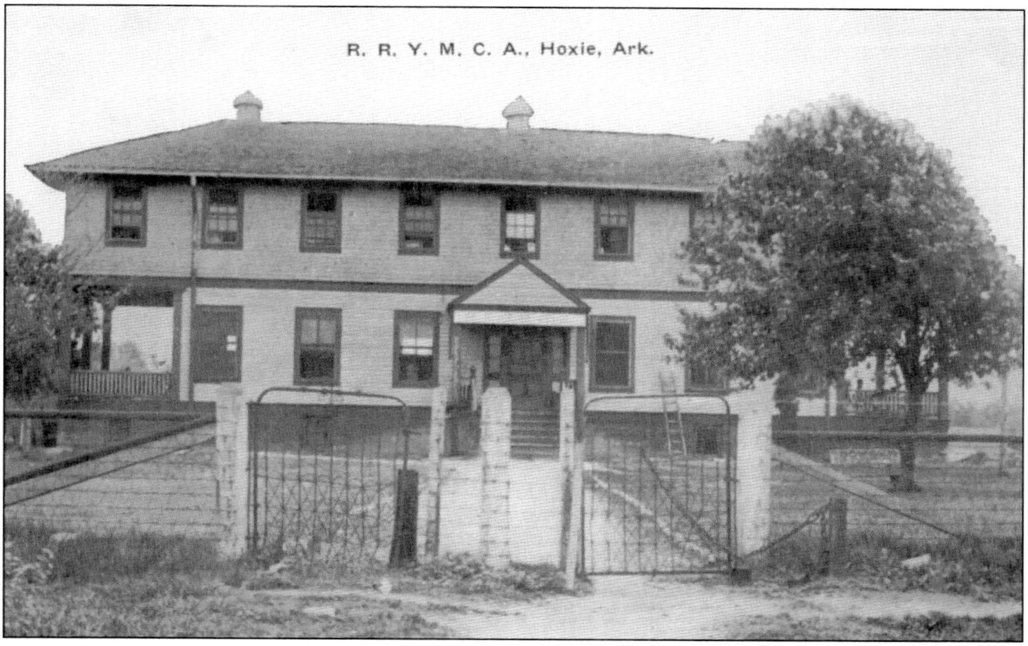

In 1904, by the generosity of railroad heiress Helen Gould, daughter of railroad tycoon Jay Gould, a $15,000 Railroad YMCA building was erected in Hoxie to provide wholesome overnight lodging and a meeting space for railroad workers. Helen later visited Hoxie on an inspection tour. Other amenities included a reading room, cafeteria, and recreational equipment. The YMCA was located south of the roundhouse, near the tracks. (JBW.)

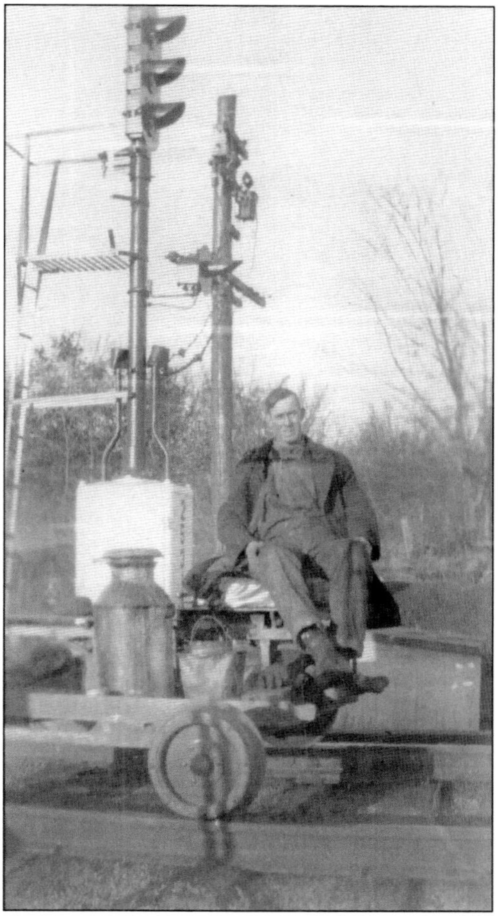

In addition to the passenger terminal, the Frisco Railway had a freight terminal in Hoxie. Coupled with the Iron Mountain roundhouse, Hoxie's population grew from a few hundred to over 2,000 in just a few short years. Hoxie benefited greatly from the higher wages and culture brought from immigrants. Jim Kapales, who emigrated from Greece in 1908, is shown on a speeder in Hoxie. (JKJ.)

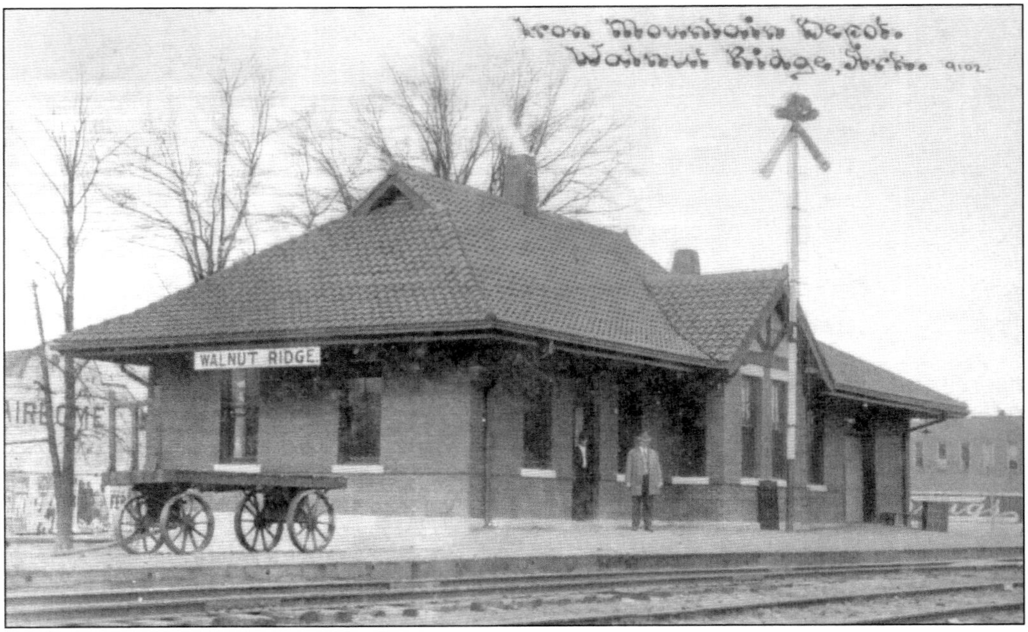

The Walnut Ridge Iron Mountain Depot was built in 1908, replacing the two-story railroad hotel. This Mediterranean-style station had a ticket office, segregated waiting areas, and a freight section. Beautifully restored in 1995, the depot now serves as the chamber of commerce office and an Amtrak passenger station. It is listed in the National Register of Historic Places. The Airdome, an open-air theater, is visible on the left. (JBW.)

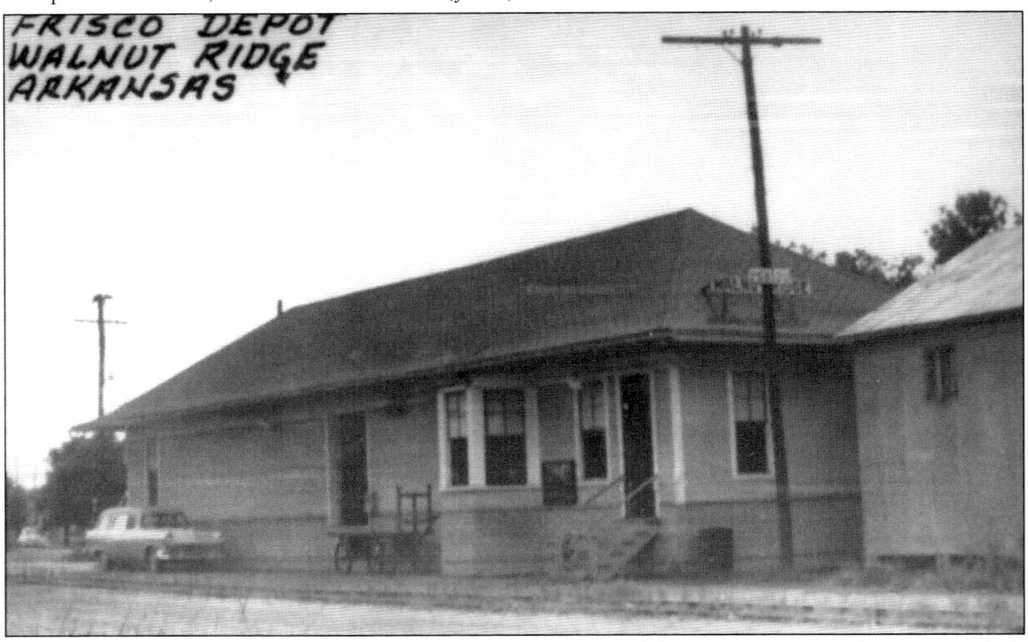

The Hoxie, Pocahontas & Northern Railway was completed from Hoxie to Pocahontas in 1896. In 1907, this railway became part of the Frisco, extending its reach from Hoxie to St. Louis, trying to compete with the Iron Mountain route to the same destination. The former railbed is now a paved walking and biking trail connecting Hoxie to Walnut Ridge. The depot, which was on Main Street, no longer exists. (JBW.)

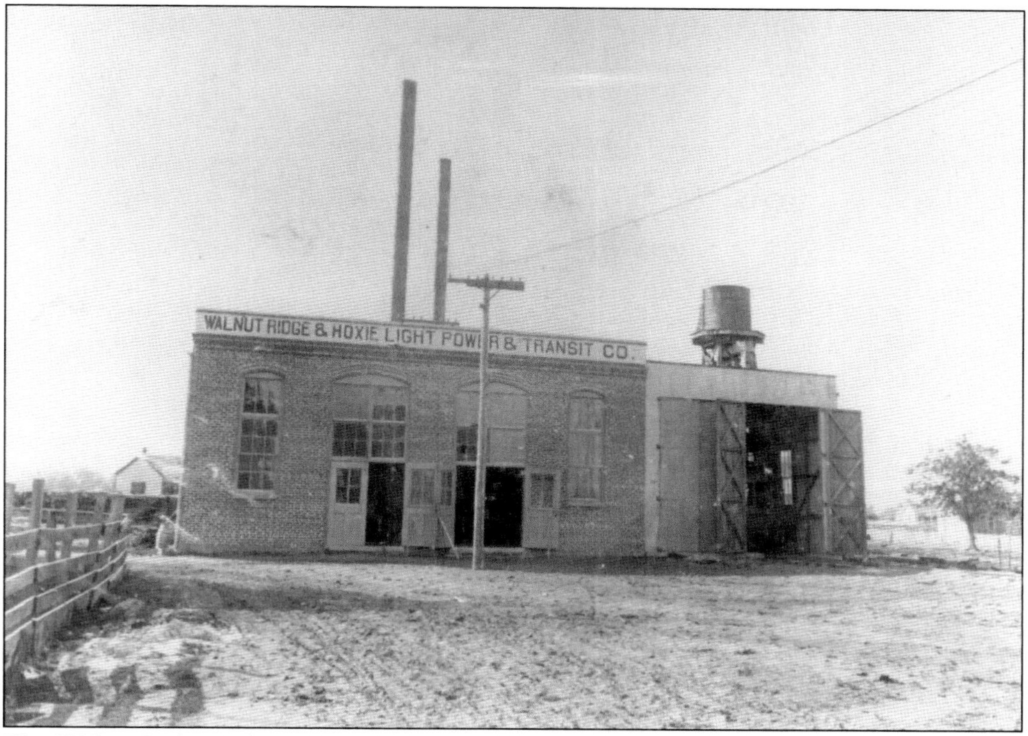

The Walnut Ridge and Hoxie Light, Power & Transit Company began operation in July 1904, running an electric streetcar line between Walnut Ridge and the Hoxie roundhouse. It also furnished electric lights and various forms of electricity. The streetcar made a round-trip every half hour along its two miles of track. In 1905, the line logged 225,668 total passengers—over 600 passengers a day. (AHC.)

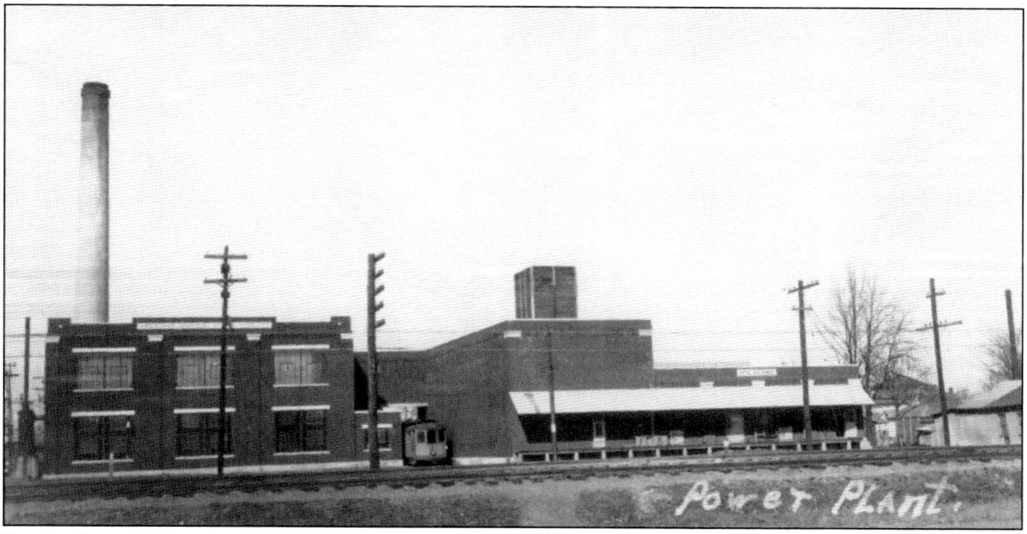

By the late 1920s, the Walnut Ridge and Hoxie Light, Power & Transit Company had changed its name to the Arkansas and Missouri Power Company and expanded to include an ice plant, visible on the near right. One of the three operating streetcars is visible in the repair shop near the center. The only existing part of the power plant today is the tall, concrete smokestack on the far left. (JMS.)

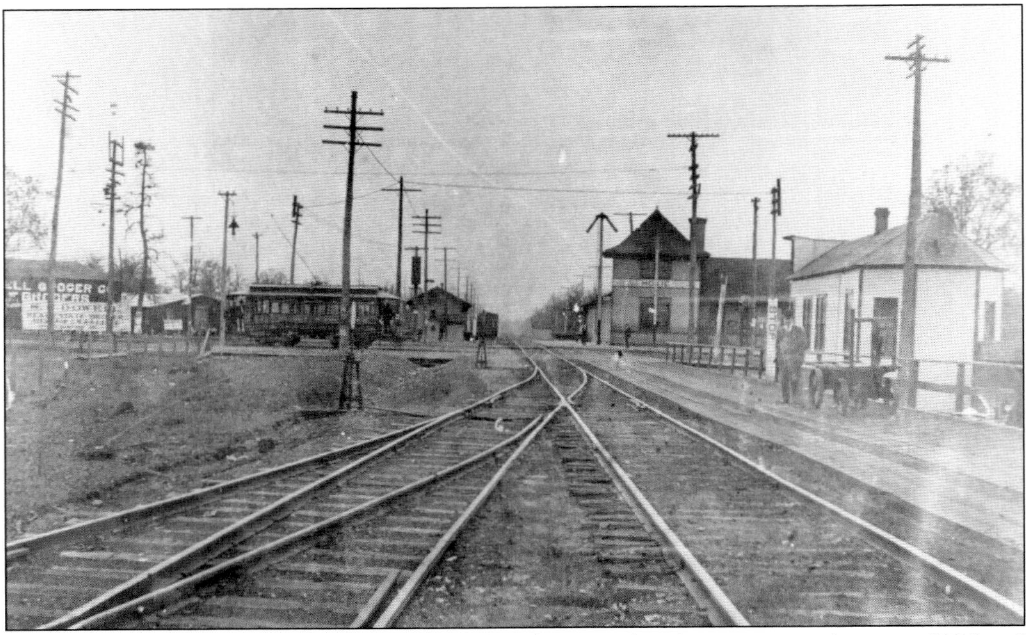

The small, white building on the far right of this photograph, taken sometime between 1906 and 1912, is Hoxie's first post office. The streetcar, approaching from the left, is about to cross the Frisco tracks and past Union Station on its way south to the roundhouse. The Plunkett-Jarrell Wholesale Grocer building is on the far left, partially obscured by a billboard for S.C. Dowell Real Estate. (JCW.)

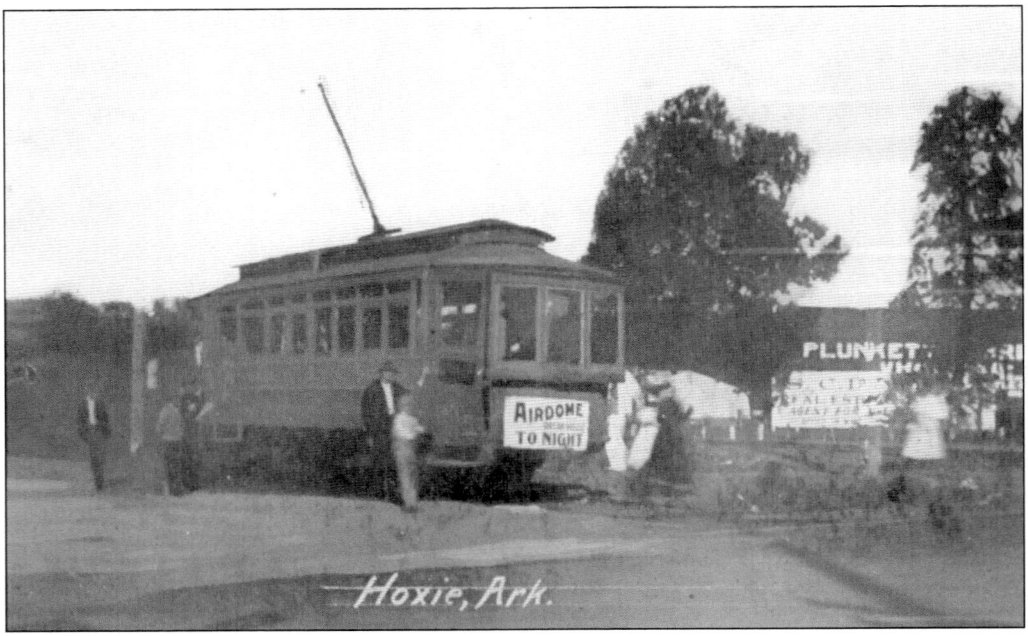

A sign advertising the Airdome Theatre is displayed on the front of the streetcar at its stop near the crossing of the Iron Mountain and Frisco railroads in Hoxie. This open-air theater, located in Walnut Ridge, allowed customers to sit and watch a movie in the summer when the indoor movie theaters were stifling hot. A forerunner to drive-ins, the Airdome was only in business about five years. (JBW.)

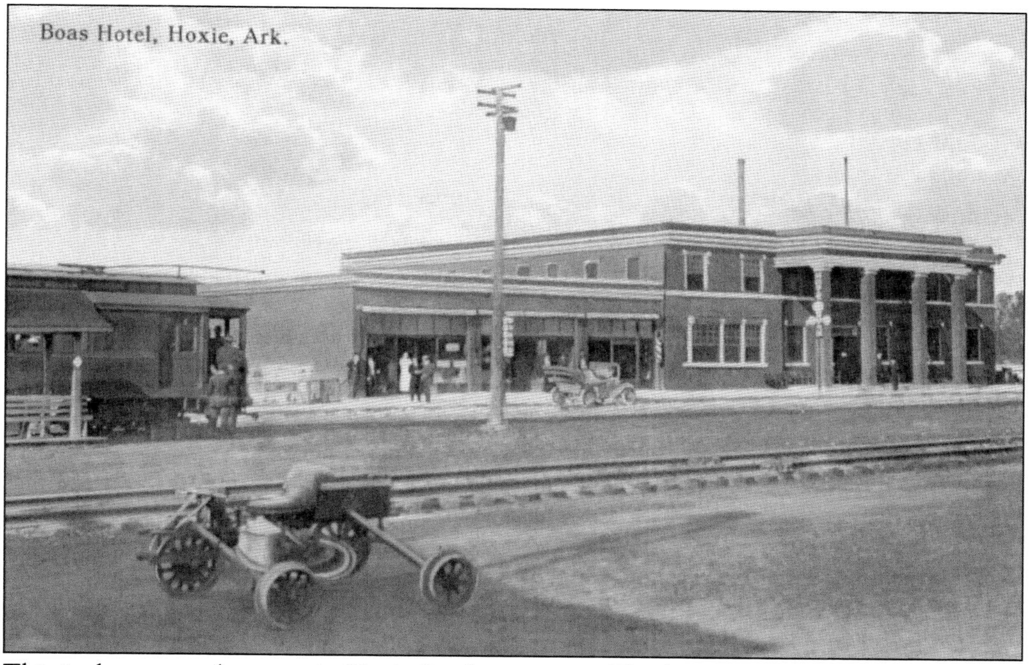

This is the next-to-last stop in Hoxie for the streetcar. The last stop was just south, near the roundhouse. Pictured in 1914, the second Boas Hotel was only one year old. To the left of the hotel are Pringle's Drugs, the new post office, and a barbershop. The velocipede in the foreground was used by railroad inspectors to travel quickly to check sections of railroad track. (JCW.)

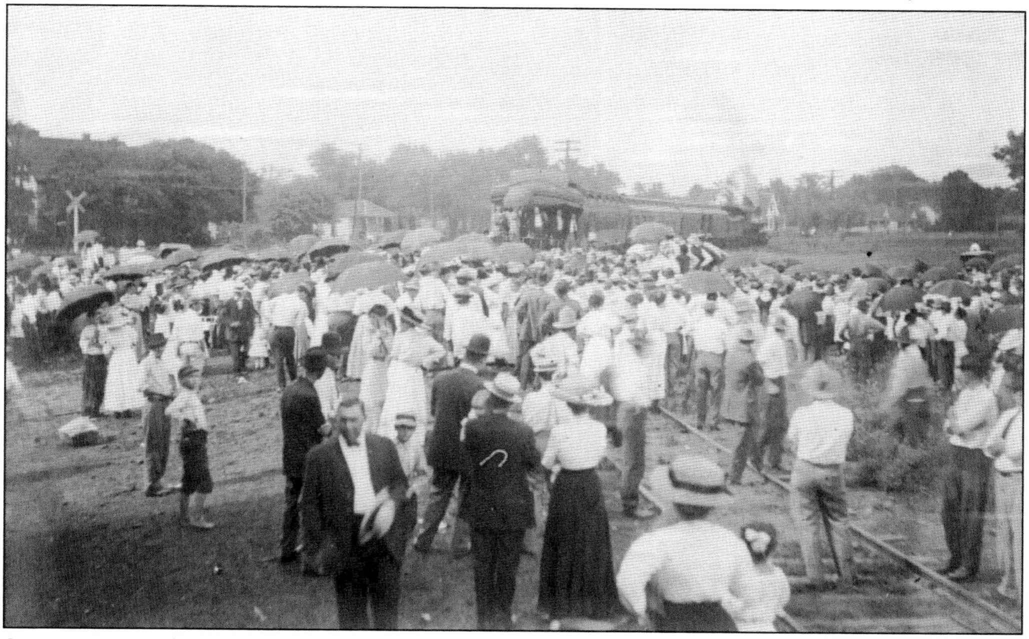

Spectators watch as the Donaghey-Bryan special train leaves Hoxie. Gov. George W. Donaghey and William Jennings Bryan toured Arkansas in September 1910, proposing an amendment to the state constitution. The five-day trip covered 1,750 miles and included 55 speeches. The train is headed north on the Iron Mountain Railroad toward Walnut Ridge. The Harry and Ida Boas home, still standing, is visible in front of the locomotive. (AHC.)

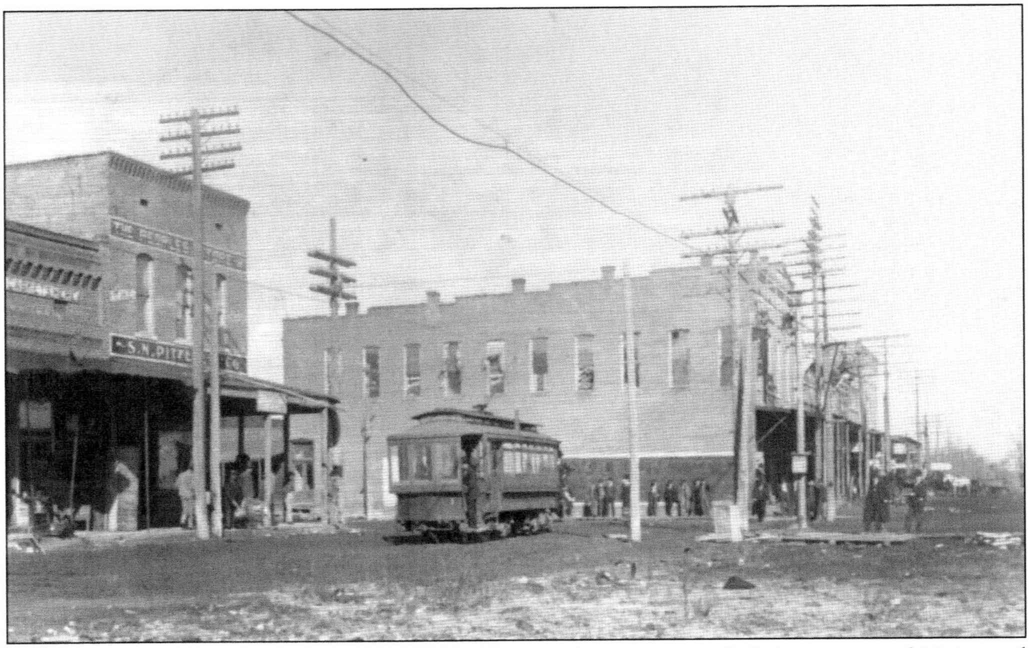

Heading south to Hoxie around 1912, the streetcar has just rounded the corner of Main and Southwest Front Streets. The two buildings on the left were a general store and warehouse owned by S.N. Pitzele and Company. Namesake S.N. Pitzele was struck by a train and killed in 1902 while walking from his home to his store. The store kept his name until it was destroyed by fire in January 1931. (AHC.)

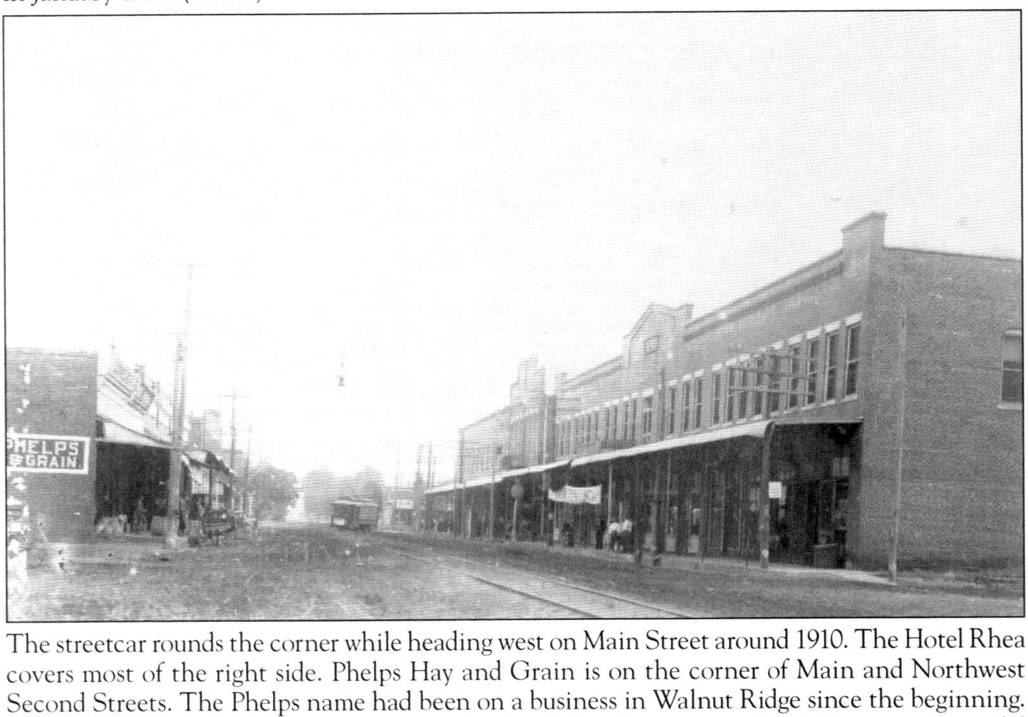

The streetcar rounds the corner while heading west on Main Street around 1910. The Hotel Rhea covers most of the right side. Phelps Hay and Grain is on the corner of Main and Northwest Second Streets. The Phelps name had been on a business in Walnut Ridge since the beginning. Zacheus Phelps started a general store in 1876 with his three sons, who all became successful businessmen and leaders of the town. (JBW.)

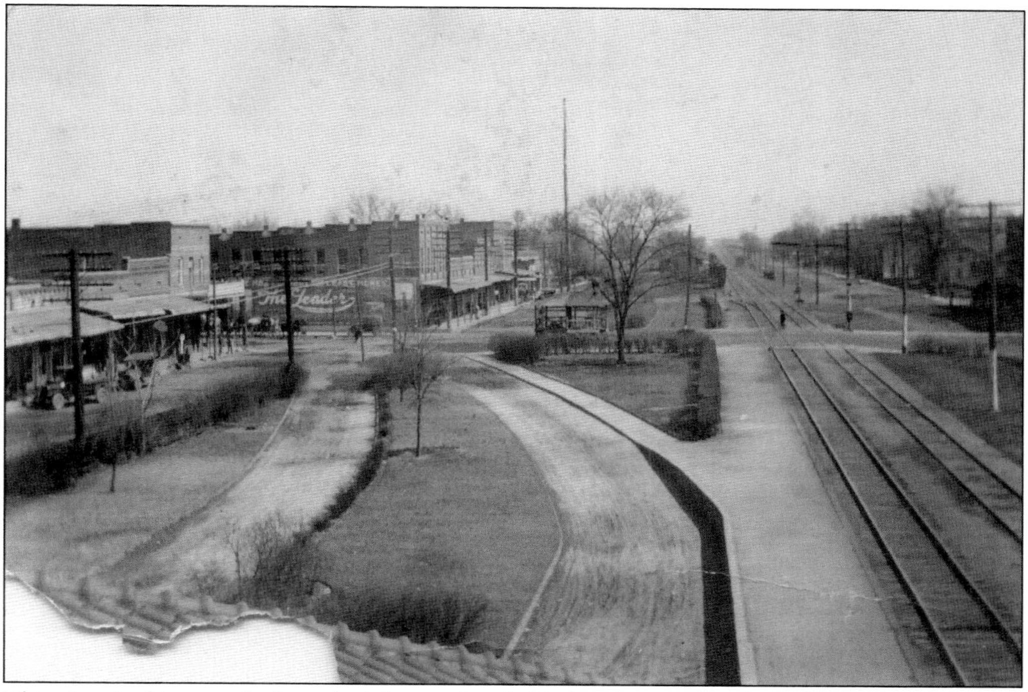

This view, looking north along the Missouri Pacific Railroad, was taken from the roof of the Walnut Ridge depot, its clay tiles visible at the bottom. A gazebo sits in the middle of Main Street. North of the gazebo, along the tracks, is the old freight depot. This depot, at the intersection of Hazel Street, is the location of the first depot in Walnut Ridge, cleared by W.M. Ponder. (JCW.)

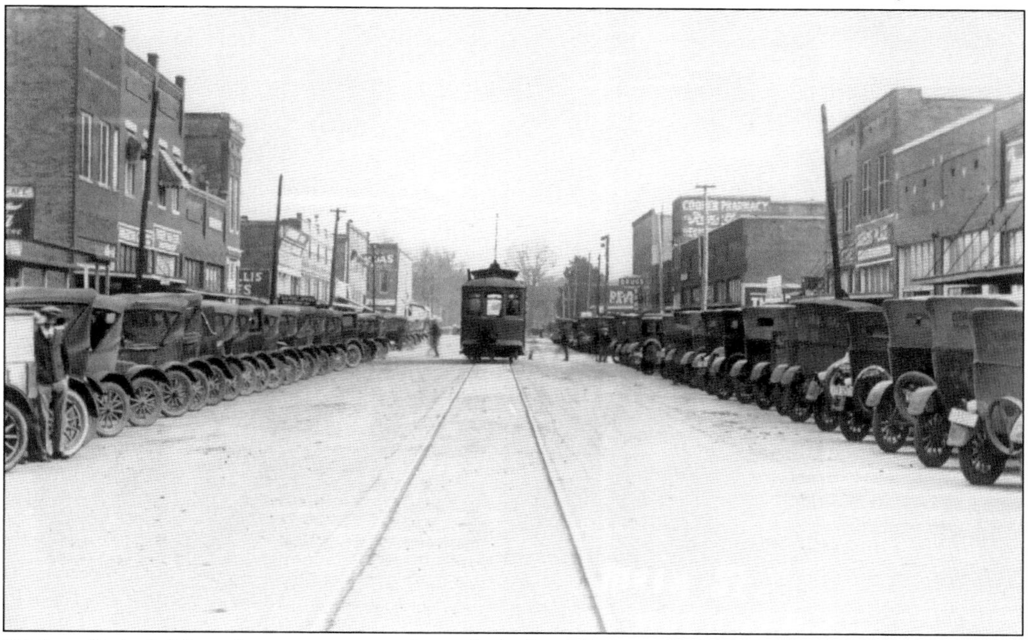

Walnut Ridge's Main Street was quite the sight before the Great Depression. At least 50 Model Ts line both sides of the road in 1926. The streetcar is sitting at the intersection of West Main and Second Street (now Abbey Road) to let passengers on and off. The streetcar ran on electricity; a wire is visible above the streetcar in this picture. (JMS.)

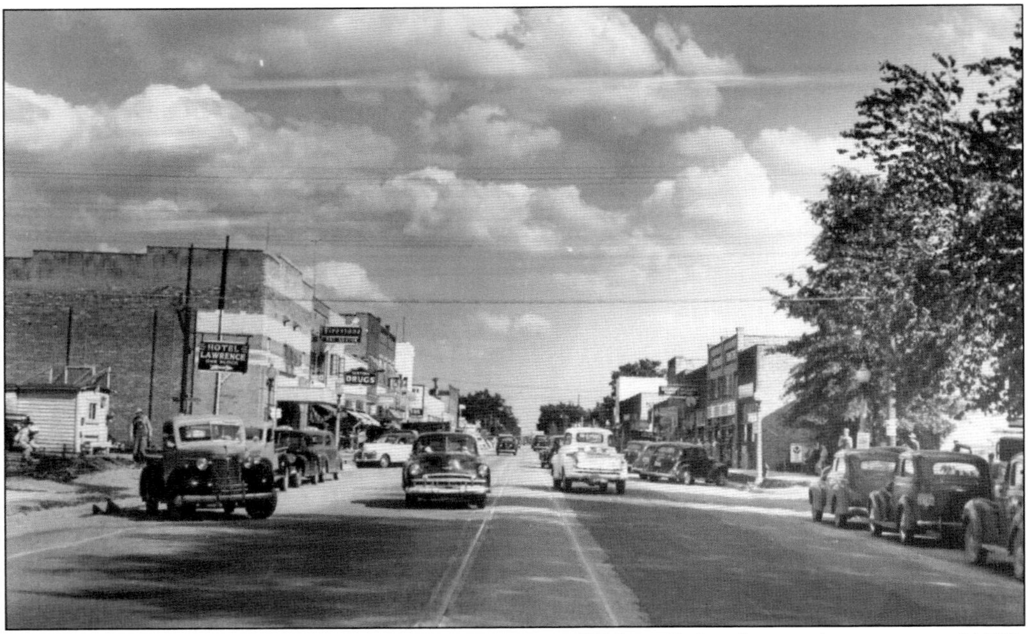

The streetcar tracks are still visible on Main Street in Walnut Ridge during the summer of 1950, but the service had been discontinued since the late 1920s. In its place, several taxicabs are lined up in front of the Sharum Theater on the left. B B Cab Company was owned by Bunk Hodge and Ben Dickerson, and the small white building was their cab office. (BS.)

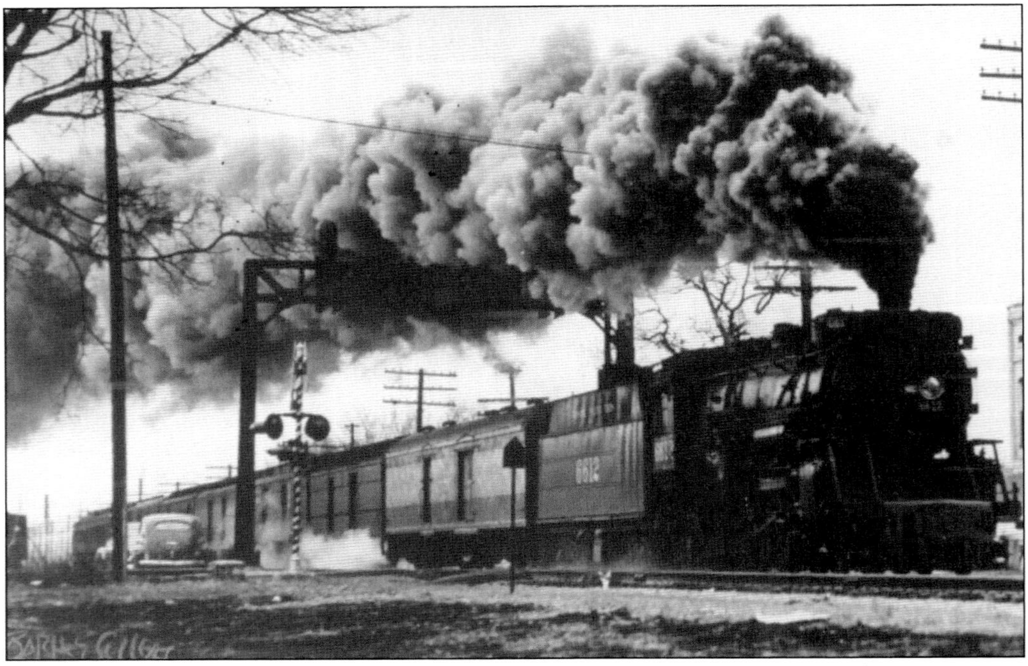

A Missouri Pacific locomotive steams south through Walnut Ridge in 1948 at the Main Street crossing. This may have been one of the last of its kind to regularly pass through, as steam engines were replaced that same year by streamlined diesel locomotives. This picture, taken by Barney Sellers, was later used as part of a limited edition painting, in which it was superimposed in front of the Iron Mountain Depot, while heading north. (BS.)

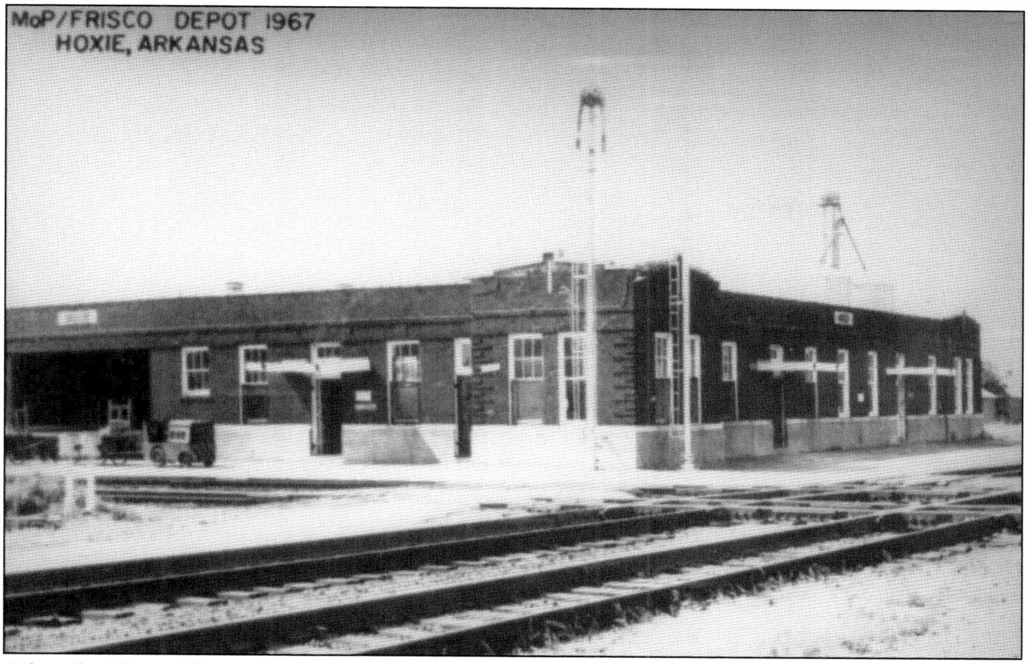

After the Hoxie Union Station burned in 1924, a larger brick depot was built to service the Missouri Pacific and Frisco railroads. Shown in this photograph from the 1960s is the third and final depot to serve Hoxie in this same spot. Passenger service was discontinued shortly thereafter, and the depot was demolished in the early 1970s. (JBW.)

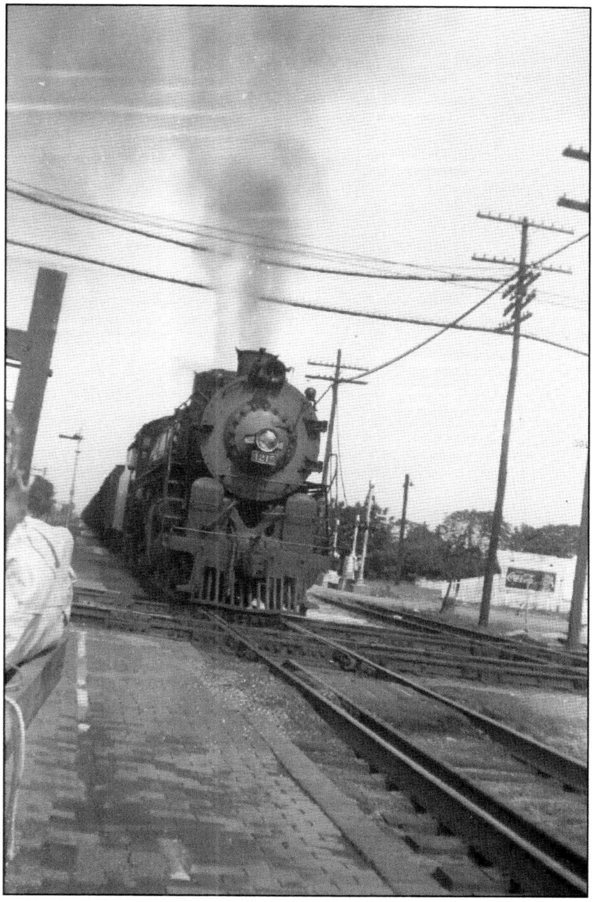

This Frisco locomotive is heading east at the intersection of the Missouri Pacific Railroad at Hoxie in this 1937 photograph. At left, bags are waiting on a cart outside the depot. A Coca-Cola billboard adorns a fence next to Warner's Drug Store on the right. Behind the picket fence was Lucian Warner's private tennis court, illuminated at night by the light pole between the locomotive and the fence. (SB.)

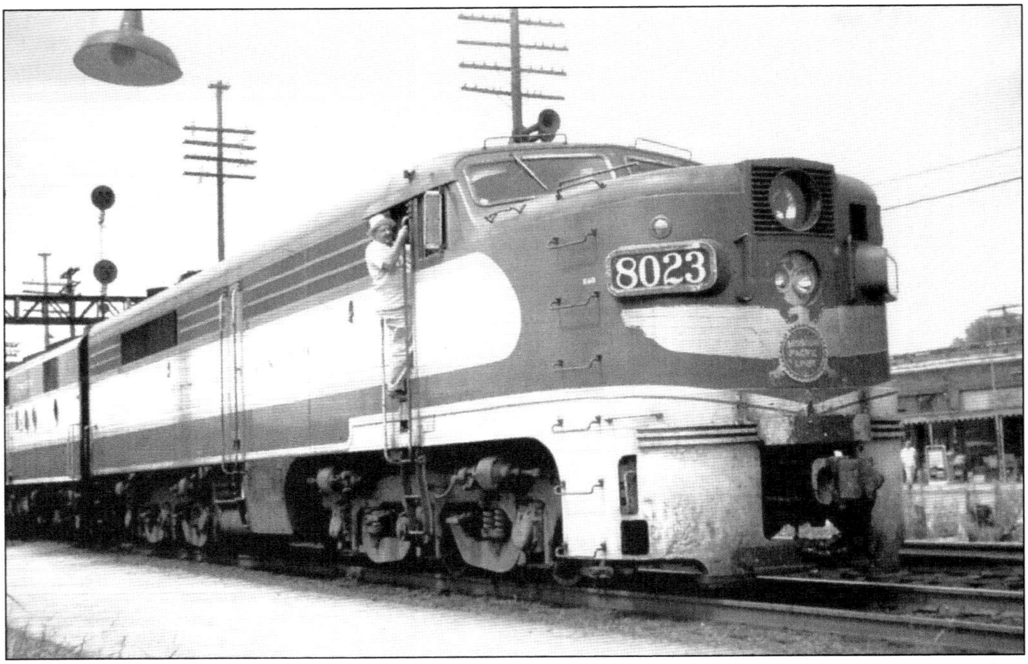

The Missouri Pacific Railroad wanted a symbol for its new streamlined diesel locomotives that represented "speed and bright modernness." The Screaming Eagles series answered that wish. Superseding the old Sunshine Special in 1948, the Texas Eagle train made daily passenger stops in Hoxie until replaced by Amtrak in 1971. The Texas Eagle is seen here on a stop in Hoxie in 1960. Sears Drugs and the post office are in the background. (MPHS.)

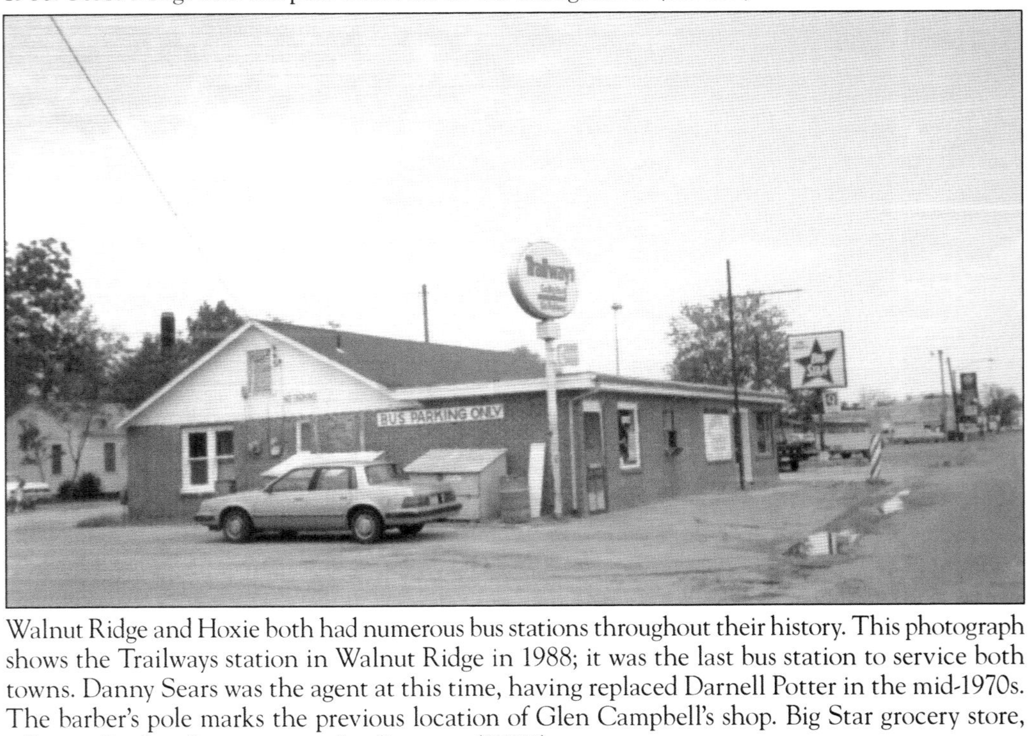

Walnut Ridge and Hoxie both had numerous bus stations throughout their history. This photograph shows the Trailways station in Walnut Ridge in 1988; it was the last bus station to service both towns. Danny Sears was the agent at this time, having replaced Darnell Potter in the mid-1970s. The barber's pole marks the previous location of Glen Campbell's shop. Big Star grocery store, offering Quality Stamps, is in the distance. (JCW.)

Four

EDUCATION

When Walnut Ridge was founded, there was no law that mandated school attendance. Schools at that time were supported by tuition fees and other private funds. This changed after Reconstruction, when Arkansas adopted its current constitution in 1874. It contained a mandate for "a general, suitable, and efficient system of free schools, whereby all persons in the state between ages of six and twenty-one may receive gratuitous education." In order to support the new free schools, a highly unpopular two-mill property tax was initiated statewide.

Founded in 1874, Walnut Ridge grew quickly and the leaders determined a school was needed in town. In 1878, Walnut Ridge School District No. 19 was formed from the Old Walnut Ridge School District No. 16. The location of the first school building is not known, but by 1897, the public school building was a two-story wooden structure located at Southeast Third and Elm Streets. It was replaced in 1907 with a two-story brick building on the current campus.

Hoxie School District No. 46 was established in 1887 from the Surridge School District No. 15, which was west of Hoxie on Village Creek. The location of the first building is unknown, but an old newspaper picture shows it was a log house. Soon after, a two-story redbrick building was erected at the corner of Annie and Lawrence Streets, replaced by another two-story brick building at the corner of Lawrence and Lindsey Streets in 1908 to accommodate the growing population.

In these early years, there were many small communities near Hoxie and Walnut Ridge that had their own schools. The high school students were consolidated with either Hoxie or Walnut Ridge and the grade schools, known later as wing schools, were in the original communities. By the 1960s, all of the wing schools were eliminated. Of the 80 school districts present in the county in 1900, there are only four today. Hoxie and Walnut Ridge are the only schools in eastern Lawrence County.

The schools in Hoxie and Walnut Ridge have always had strong support from the community, both in academics and athletics. The friendly rivalry between the Bobcats and the Mustangs continues to this day.

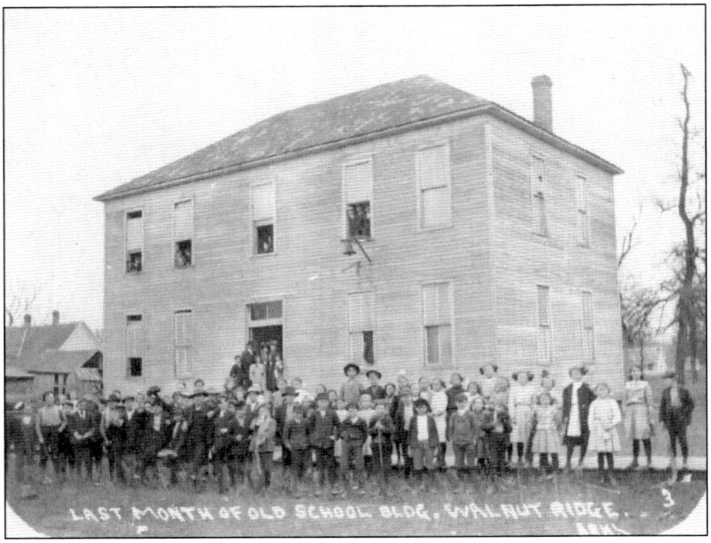

The Walnut Ridge School District was formed in 1878. Possibly its first schoolhouse is shown during the spring of 1907, the last term for this building. A wooden structure, it was located on the corner of South East Third and Elm Streets. It was on the opposite side of East Main Street from the original location of the Walnut Ridge Courthouse, where Main Street Church of Christ is today. (JMS.)

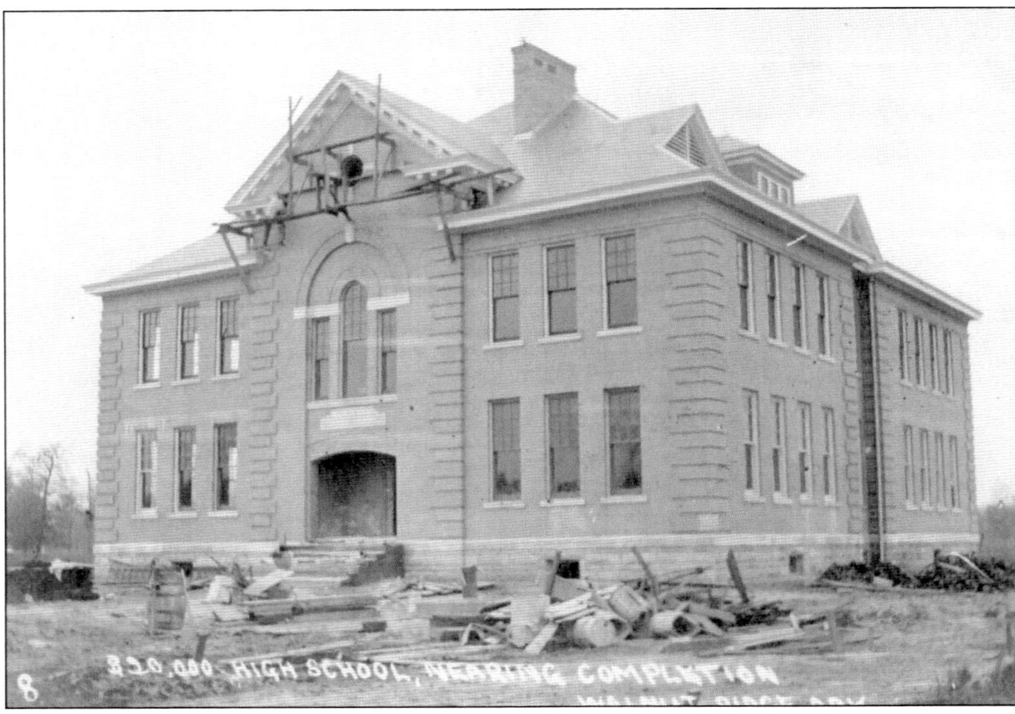

The finishing touches are being made on the new Walnut Ridge School on the same spring day in 1907. Scaffolding is visible under the front gable, and building materials are scattered around the yard. This is the first building erected on the current campus site. Students who left the old wooden building in the spring started classes here in the fall of 1907. (JBW.)

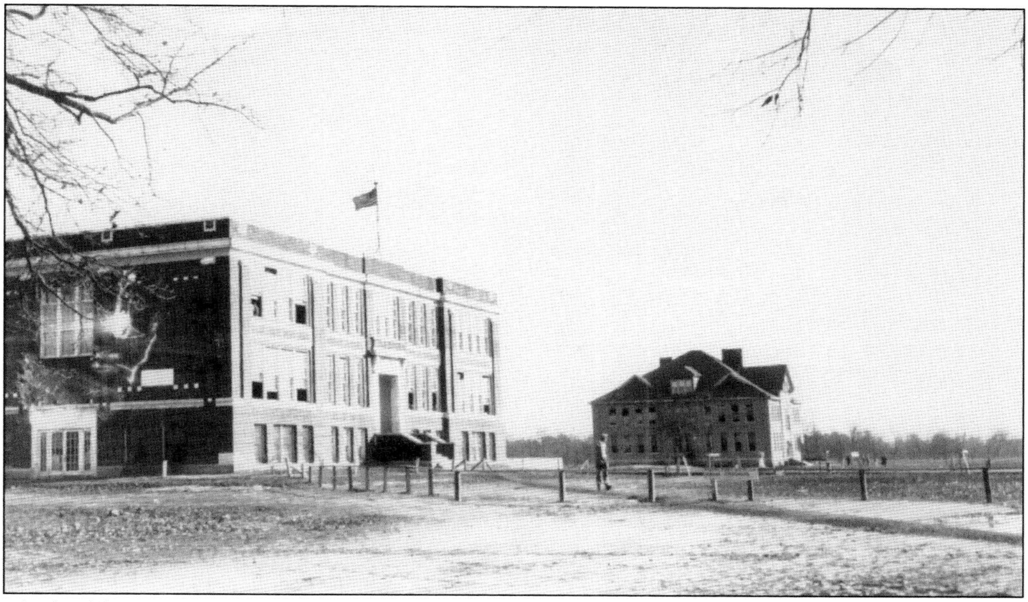

The building on the left is the second erected on the current school campus. Constructed in 1923 by the contracting firm Ring and Carty, it served as the new high school. The building in the background, constructed in 1907, then served as the grade school. Capt. J.M. Medearis delivered the dedication address, which was attended by Gov. Charles Brough. This building was destroyed by fire on December 12, 1957. (JMS.)

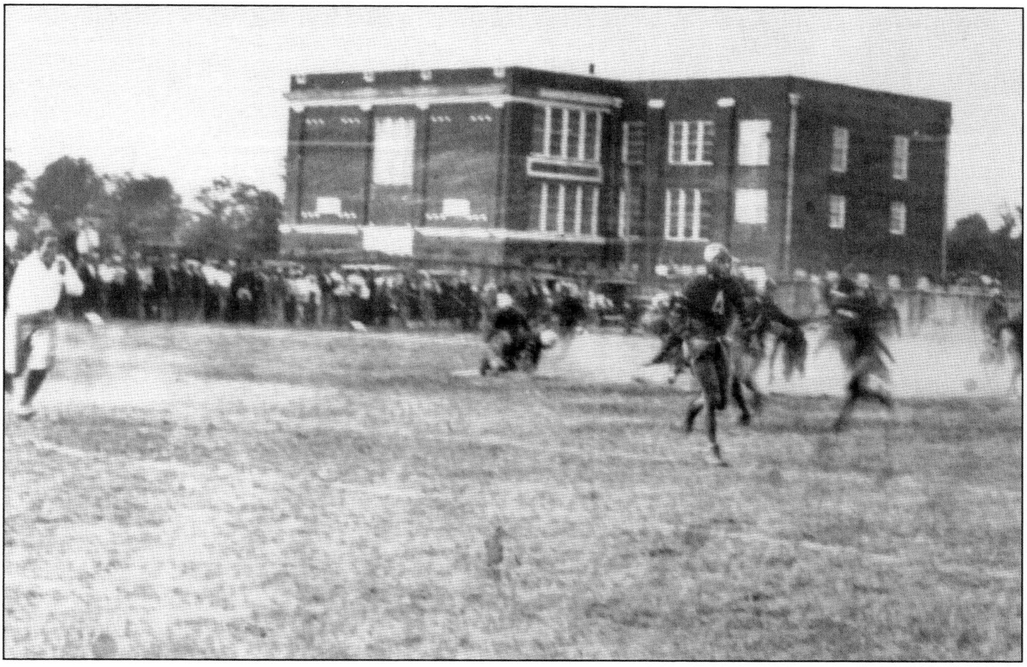

A football game is played in the 1920s at Walnut Ridge. The photograph is marked Hoxie, but the building in the background is clearly the back of the Walnut Ridge High School, leading one to believe this may be an early game between the two schools. Football was discontinued at Hoxie in 1947 to allow for a split schedule for picking cotton. The rivalry resumed in the fall of 1969. (LCHS.)

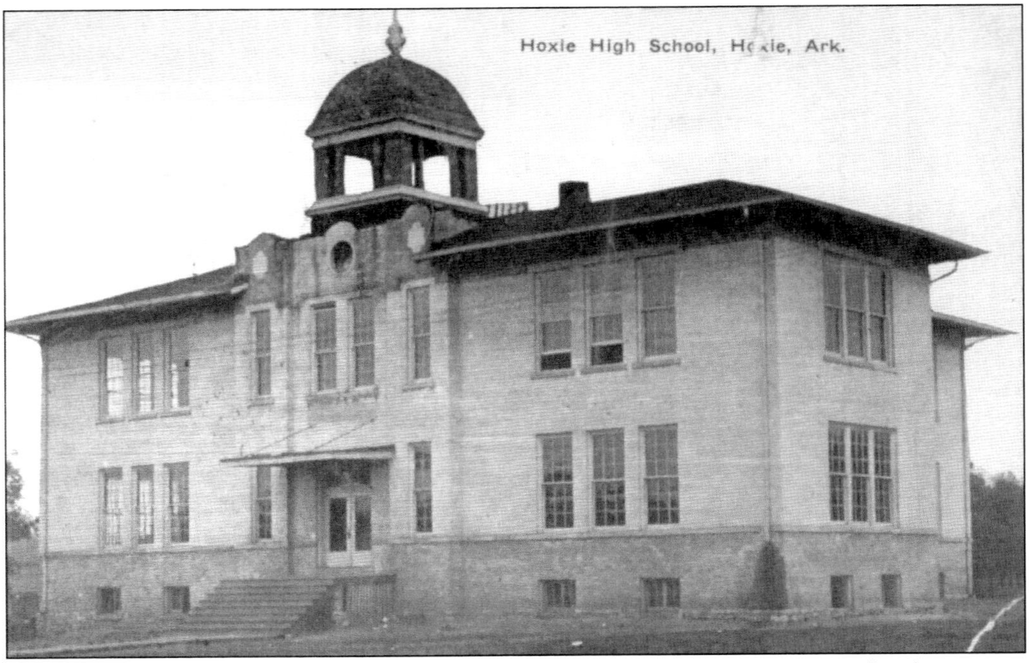

The Hoxie School District was formed in 1887. Its first building was a two-story redbrick structure located at the corner of Annie and Lawrence Streets, which was shared with the Methodist church. In 1908, a new school building, pictured here, was erected at the corner of Lindsey and Lawrence Streets. It was heavily damaged by tornadoes in 1913 and 1927 and was destroyed by fire in 1941. (JBW.)

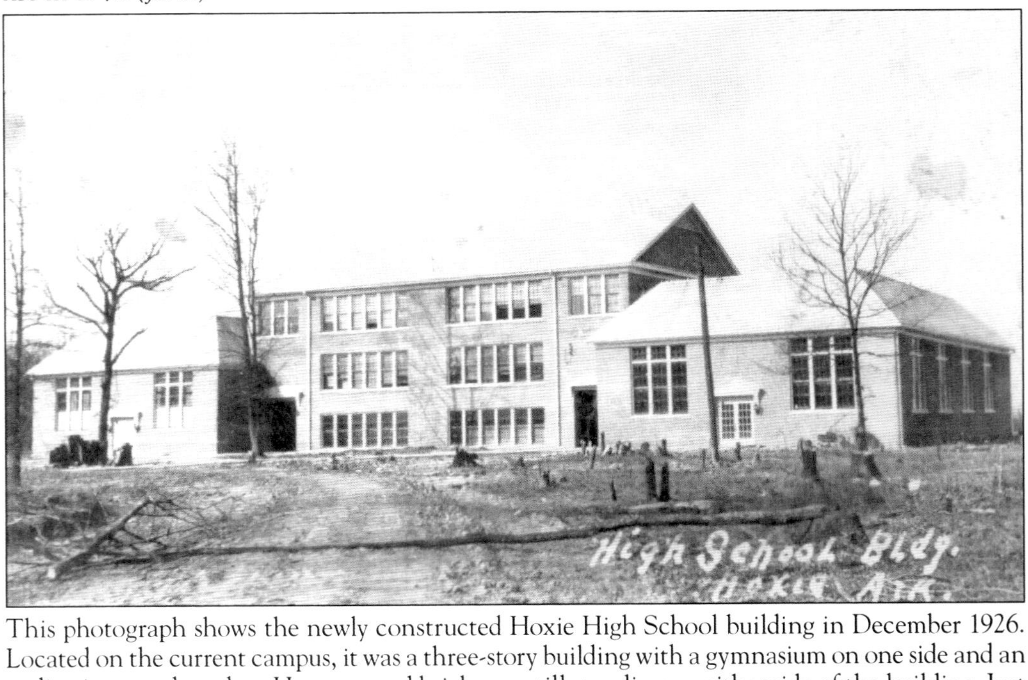

This photograph shows the newly constructed Hoxie High School building in December 1926. Located on the current campus, it was a three-story building with a gymnasium on one side and an auditorium on the other. Here, unused bricks are still standing on either side of the building. Just five months later, it was damaged by a tornado; two children were killed instantly. The structure was destroyed by fire in 1941. (JBW.)

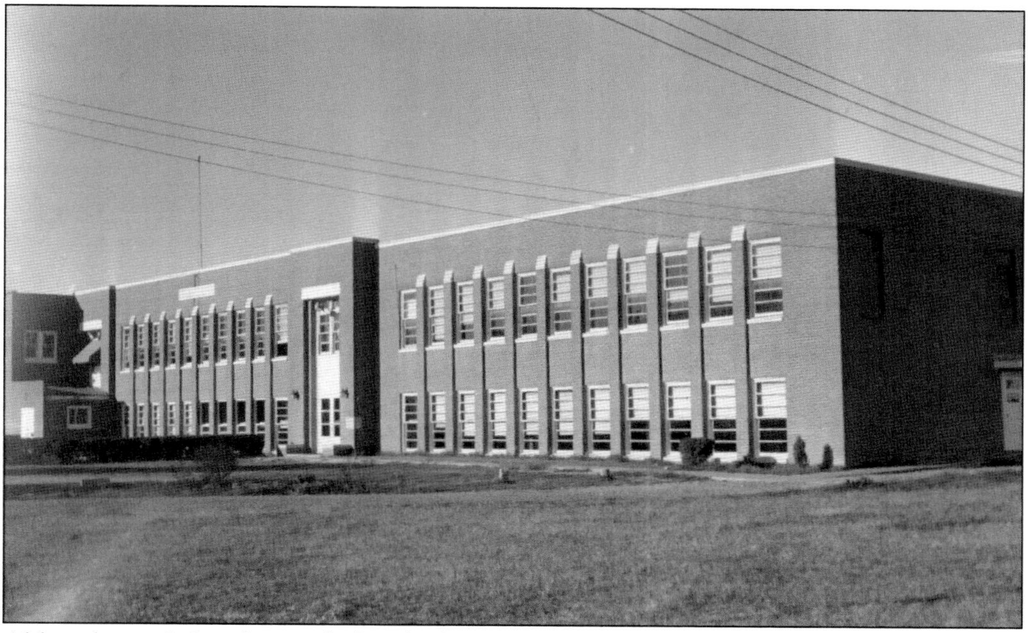

Although greatly handicapped after the fires of 1941, school continued in churches and homes. In 1943, a new high school was completed on the Hoxie campus. A year later, an adjacent gymnasium was added. Shown here during the 1955 integration, this became the junior high school building in 1971, when a new high school building was constructed. It was destroyed by fire in December 1972. (UM.)

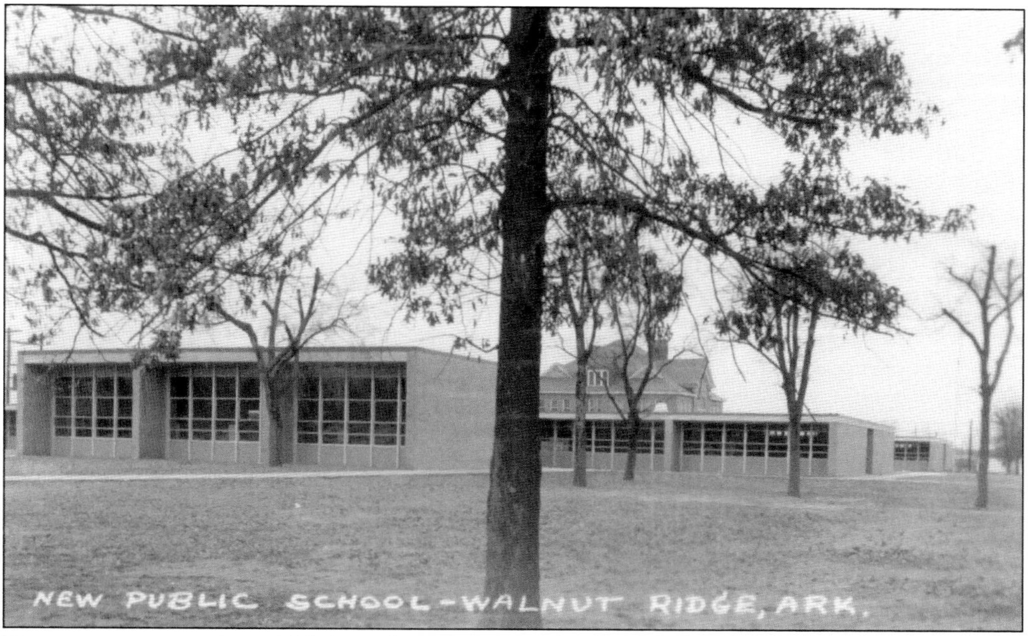

Two years, one month, and 25 days after a disastrous fire destroyed the Walnut Ridge High School in December 1957, the final two buildings of the new school were occupied. Students from the junior high were the last to move from the old grade school to the new buildings in the spring of 1960. The original two-story building, erected in 1907, looms above several wings of the new school in the background. (JBW.)

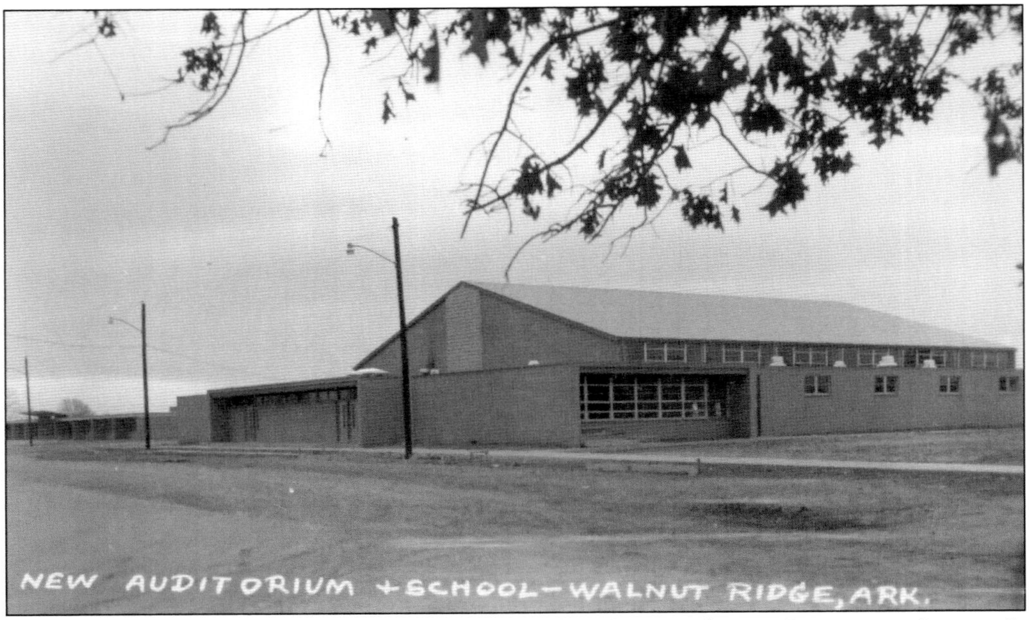

$750,000 was spent on the new school campus, including the new Sharum Gymnasium (pictured), which was the last building completed. Superintendent Van Ellis and Assistant Superintendent Rainwater moved into their new offices, located at the northeast corner of the gymnasium, in February 1960. Prior to this, they maintained an office downtown in the city hall. (JBW.)

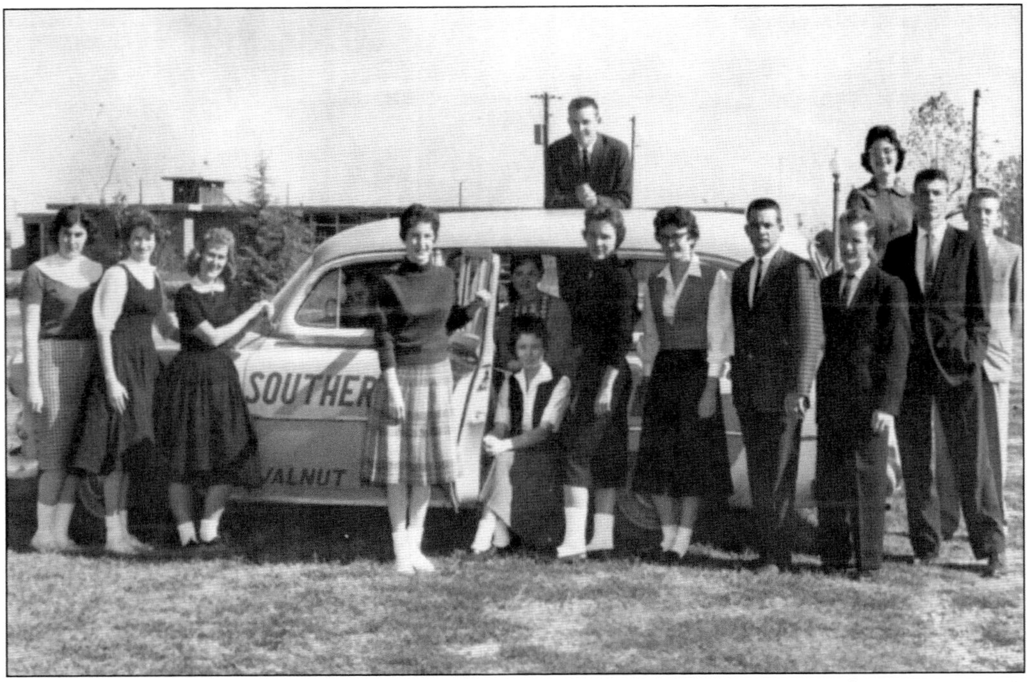

In June 1941, Dr. H.E. Williams established Southern Baptist College in Pocahontas. In 1946, a portion of the school burned, and Williams petitioned the City of Walnut Ridge to use 122 acres on the recently acquired Army airfield, which included 157 apartment units and six other buildings. Walnut Ridge granted the request for land in May 1946, and it has been the college's home ever since. (WBC.)

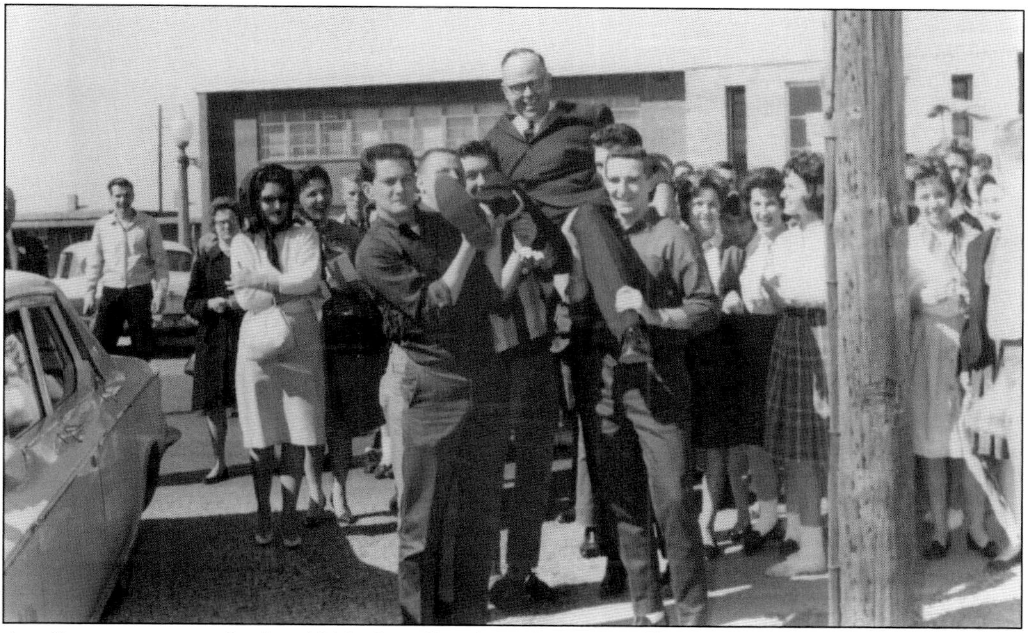

A milestone was reached in 1948 when Southern Baptist College was included in the budget for the Arkansas Baptist State Convention, which later officially adopted the school. By 1962, the college was accredited by the North Central Association. Students and faculty celebrate this second milestone by hoisting Dr. H.E. Williams on their shoulders. The university was renamed Williams Baptist College in 1991 in honor of its founder. (WBC.)

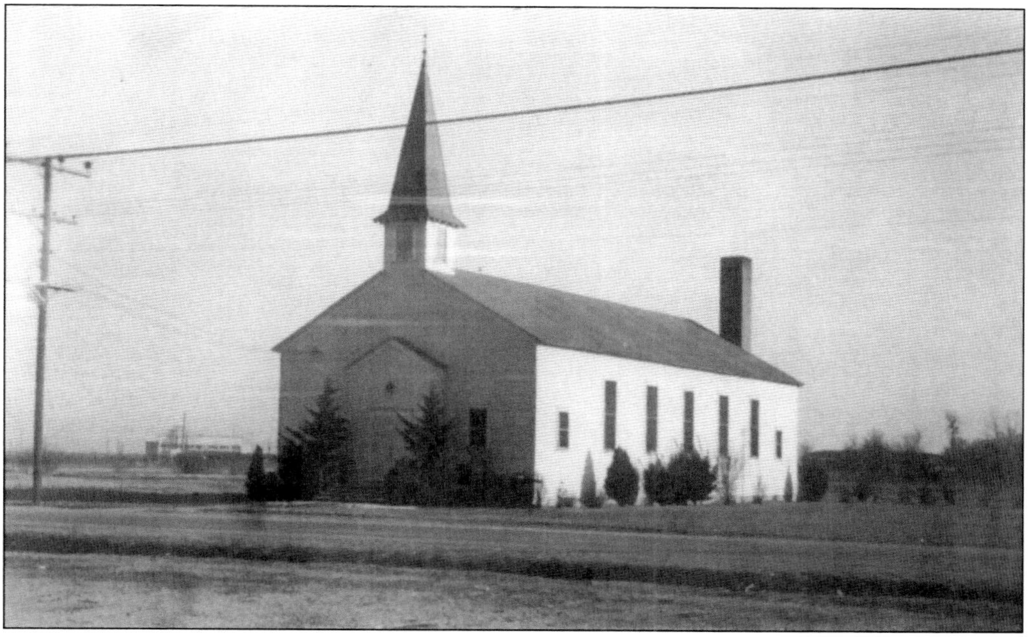

Built in 1942 at the Walnut Ridge Army Air Field, this white wooden chapel served as a place of worship for air cadets and soldiers stationed here during World War II. After becoming the home of Southern Baptist College, the chapel was moved to its current site on Fulbright Avenue next to the library and updated with a brick facade. It is now used for theater performances and lectures. (WBC.)

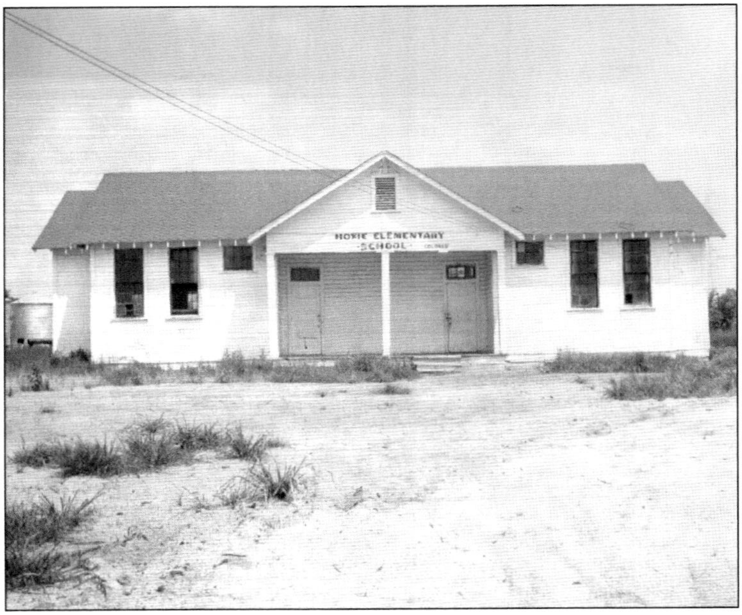

One of the first black schools in Hoxie was located in the southern part of town on Pecan Street. Later, the old Whittaker School building was moved near Highway 63, east of the Missouri Pacific Railroad tracks for use as a grade school. The grade school had outdoor toilets, wood-burning stoves, a leaking roof, and no running water. High school students were sent 30 minutes away to Jonesboro. (UM.)

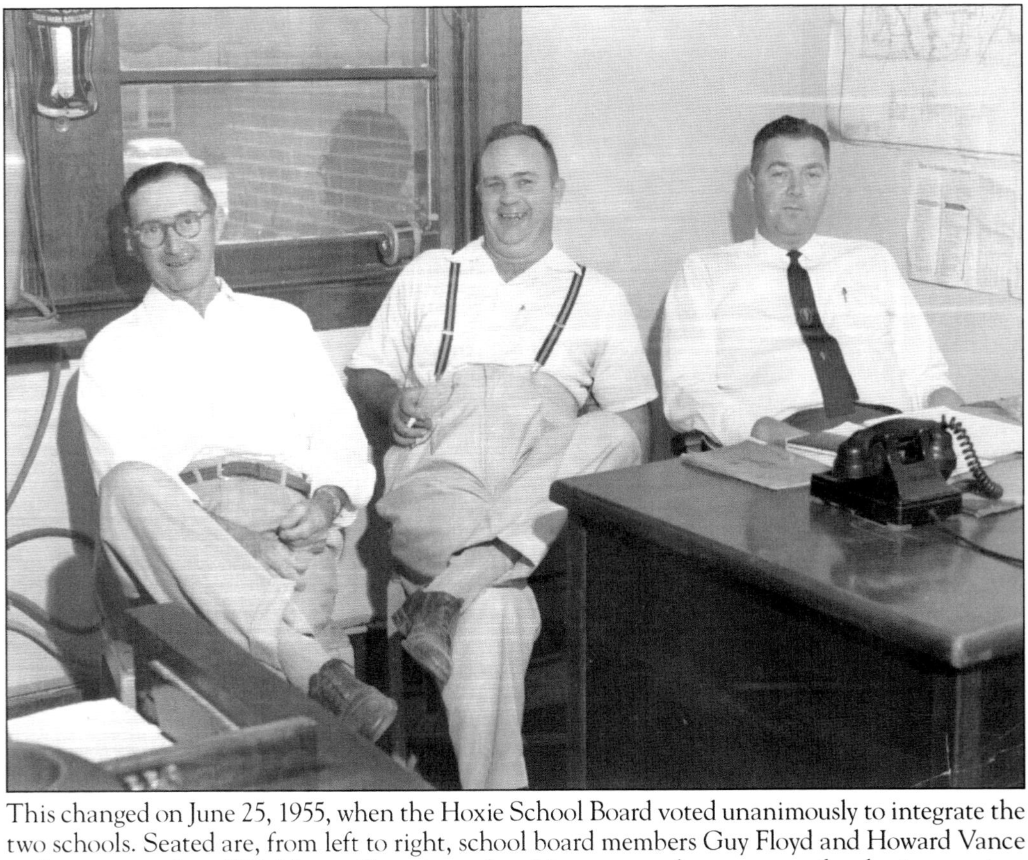

This changed on June 25, 1955, when the Hoxie School Board voted unanimously to integrate the two schools. Seated are, from left to right, school board members Guy Floyd and Howard Vance and superintendent K.E. Vance. Superintendent Vance gave three reasons for the integration: it was right in the sight of God, it obeyed the law, and it was less expensive for the district than bussing students to Jonesboro. (UM.)

Twenty-five black students peaceably entered Hoxie School on July 11, 1955, and the day's events were recorded by photographers from *Life* magazine. Joyce Green, a third-grade teacher, is shown teaching reading to Louis Ruffin (left) and Bobby Ruffin (right) during one of the first days of integration. When the *Life* publication arrived on shelves two weeks later, it raised the ire of outside segregationists, who descended upon Hoxie in force. (UM.)

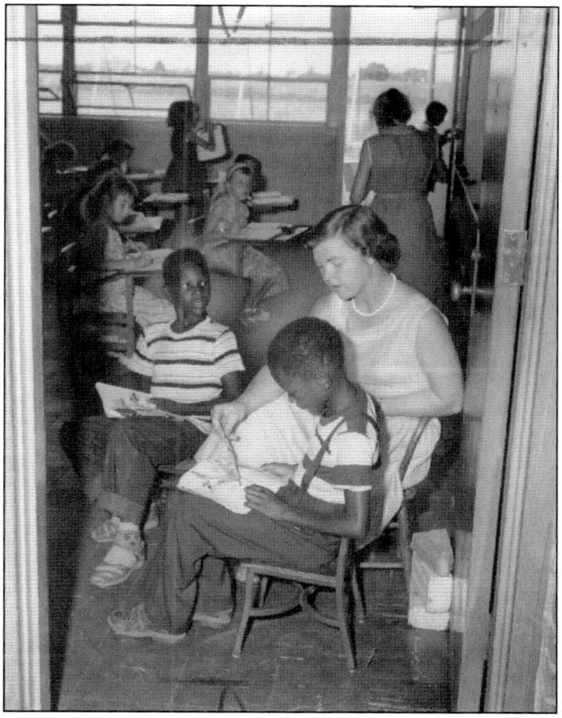

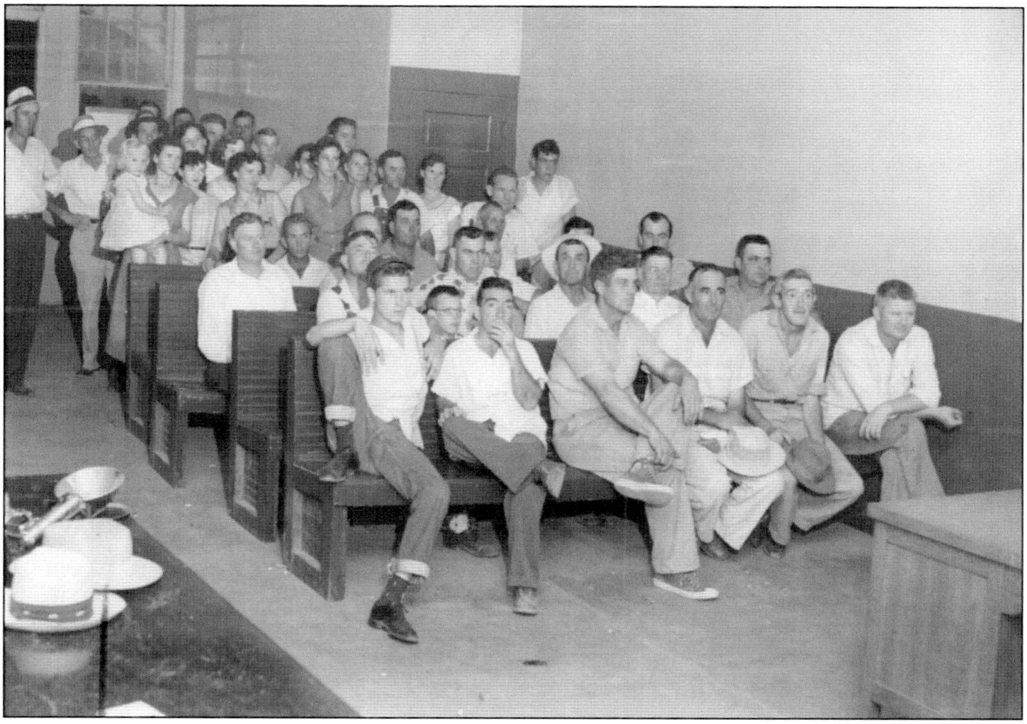

A local segregationist group quickly formed and called for boycotting Hoxie School. On August 9, 1955, this group presented a petition to the school board requesting a reversal in integration. On August 15, 1955, Hoxie citizens are shown in the city hall awaiting the decision of the school board. A courier was later sent, informing citizens of the petition's rejection. (UM.)

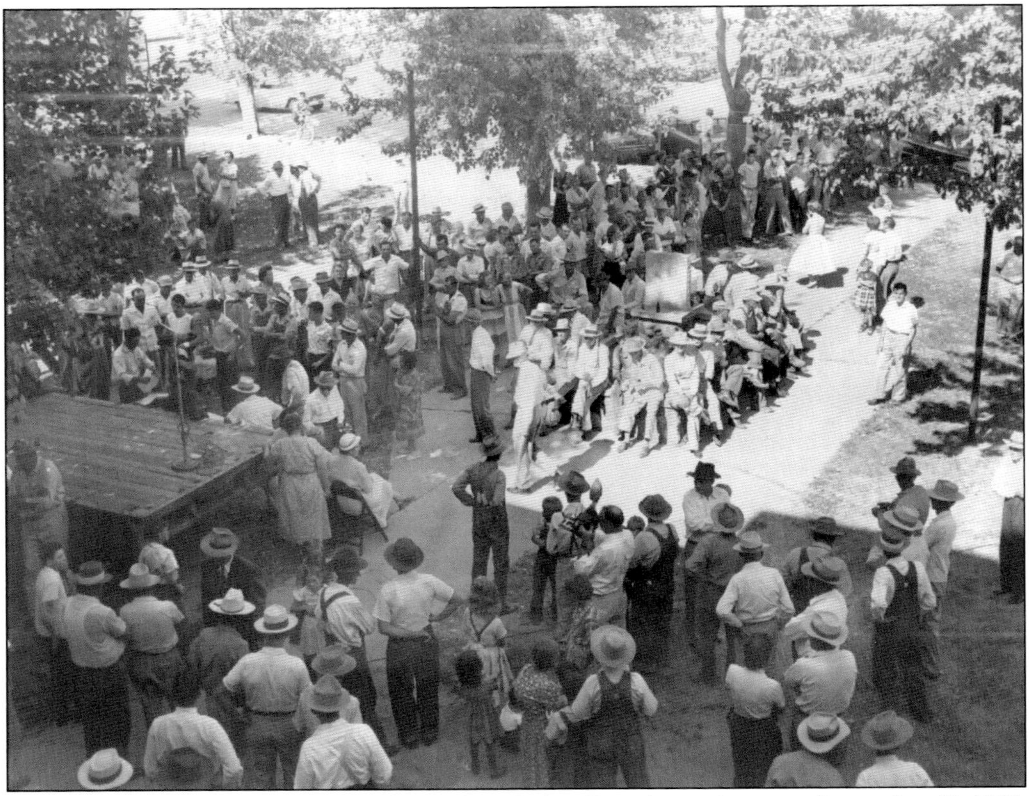

A segregationist rally was held on the Walnut Ridge Courthouse lawn on September 17, 1955, with hundreds in attendance. Afterward, school board members and parents were intimidated so badly that school attendance declined by 50 percent. The school board filed suit against the Hoxie segregationist group, asking for a restraining order to keep members from interfering with the integration. After several hearings, a federal judged ruled in favor of the school board in January 1956. (UM.)

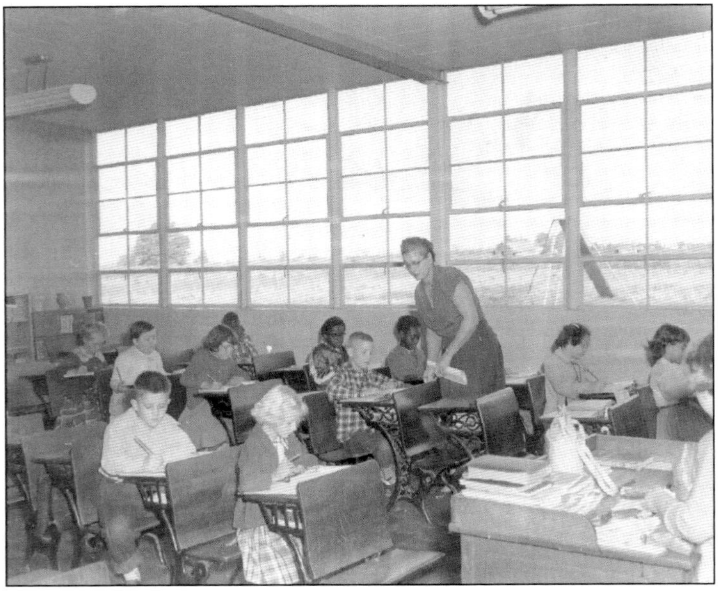

In October 1956, the Hoxie segregationist group lost its appeal, ending the fight. Two schools in Arkansas had integrated without incident prior to Hoxie, but Hoxie was the first successfully contested integration in the state, two years prior to the more famous case at Central High in Little Rock. Vera Floyd is shown with her fourth-grade class in the fall of 1955. (UM.)

Five

AGRICULTURE

Agriculture has always been a major industry in the Walnut Ridge–Hoxie area, even before the towns were even established. The Swamp and Overflow Act of 1850, which reverted federal lands to the state to sell, brought the first land speculators and small farmers to this area. John A. Lindsey and John Arendale were two of the foremost early landowners. Lindsey and his son Asa sold land that would later become Hoxie to Henry and Mary Boas in the 1870s.

In between low swamp areas, settlers started clearing the land on the high sandy ground for farming. In the early 1900s, ditches were dredged, connecting the swamp land to natural drainage sources. This opened up for cultivation tens of thousands of acres that had previously been too swampy. Corn, hay, wheat, and cotton were raised, but cotton was the cash crop. Cotton was king in this area from the 1860s to the 1980s, when rice and soybeans became the major crops. Therefore, cotton gins have been part of Walnut Ridge and Hoxie since the beginning. Though sawmilling was the major initial industry, when the forest was depleted, the cotton industry became the leading commerce, with Phoenix Cotton Oil Company and the Federal Compress.

Rice was first grown north of Walnut Ridge in 1909 by S.C. Dowell but did not become popular until after World War II. John and Raymond Recker, Robert Smith, and Martin Whitlow were some of the early rice growers in the 1940s. Allotments on rice limited the number of farmers who could grow it, but in 1973, the allotments were lifted and any farmer could raise as much as he wished.

Some early farm equipment dealers in Walnut Ridge were the Graff brothers in the 1890s, who were agents for well-known farm equipment companies. In the 1930s, the Baltz family started the Lawrence County Implement Company, which carried the International Harvester brand. Robert Smith Sr. and Earl Smith owned the John Deere dealership starting in the 1940s, and C.W. Rose owned the Allis-Chalmers dealership, selling tractors and farm supplies. In Hoxie, Cox Implement sold Massey Ferguson equipment.

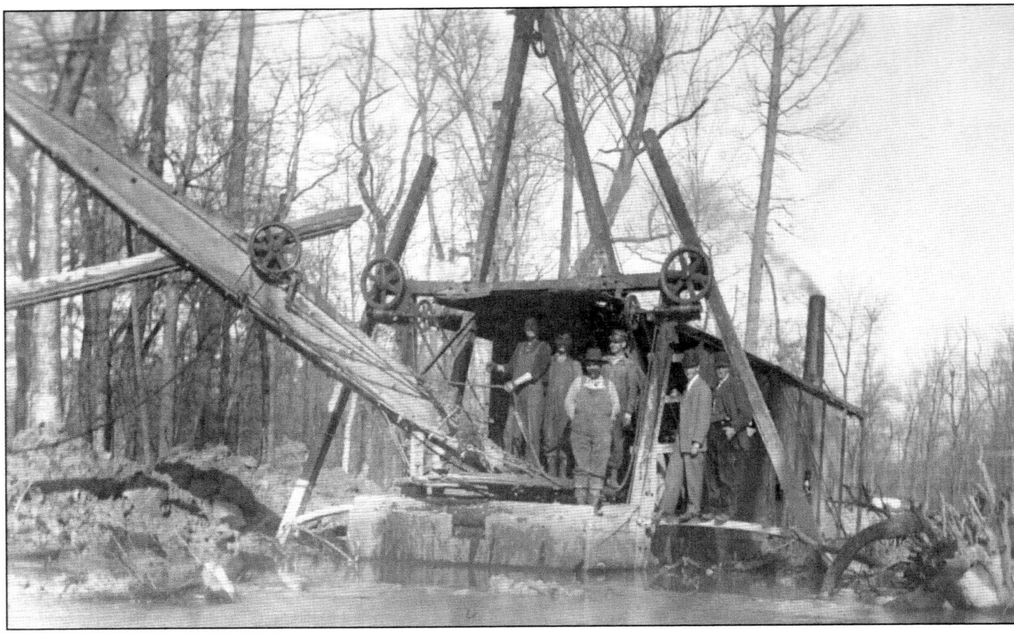

The eastern half of Lawrence County was practically unsettled prior to 1870, due to swampy conditions. In the early 1900s, over 41 miles of ditches were dredged. Suddenly, 50,000 acres of farmland once considered too low for cultivation held the garden spot of the county. A.C. Miller, second from right, was vice president of the National Drainage Company. He poses with a dredge boat crew in Hoxie in 1912. (JBW.)

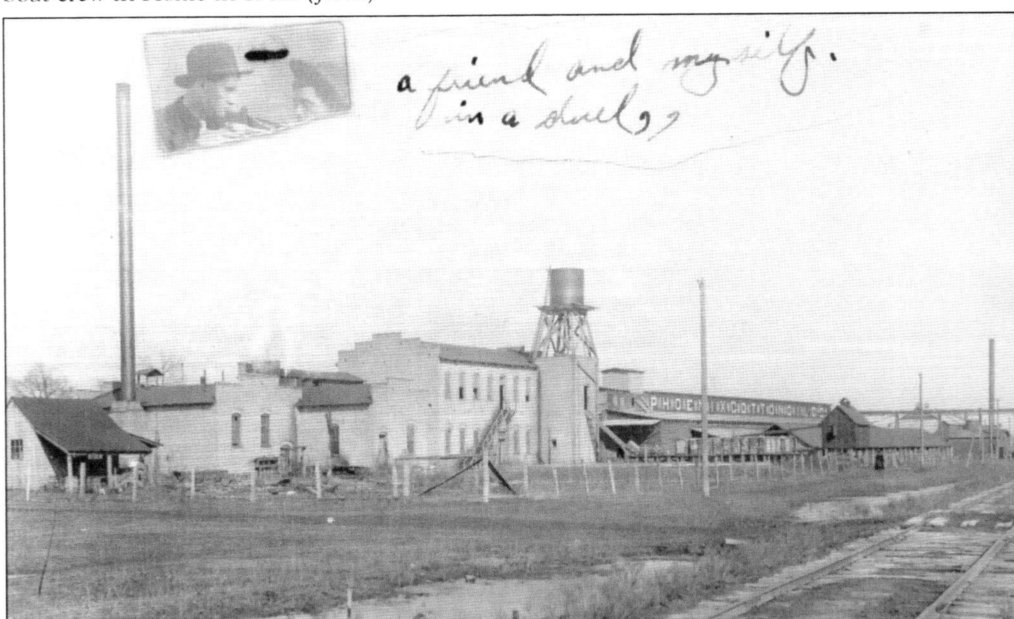

The Phoenix cotton gin was the largest in Walnut Ridge. The gin, with the Phoenix Cotton Oil Company, stretched three blocks from Elm Street to Free Street along the west side of the Hoxie, Pocahontas & Northern Railroad tracks, visible on the far right. This view from the south shows the oil company on the left, the seed house in the middle, and the cotton gin on the far right. (JBW.)

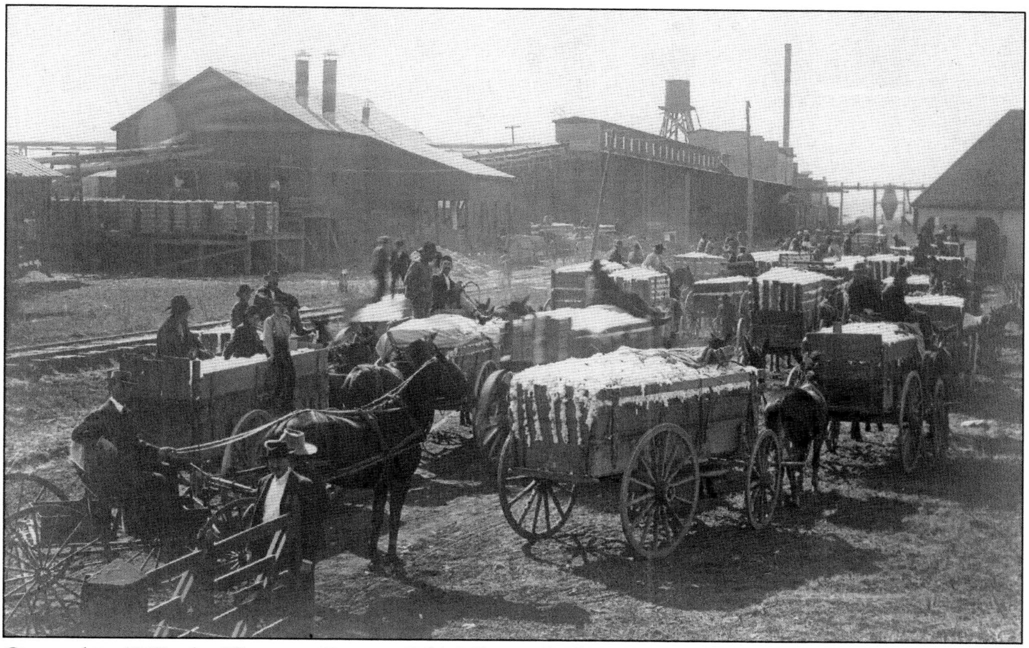

Opened in 1903, the Phoenix Cotton Oil Mill was the largest institution built in Walnut Ridge to this point. Based in Memphis, Tennessee, it provided well-paying jobs year-round, not just during cotton season. Housing was constructed on-site to accommodate black workers. This view from the north shows cotton wagons lined up near the gin. The water tower and chimney of the oil mill are in the distance. (JBW.)

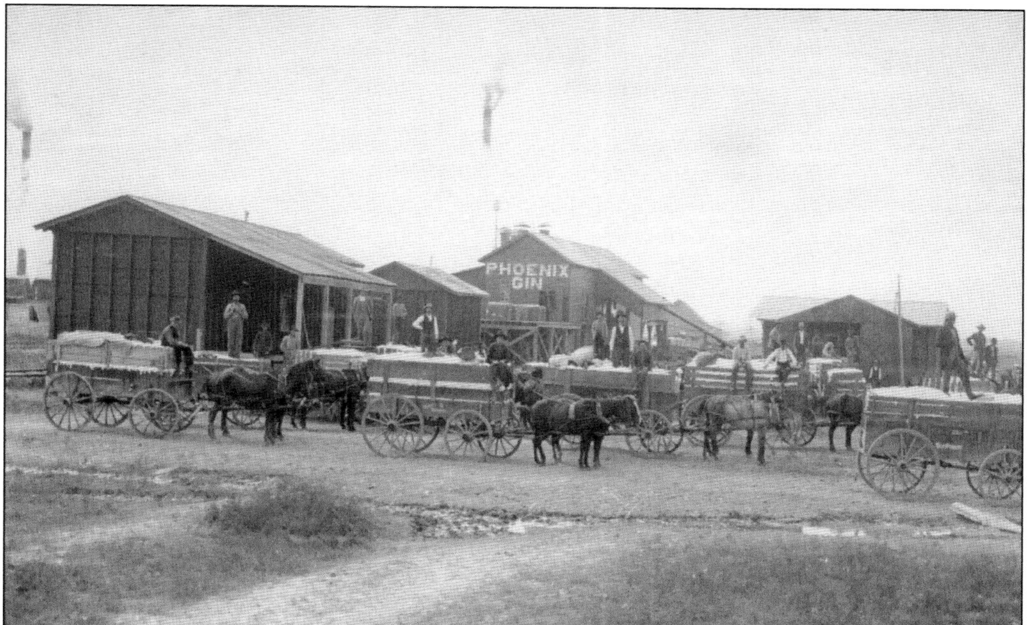

This view shows a close-up of only the Phoenix cotton gin. Wagons stamped with owner names are full of cotton, while farmhands pose for the camera. With the Hoxie Iron Mountain Railroad shops and roundhouse constructed at the same time as the huge Phoenix cotton complex, both towns experienced the largest economic and population gain in their histories. (JMS.)

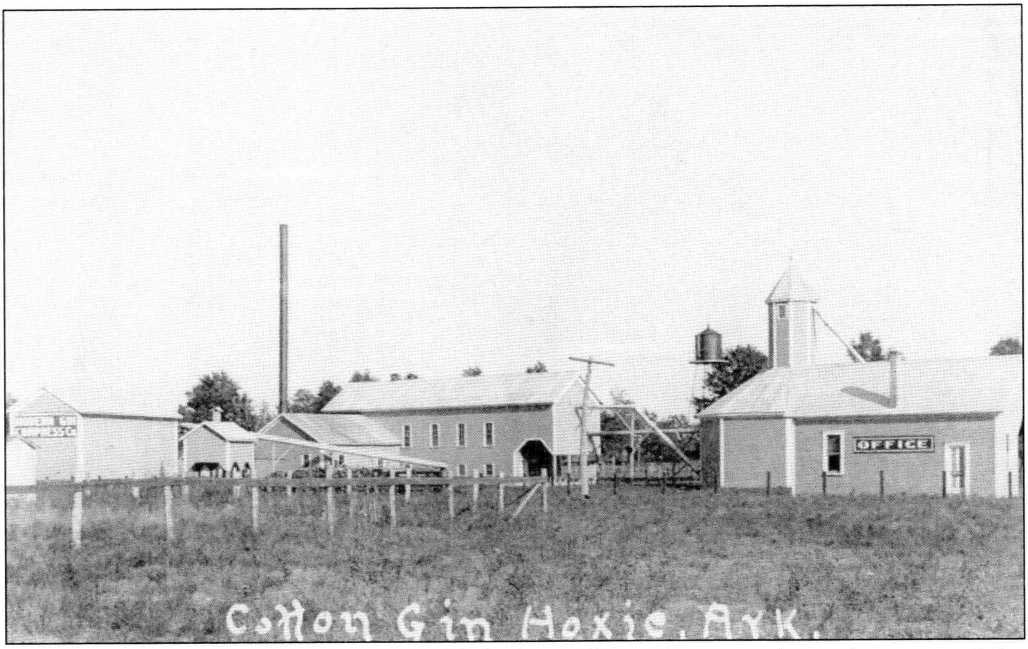

Modern Cotton Gin and Compress, established in 1909 in Hoxie, was located just east of the Union Station Depot, where Southeast Second Street dead-ends into the Frisco tracks. Located adjacent to the railroad spur that connected the Iron Mountain to the Frisco, the business was in the perfect place to ship compressed bales of cotton in any direction. By 1928, the cotton gin was no longer there. (JBW.)

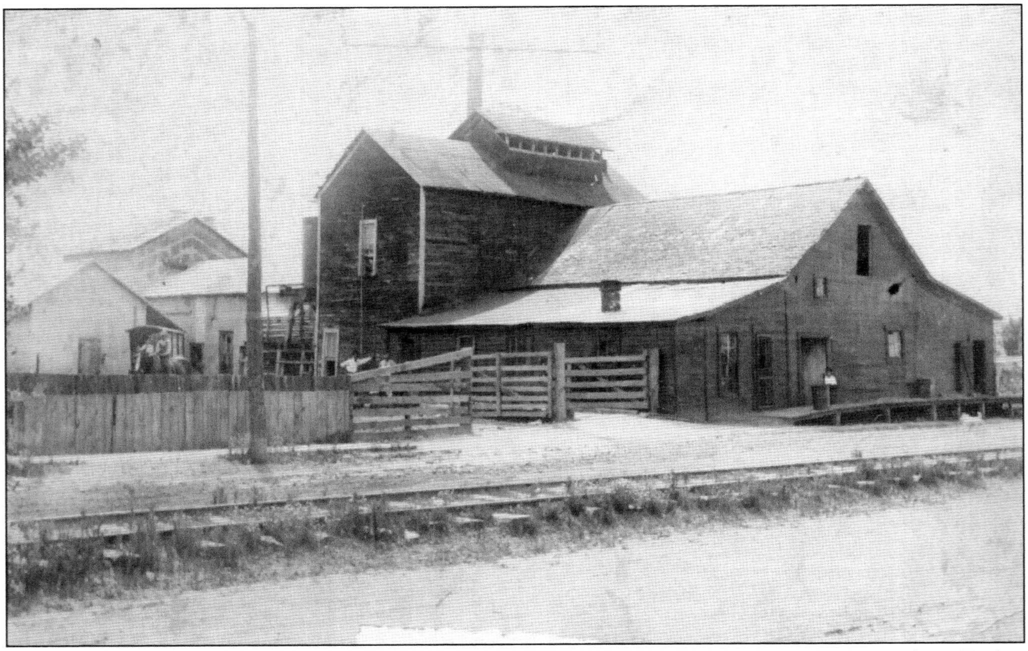

In 1901, W.R. Lane bought land next to the Frisco Railway along Main Street in Walnut Ridge and built the Crystal Ice House and Distillery. By 1908, a cotton gin was added here. This picture shows the icehouse in the foreground, with streetcar tracks visible in front. A wagon with "Crystal Ice" stenciled on the side is in the background, in front of the cotton gin. (BLB.)

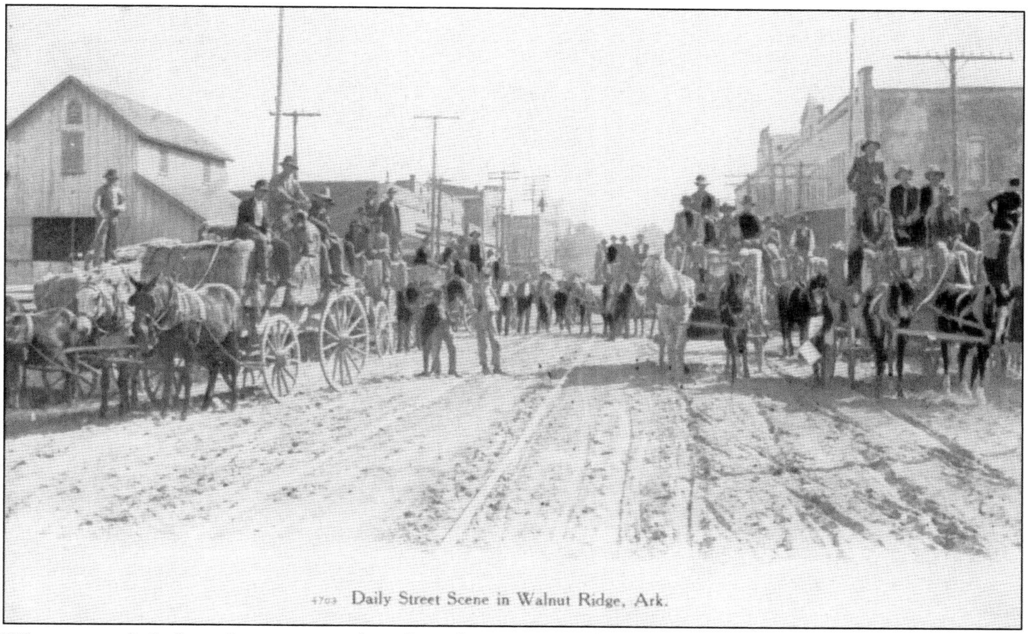

Wagons with bales of cotton are lined up facing west along Main Street around 1907, with the streetcar tracks barely visible in the dirt surface. The Hotel Rhea can be seen in the background on the right. The white building on the left sits at the location of the first steam gin in Lawrence County, built by W.M. Ponder. It was located where First National Bank sits today. (JCW.)

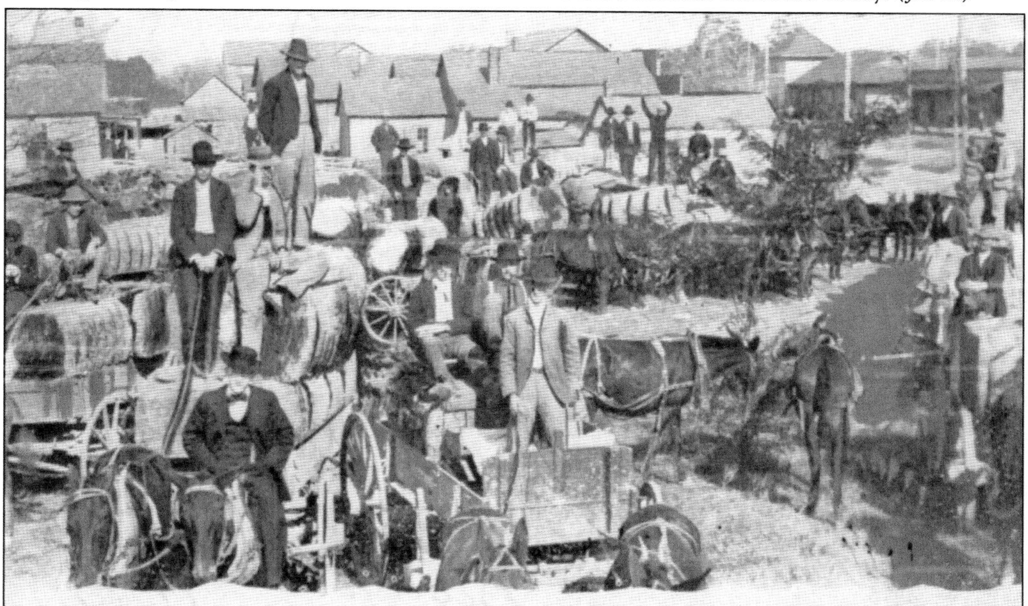

This picture in Hoxie was taken the same day. The white wooden buildings in the background are businesses along Texas Street between Memphis and Case Streets. The wagons are located near where the post office is today. The two buildings in the top right corner are Union Station and the Van Noy restaurant. By 1914, all the wooden buildings had been replaced with brick ones. (JBW.)

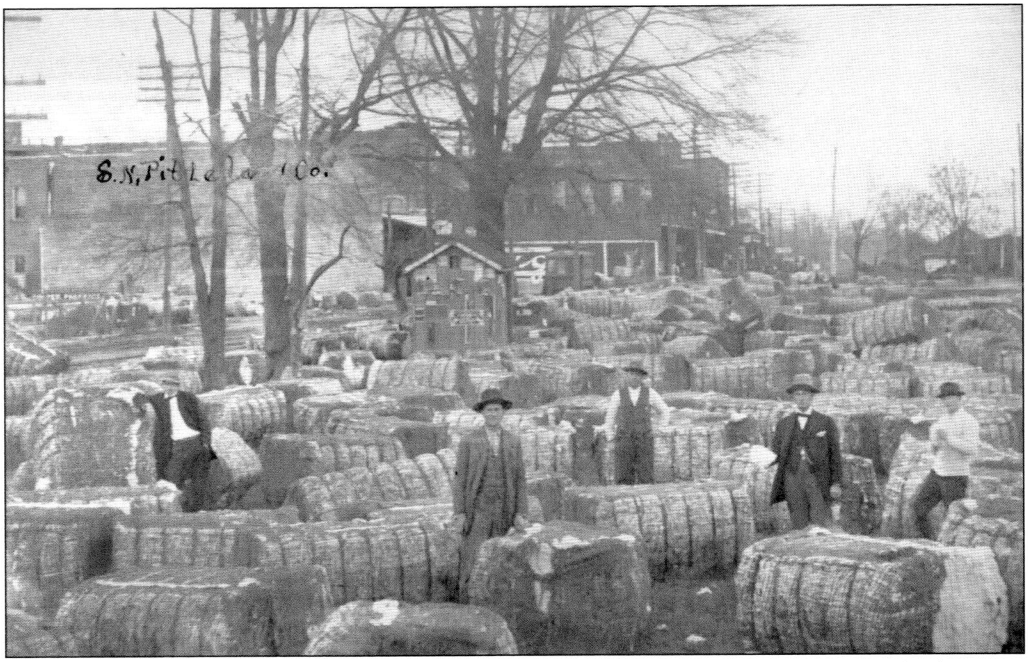

Some of the most impressive street scenes in early times are those surrounding the harvest. Taken in November 1908, these 700 bales of cotton awaited shipment in the front yard of the Iron Mountain Depot, which had just been built the same year to replace the old Iron Mountain Hotel. Visible in the background is the Hoxie and Walnut Ridge streetcar rounding Main Street and heading toward Hoxie. (JBW.)

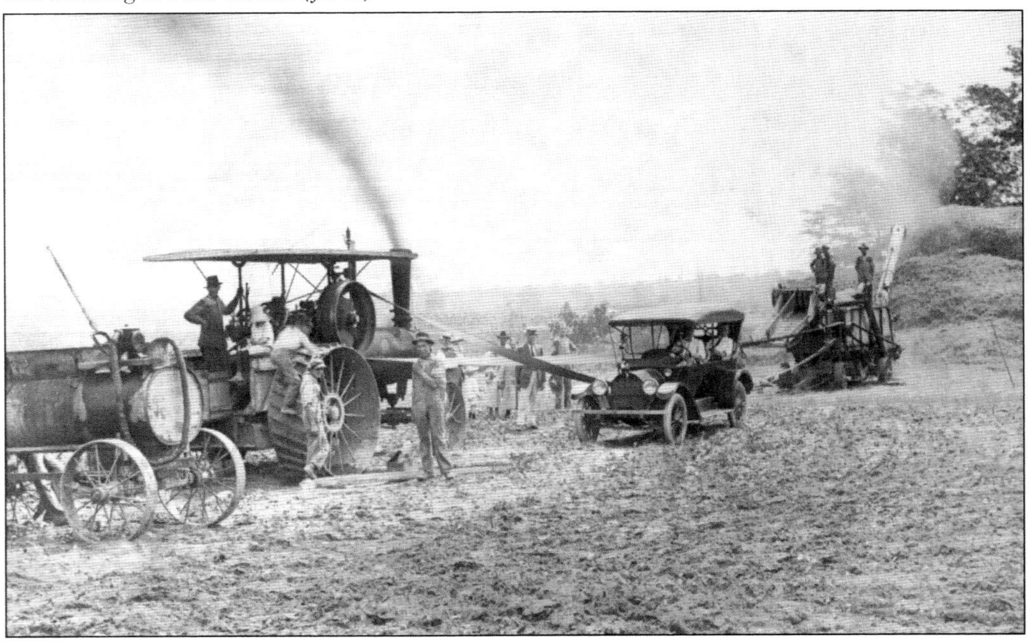

Rice farming in this area did not become popular until later years, but it was grown long before. Swan C. Dowell planted the first rice crop on a small tract of land in Walnut Ridge in 1909. His experiment went so well that he planted 50 acres the next year and harvested 5,000 bushels. Several men in coats and ties are visiting a Dowell farm in a 1913 Case automobile. (BCAS.)

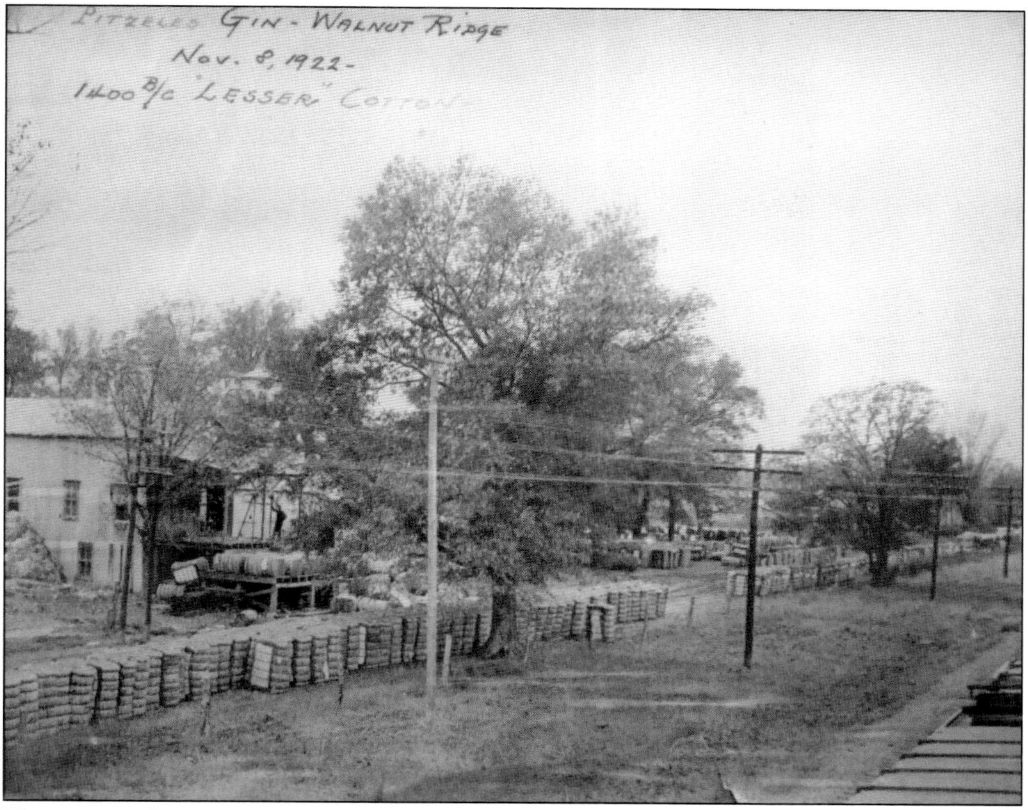

This image taken on November 8, 1922, shows 1,400 cotton bales lining Northeast Front Street near the intersection of Hill Street in front of the S.N. Pitzele Cotton Gin. They are awaiting shipment on the Iron Mountain Railroad. Boxcars can be seen on the tracks at the far right. The Pitzele Farm Center is still located here today. (BH.)

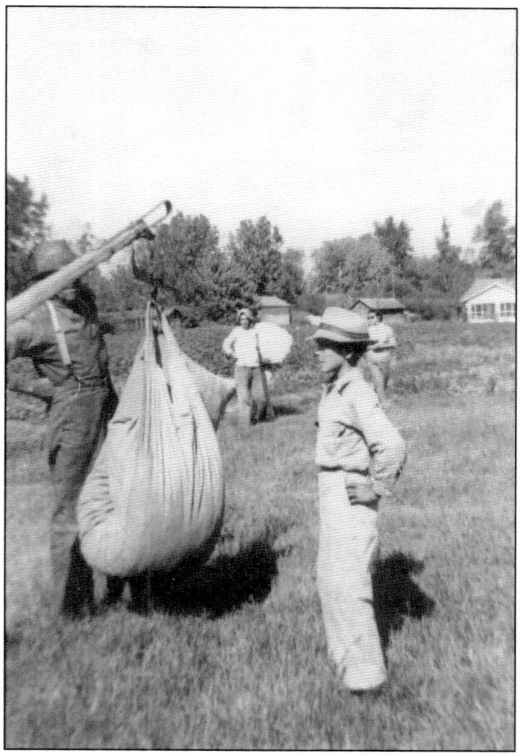

When cotton was king, most schools in Lawrence County held a summer term, which lasted six to eight weeks, starting after the Fourth of July. This allowed students to help with the fall harvest and earn some money. Everyone but the wealthy picked cotton; even people from town would find a nearby cotton patch. A young boy has his cotton sack weighed in Hoxie in this 1945 image. (JBW.)

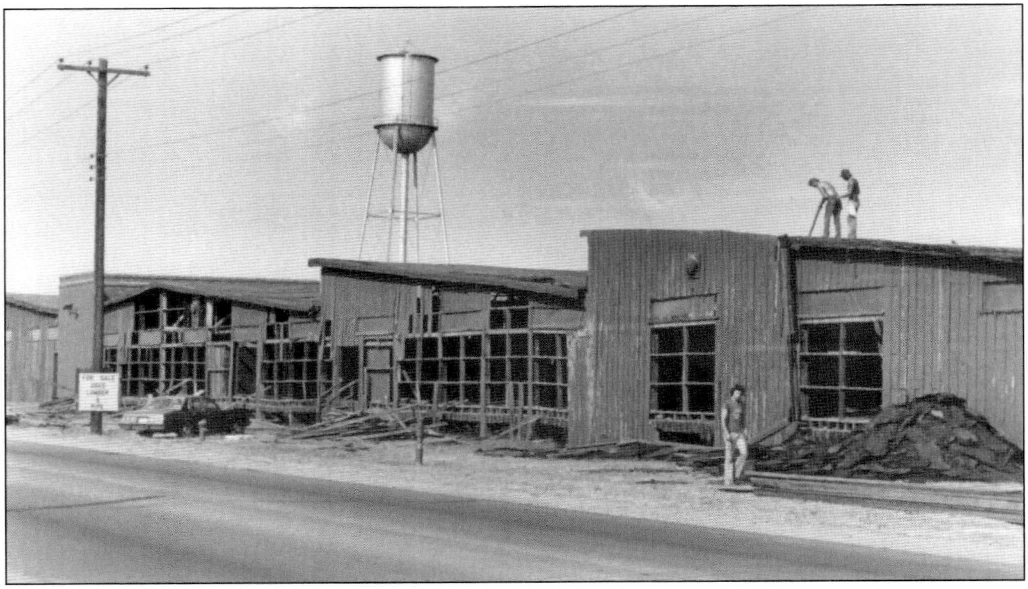

The Hoxie and Walnut Ridge Compress Company, owned by Lesser and Goldman Company, was founded in the early 1900s. In 1926, the Federal Compress and Warehouse Company bought 14 compresses, including this one. Along Highway 67, between Midway Road and Georgia Street, locals could set their clocks to the daily noontime steam whistle. Although the company has been gone since 1980, many still refer to Midway Road as Compress Road. (CR.)

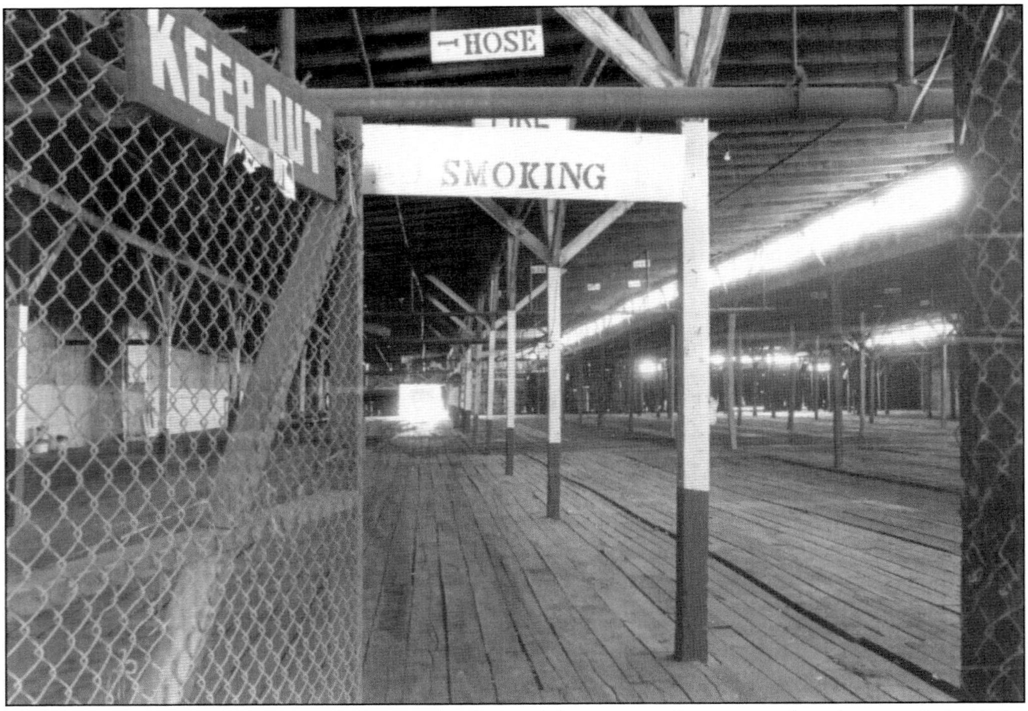

This is a view of an empty warehouse at the Federal Compress after it was shut down in July 1980. It was one of 11 warehouses in the massive building. At its peak, the compress handled 60,000 bales of cotton in a season, each weighing an average of 500 pounds. The facility continued to operate as a warehouse for several years, and a portion is still in use today by Farm Service, Inc. (CR.)

Harry Clark is shown standing next to a large cotton press in 1980, just prior to dismantling portions of the complex. Operated by steam, the press put millions of pounds of pressure on a bale of cotton, reducing it to a fraction of the size. This allowed more cotton to be transported in a single boxcar. Clark began working at the compress in 1944 and operated this machine for 12 years. (CR.)

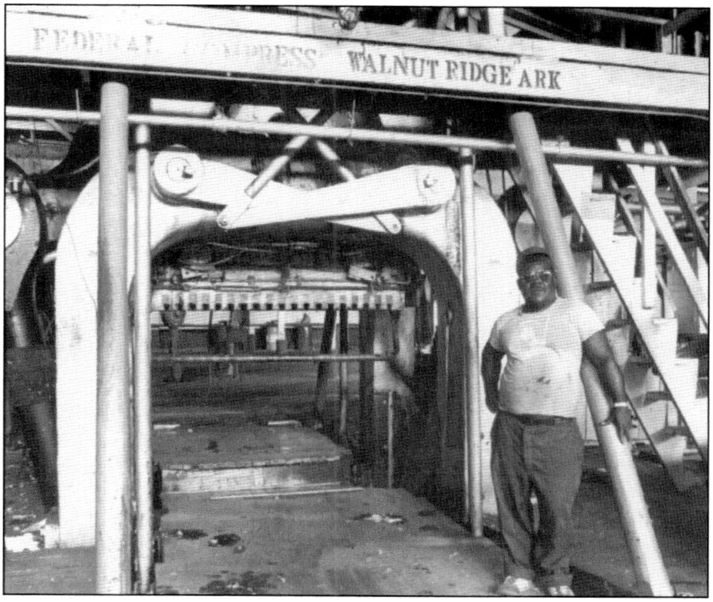

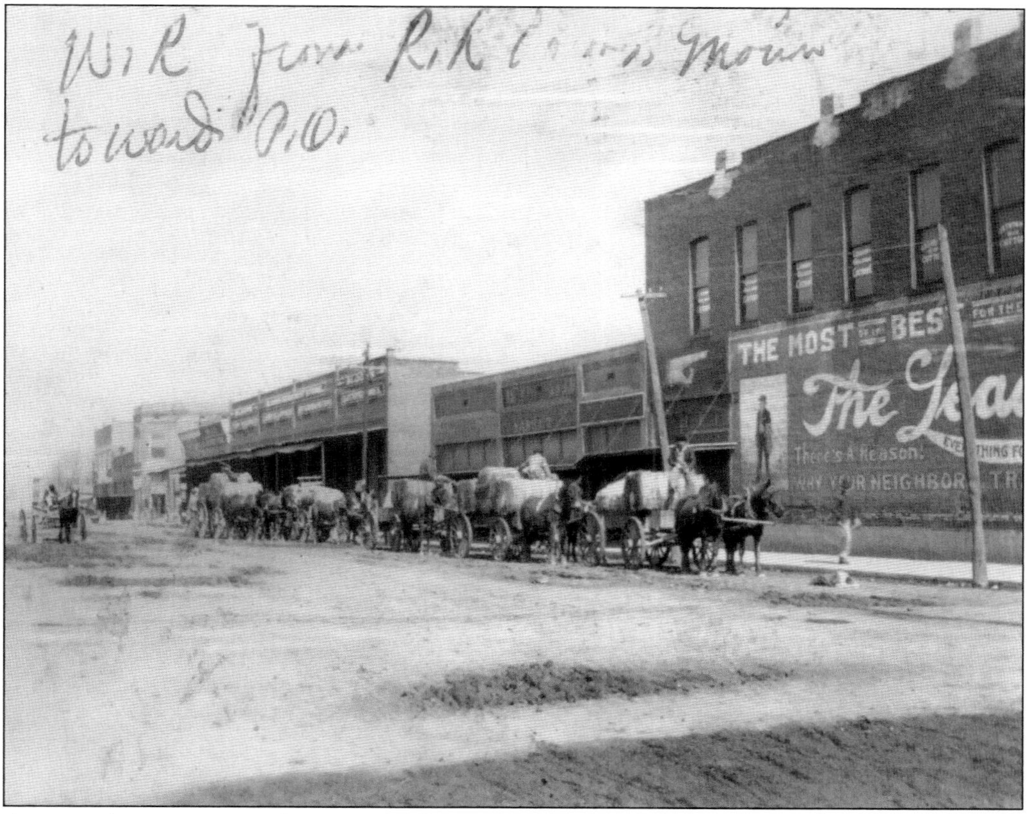

A team of cotton wagons lines up on West Main Street in Walnut Ridge in 1921. The building with the mural is on the corner of Main and Front Streets. It housed the offices of two cotton buyers—G.S. Tiffany and Company and Lesser and Goldman Cotton—whose names are visible in the upper windows. The wagons are also in front of Bloom's Department Store and F.E. Holloway Cash Grocery. (JCW.)

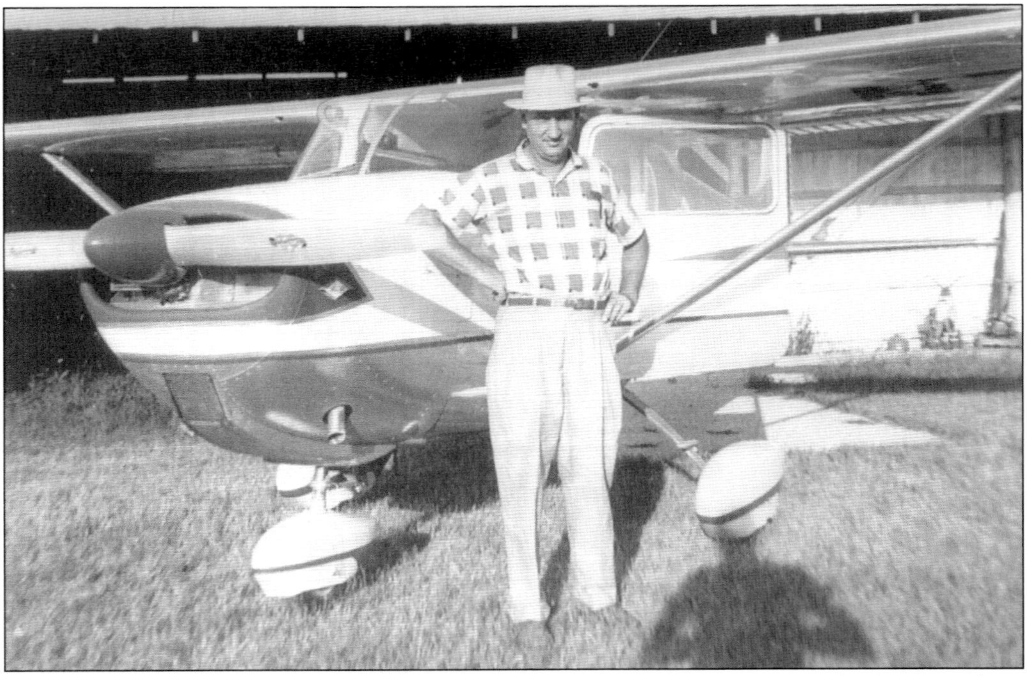

In 1943, early rice farming pioneer John Recker moved to Arbor Grove, just south of Hoxie, where he used German prisoners of war from Walnut Ridge Army Air Field to help clear his land. In 1947, he and his brother Raymond opened Recker Brothers Rice Dryer in Walnut Ridge. It later became Lawrence County Rice Dryer. Here, Recker stands on his farm in front of his private airplane. (PRS.)

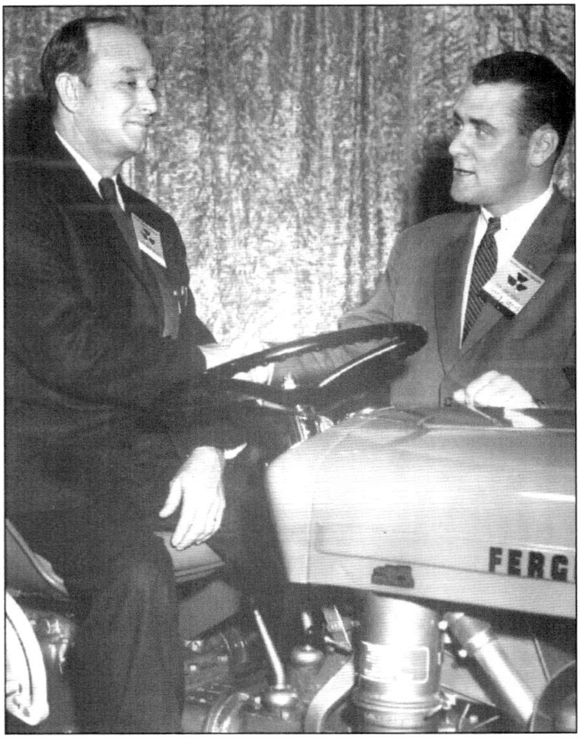

There have been numerous agricultural equipment companies serving the Hoxie and Walnut Ridge farming communities, starting with the Benjamin and Fritz Graff Harness and Implements House on Front Street in Walnut Ridge in the 1880s. Cox Implement Company of Hoxie, founded by Loyd and Dorothy Cox, opened in 1956 and is still in business today. Loyd (left) is shown here speaking with a Massey-Harris-Ferguson representative that same year. (JRC.)

Six

Military

Walnut Ridge and Hoxie have a long and illustrious history with the military. Residents have served in every major campaign since the Civil War and continue to distinguish themselves today. Both founders and the majority of the first businessmen and city leaders served during the Civil War, primarily for the Confederacy. W.M. Ponder, the founder of Walnut Ridge, climbed the ranks from first sergeant to colonel, fighting for the Confederacy in Prairie Grove, Helena, and Shiloh before being taken prisoner in Shreveport. One of the first postmasters of Walnut Ridge, Capt. Abner Bergen Israel, was captured and made a member of the Immortal 600, a group of Confederate officers sent to Morris Island, South Carolina, in retaliation for the conditions imposed on Union soldiers at the Confederate prison in Andersonville, Georgia.

In the late 1890s, W.K. Surridge, a marshal in Walnut Ridge, went with a contingent of men from the surrounding area to support the 4th Infantry Regiment in the Spanish-American War. Surridge was later promoted to brigadier general and appointed as the adjutant general, head of the National Guard, in Arkansas.

Company K, 153rd Infantry Regiment was established in Walnut Ridge in 1929 under the command of Capt. Boas Gibson, grandson of Henry and Mary Boas, founders of Hoxie. Gibson moved the training to Hoxie in 1933, and the company met there until deployed to Alaska in 1941 to take part in the Aleutian Islands Campaign. After returning home in 1944, they met again in Walnut Ridge. In 1957, the company was deployed to Little Rock in support of the Central High School integration. In the 1960s, Company K was replaced at Walnut Ridge with Company A, 153rd, which has made multiple tours to Iraq and the Sinai Peninsula.

Also, during World War II, Walnut Ridge was selected as a site for an Army airfield for pilot training. From 1942 to 1944, over 4,500 pilots graduated from Walnut Ridge. Graduates of Hoxie and Walnut Ridge have attended all three major service academies. The majority, three from Hoxie and four from Walnut Ridge, graduated from the United States Military Academy at West Point.

Also noteworthy, Maj. Gen. Bobby Porter, a graduate of Walnut Ridge High School, commanded the famed 82nd Airborne Division at Fort Bragg. Four-star general James T. Conway, born in Walnut Ridge, was the 34th commandant of the Marine Corps.

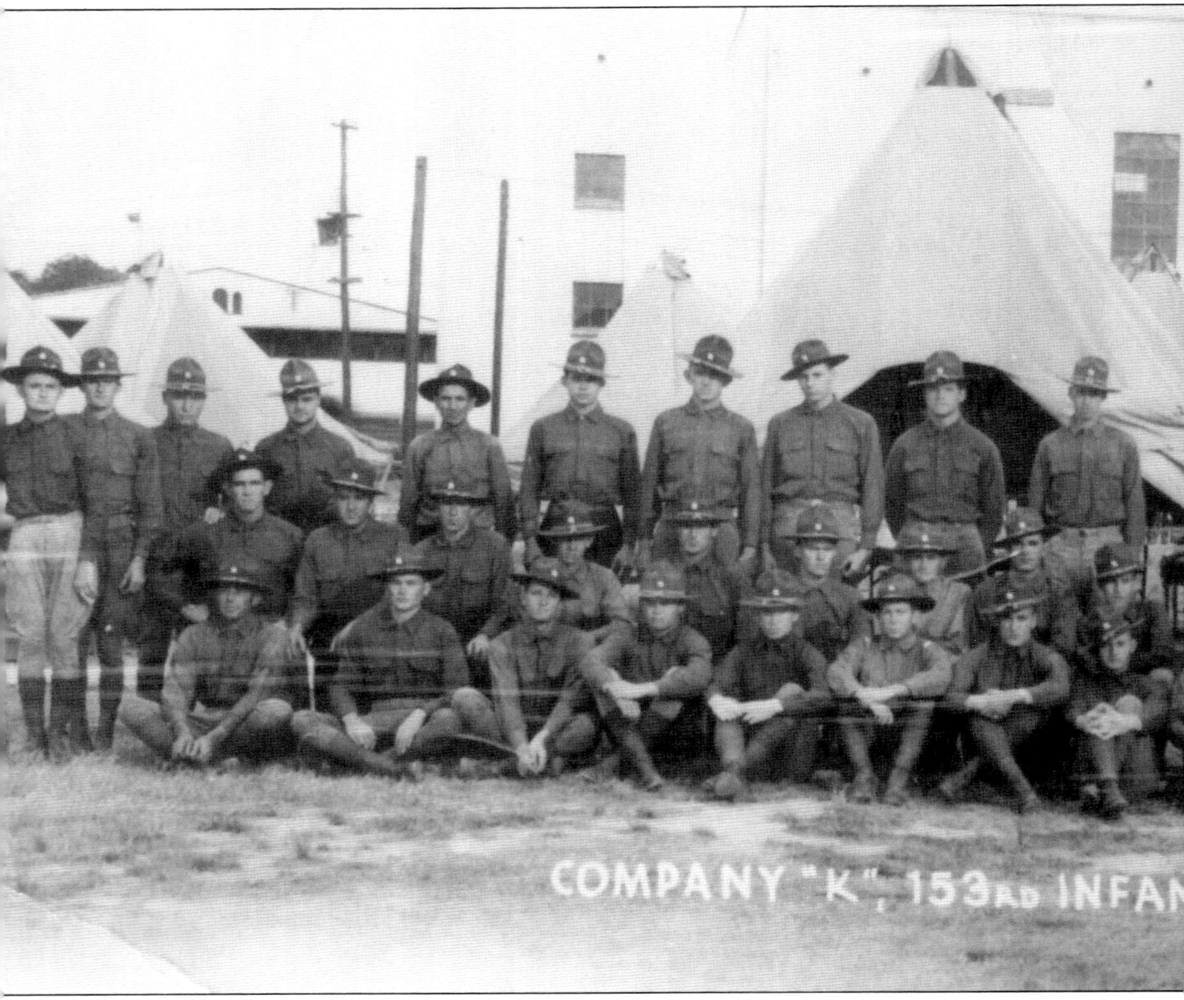

Company K, 3rd Battalion, 153rd Infantry was organized in Walnut Ridge on April 29, 1929, under Capt. Boas E. Gibson and 2nd Lt. Alfred L. King, with two officers and 67 enlisted men. The unit is shown here in 1932 at Camp Pike in Little Rock, with only the officers identified. On the back row, to the far right, is Captain Gibson. To his left is Second Lieutenant King. The unit moved

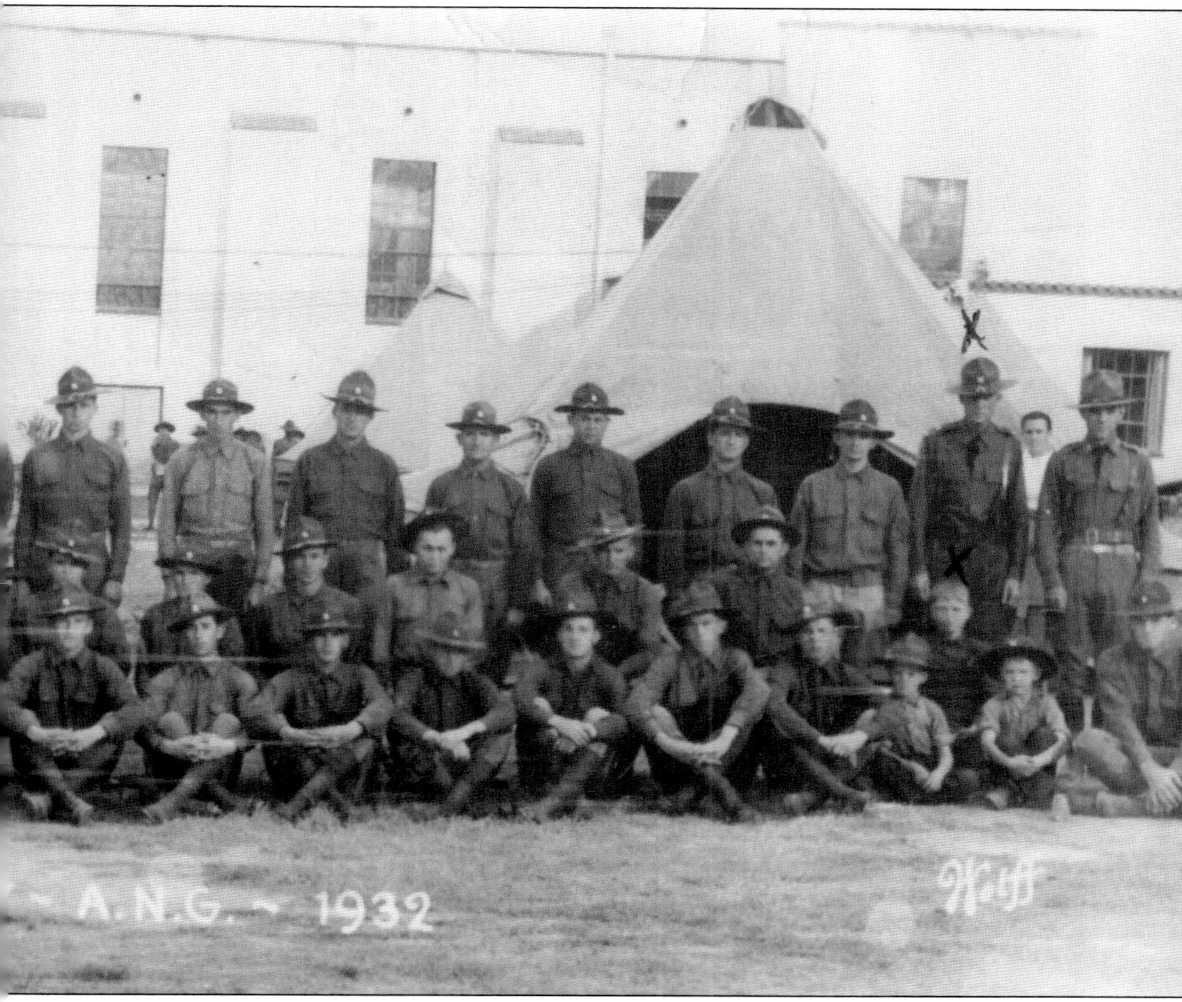

to Hoxie in 1933 and remained until deployed to Alaska in September 1941. After its return in June 1944, the entire 153rd Infantry Regiment was briefly disbanded. On September 30, 1946, Company K was reconstituted in Walnut Ridge. It met first in the United Service Organizations (USO) building on Main Street, moving to the present armory in the mid-1950s. (ML.)

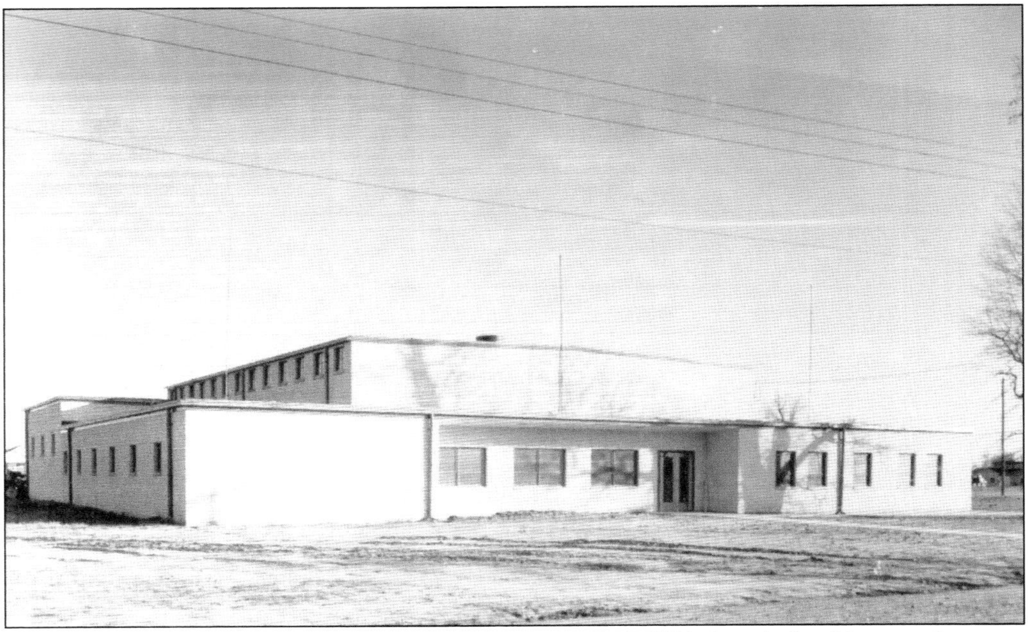

Robert National Guard Armory, named after Lawrence E. "Bill" Robert for his 30 years of service, became the new home of Company K, 3rd Battalion, 153rd Infantry when it was built in the mid-1950s. It is located in Walnut Ridge, but only a street divides it from neighboring Hoxie. The infantry regiment reorganized in 1967. The armory is now the home of Company A, 2nd Battalion. (JBW.)

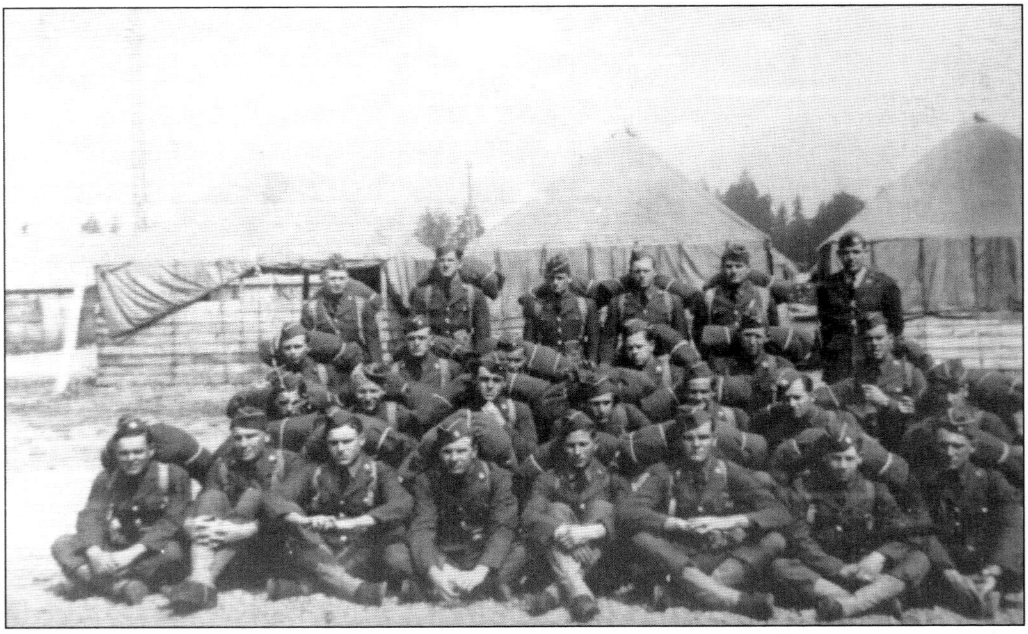

This picture of 4th Platoon, Company K was taken at Camp Murray, Washington, on September 25, 1941. The platoon contained two mortar squads and two machine gun squads. Pvt. James Sauls is sitting in the front row, second from the right. Lt. Sam Scott is standing in the last row, at far right. From here, they boarded the *President Taft*, a transport ship, landing at Seward, Alaska, four days later. (JES.)

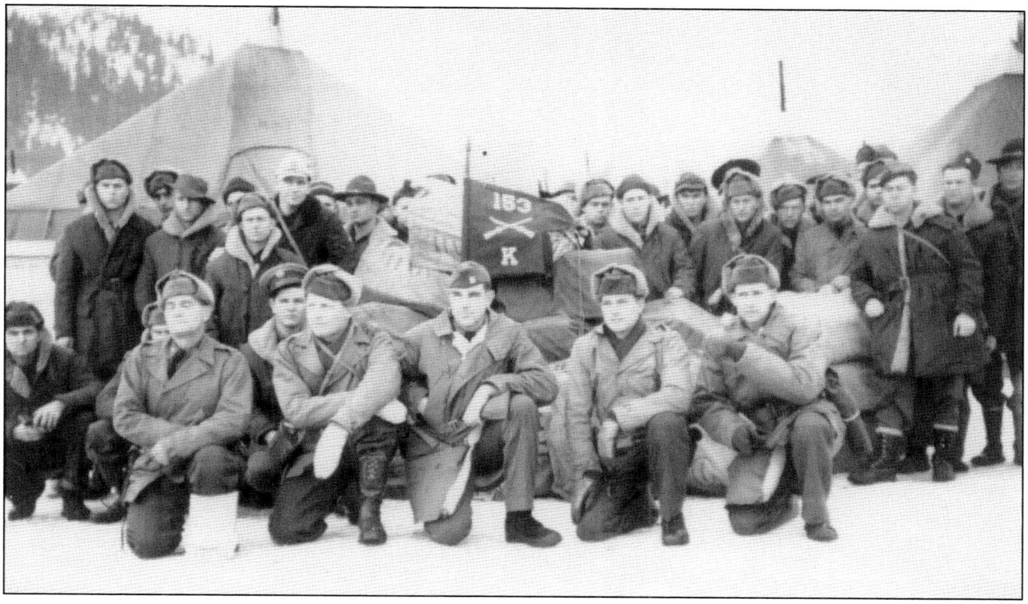

Company K was deployed to Seward, Alaska, from September 1941 to June 1944. The men were there during the occupation of Adak Island and the assault on Kiska, part of the Aleutian Islands Campaign in 1943. This picture from December 1941 shows the battalion commander with troops from Company K. Kneeling are, from left to right, Lieutenant Colonel Crawford, Capt. Julian Beakley, Lt. Sam Scott, Lieutenant Kentz, and Lieutenant Adams. (WOH.)

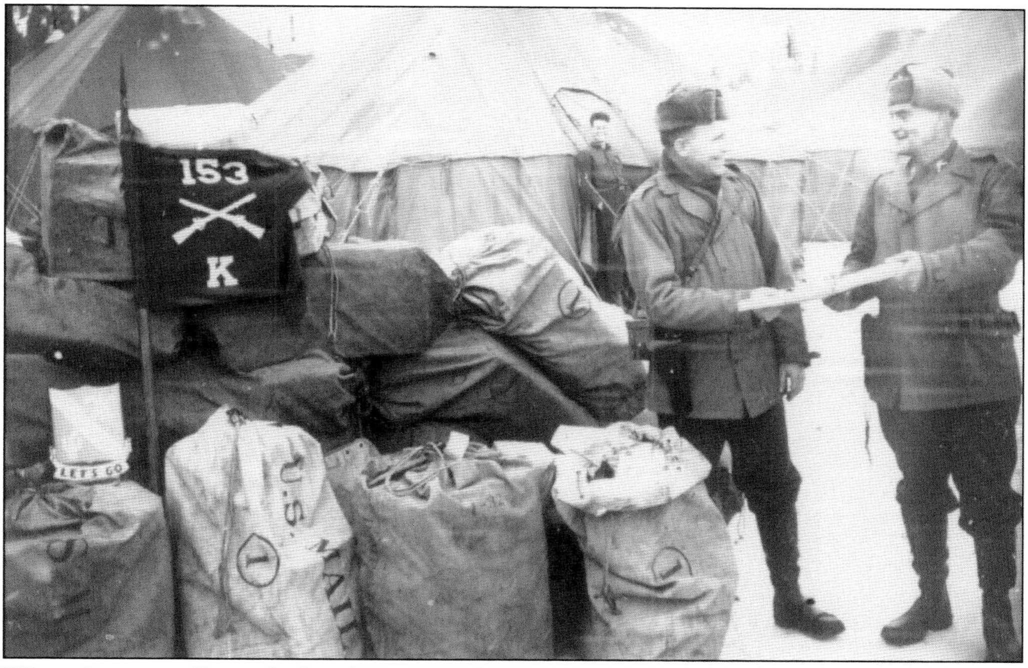

When Company K was deployed in September 1941, the United States was not at war. Things changed in early December after Japan attacked Pearl Harbor. The company guidon and crest sit above numerous cards, letters, and packages that have arrived for the men of Company K during the first of three Christmas seasons away from Walnut Ridge. Capt. Julian Beakley, left, and Lieutenant Colonel Crawford, right, hold one of the first packages. (WOH.)

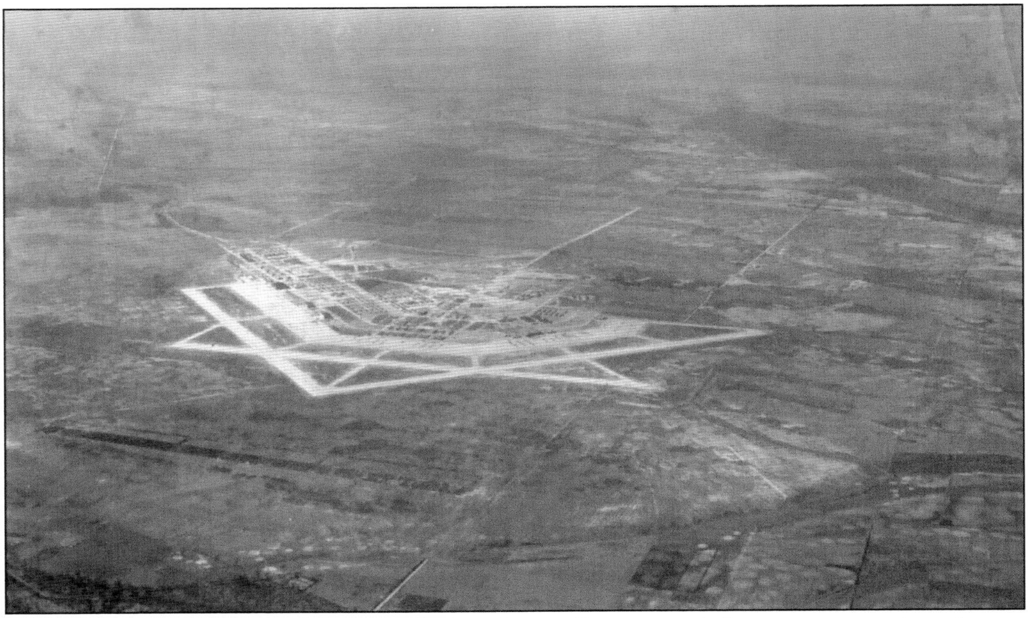

After Pearl Harbor, the need for trained pilots drastically increased, forcing construction of many new air training fields. When a proposed airfield in Dyersburg, Tennessee, was deemed infeasible, the War Department ordered selection of a new site. Walnut Ridge was favorably recommended after an aerial search of eastern Arkansas. The government purchased 3,096 acres of farmland to build three runways. Construction started June 20, 1942, and was completed by August 15. (WOH.)

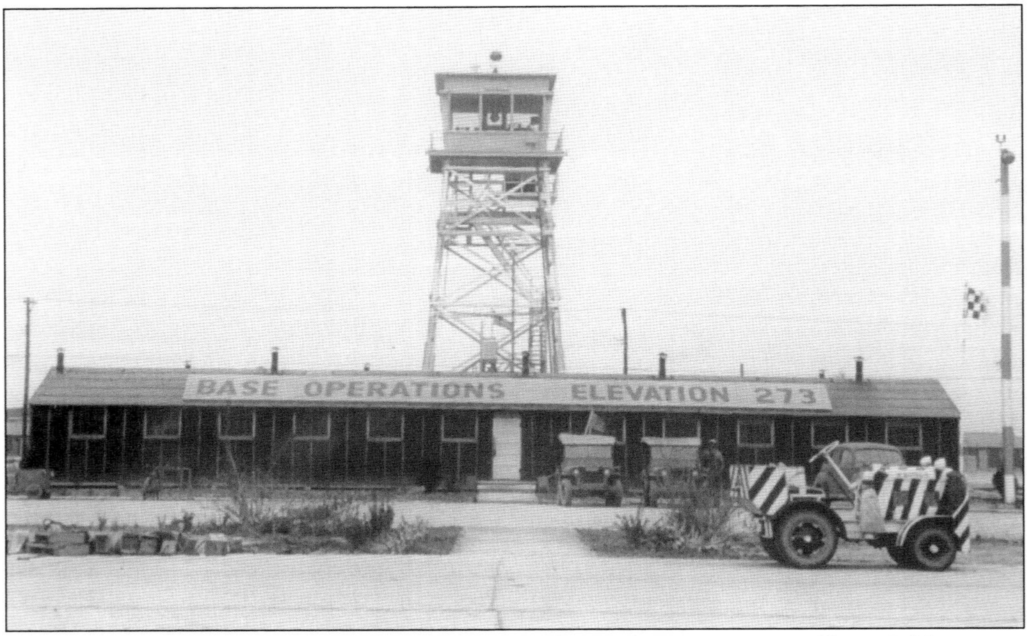

Even after the airfield was activated, there was no place to house troops or offices. Soldiers were transported back and forth from a Civilian Conservation Corps camp in Pocahontas, and the headquarters were housed in the Mize Motor Building in downtown Walnut Ridge. On September 24, 1942, all troops and offices were moved to the airfield. An elevation of 273 feet is displayed on the base headquarters building. (WOH.)

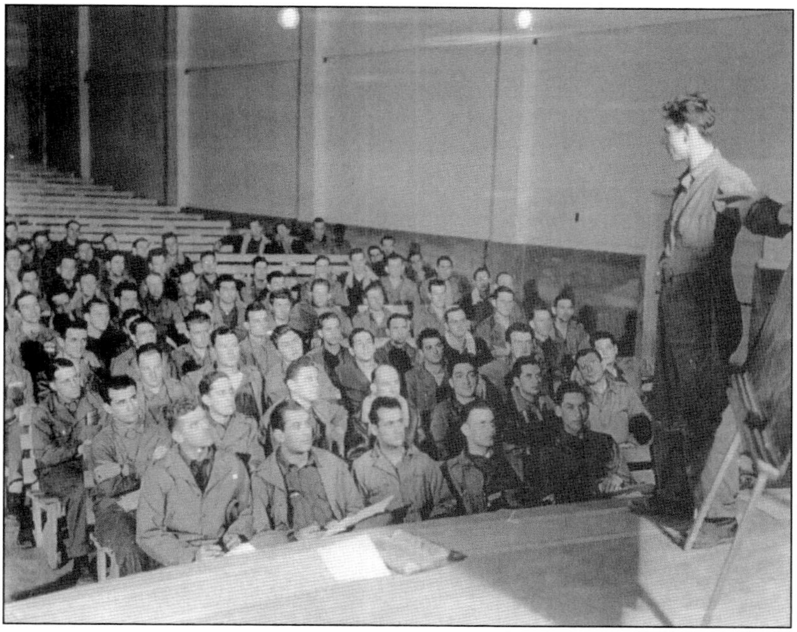

On October 3, 1942, the first aircraft arrived at Walnut Ridge—the Vultee BT-13 Valiant. A week later, the first class arrived, and on October 12, 1942, the student officers and aviation cadets of Class 43-B began training at 1:00 p.m. This picture of a ground training class was taken in January 1943. (WOH.)

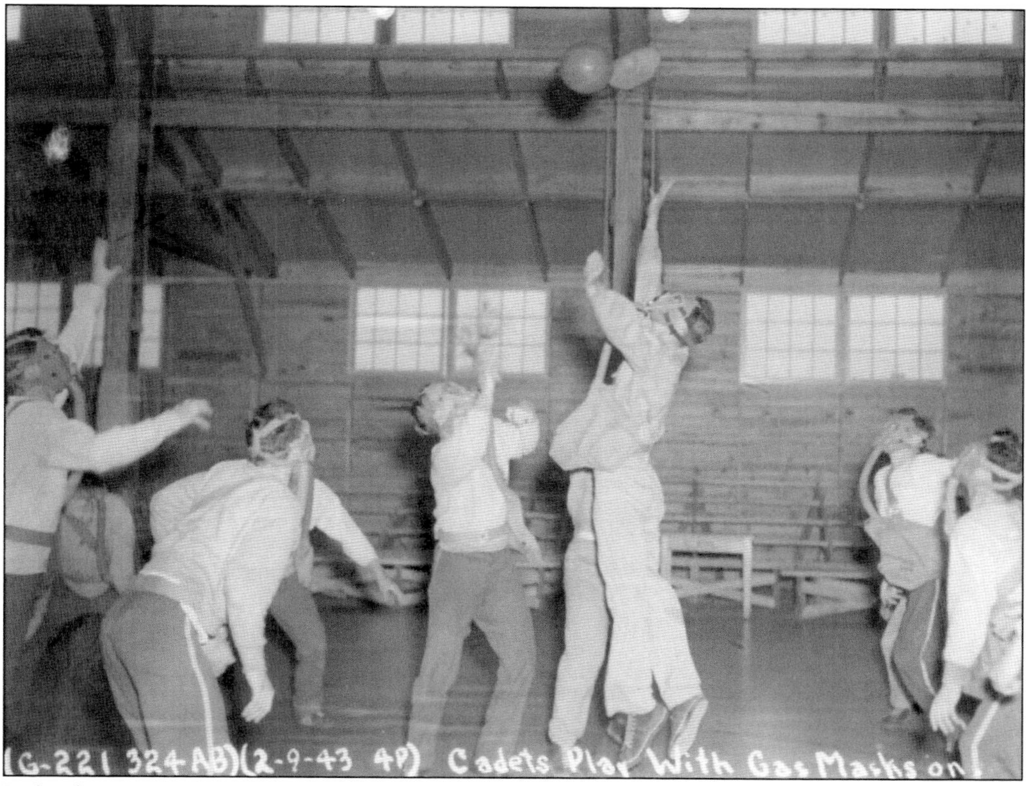

Before beginning flight school, aviation cadets spent hours a day exercising and at tough commando training. They are seen here in the Walnut Ridge Air Field gymnasium, playing basketball with their gas masks on to accustom them to wearing them during strenuous tasks. As can be seen in the quality of materials used in this building, most were intended to be temporary facilities, lasting a few years at best. (WOH.)

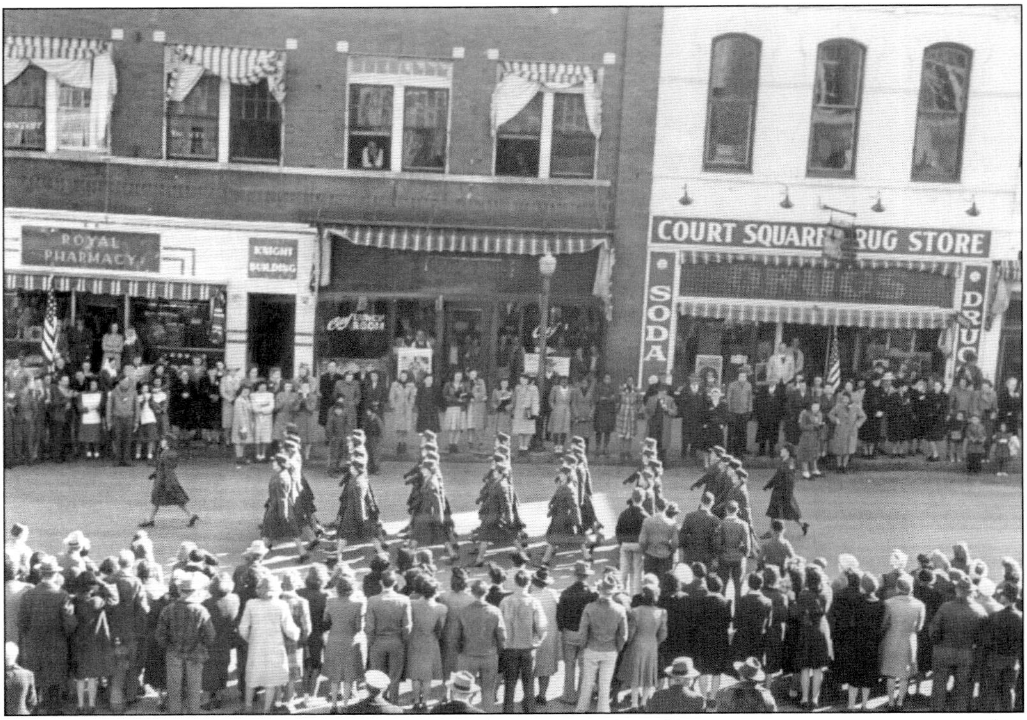

The Women's Army Corps (WAC) was created in May 1942 to allow women to serve in noncombat positions, such as radio operators, electricians, and air traffic controllers. Several WACs served at Walnut Ridge during World War II, including Third Officer Mildred Inez Bailey, who would later attain the rank of brigadier general and command the WACs from 1971 until 1975. A group of WACs from Walnut Ridge is seen here marching in an Armistice Day parade in Jonesboro, Arkansas. (WOH.)

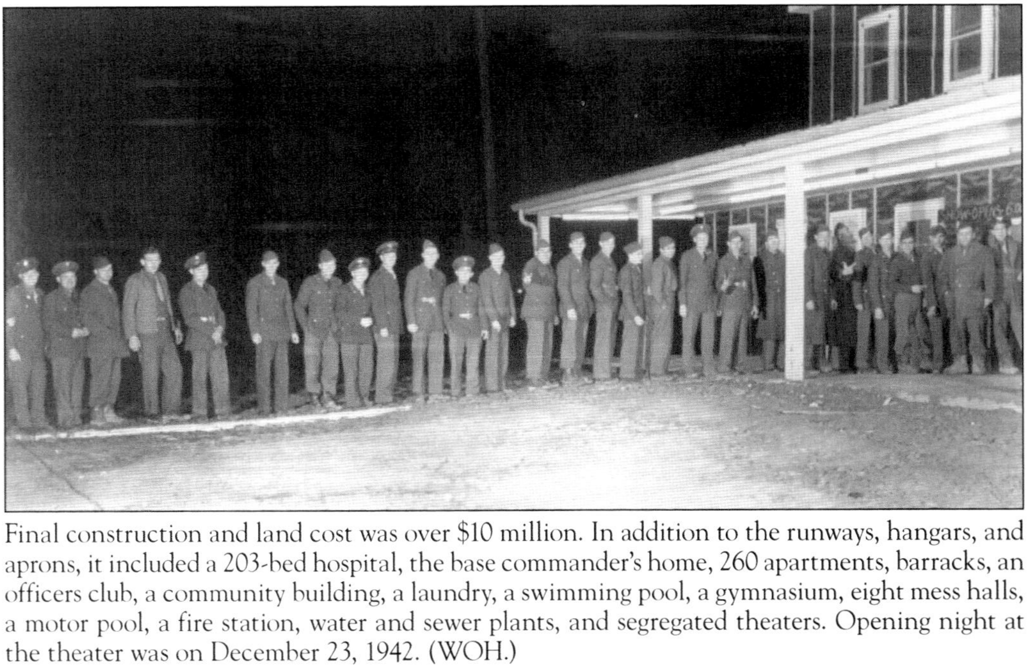

Final construction and land cost was over $10 million. In addition to the runways, hangars, and aprons, it included a 203-bed hospital, the base commander's home, 260 apartments, barracks, an officers club, a community building, a laundry, a swimming pool, a gymnasium, eight mess halls, a motor pool, a fire station, water and sewer plants, and segregated theaters. Opening night at the theater was on December 23, 1942. (WOH.)

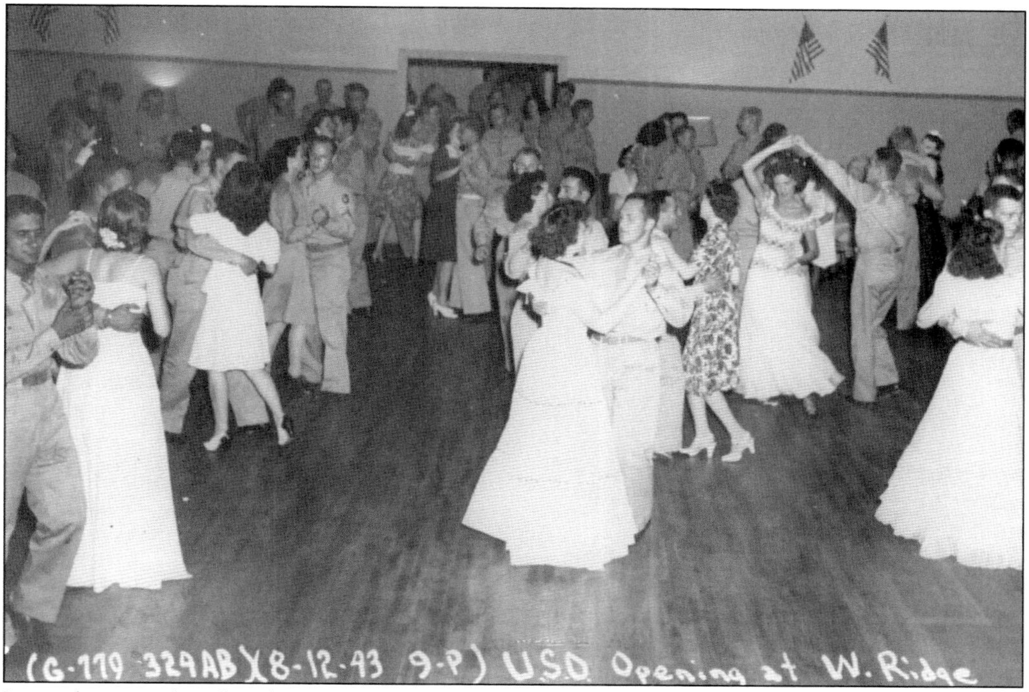

Just a few months after the construction of the airfield, Walnut Ridge was transformed from a sleepy farming community into a bustling town full of Army officers. The American Legion Hall at 218 East Main Street was rebranded a United Service Organizations (USO) building. Pictured here is the opening night dance, on August 12, 1943. After the war, this building became an armory, a community center, and a fireman's hall. (WOH.)

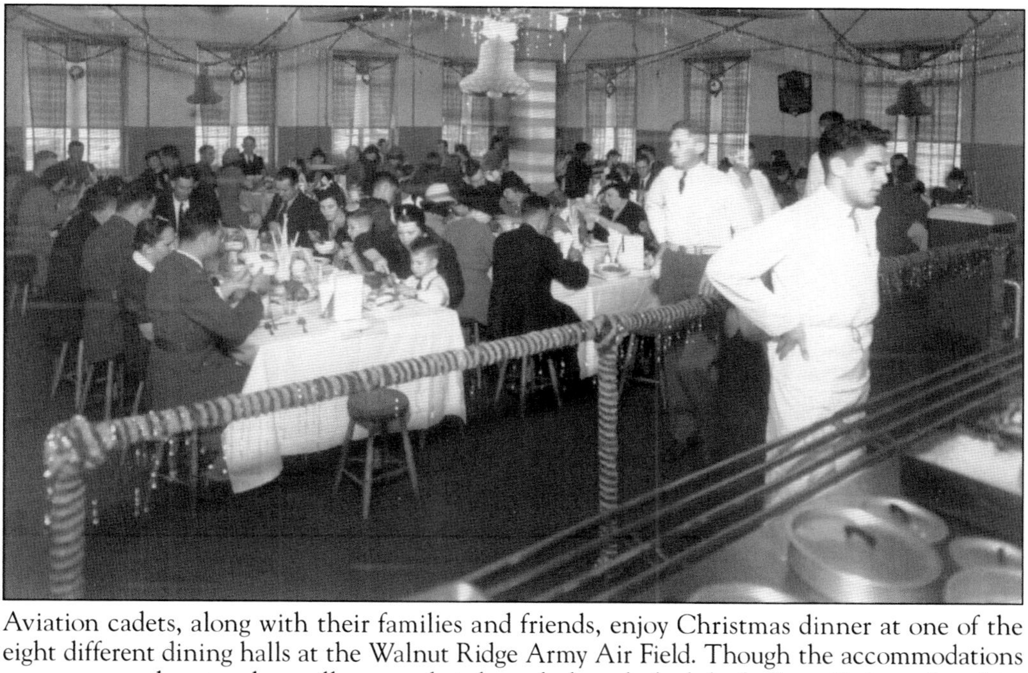

Aviation cadets, along with their families and friends, enjoy Christmas dinner at one of the eight different dining halls at the Walnut Ridge Army Air Field. Though the accommodations were meager, the attendees still put on their best clothes, decked the halls, pulled out the white tablecloths, and had a fancy feast, if even for just one day. (WOH.)

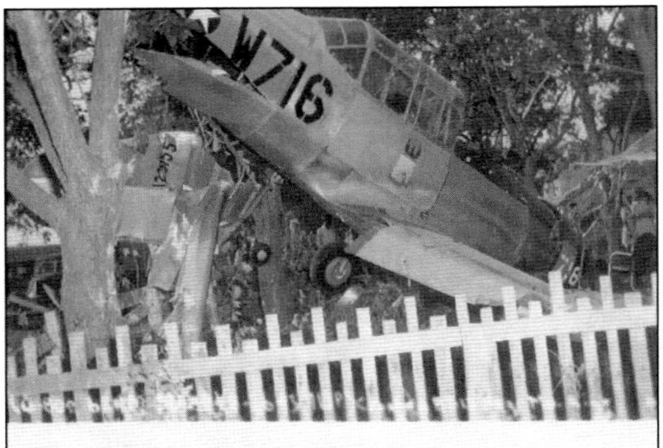

Flight training began slowly but accelerated to a rapid pace, culminating in solo flights of chandelles, lazy eights, loops, slow rolls, and spins. Subsequently, there were many accidents. The first fatal crash happened on November 15, 1942. In just under two years of training, 42 students, instructors, and passengers were killed in training at Walnut Ridge. (WOH.)

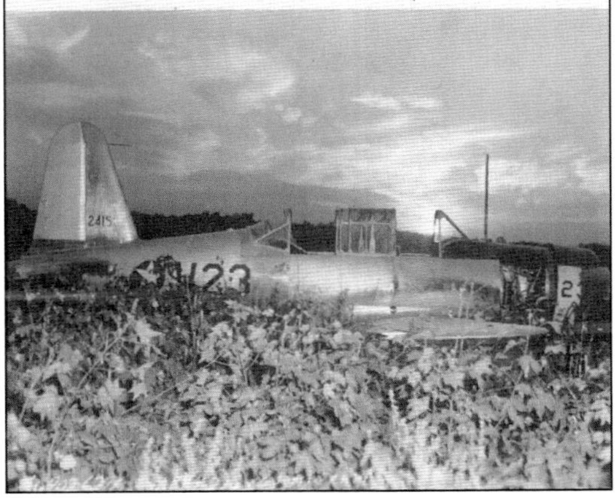

Cadets fly over the Walnut Ridge Air Field during a graduation ceremony. In just under 21 months, 5,310 students entered training and 4,641 graduated. All graduates went on to take advance training in heavier aircraft. Those who took twin-engine training became bomber or transport pilots. Those who took single-engine training became fighter pilots. The first graduation was December 12, 1942, and the last was on June 27, 1944. (WOH.)

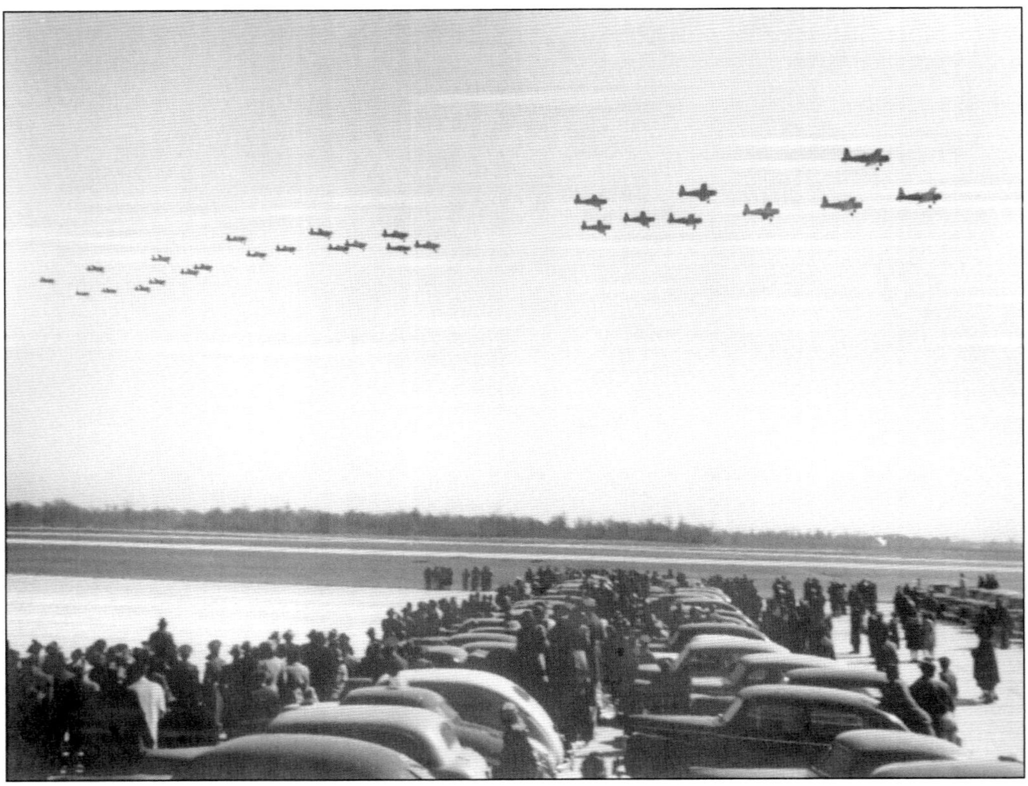

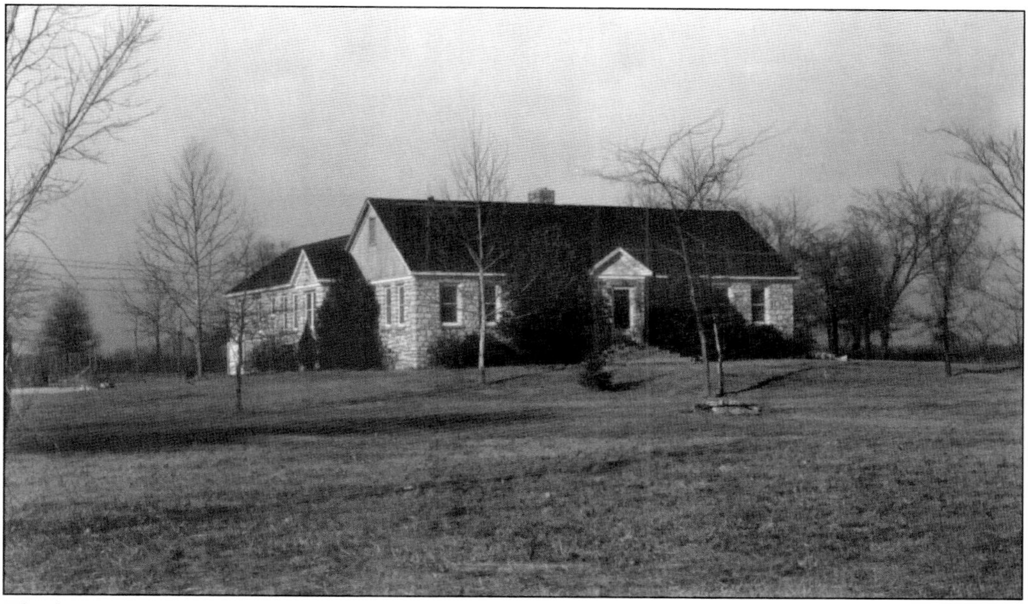

The base commander's house was constructed under the guise of being a guesthouse for military dignitaries. After an investigation, funding was halted. The commandant completed the house using materials from the demolished Civilian Conservation Corps camp in Pocahontas. Listed in the National Register of Historic Places, it was later the residence of Dr. H.E. Williams, the founder of Williams Baptist College. (WBC.)

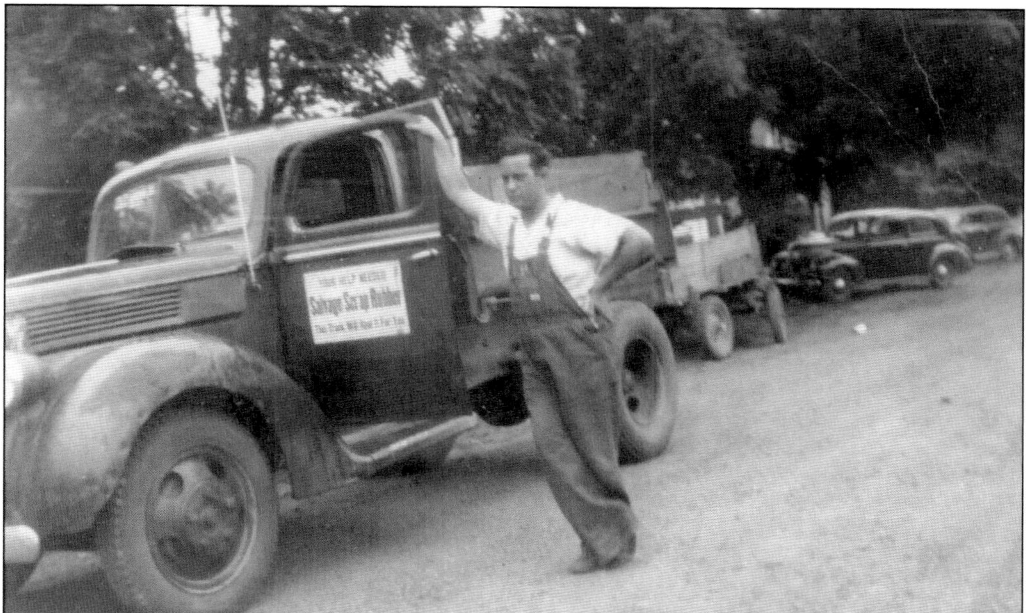

Military production factories needed every scrap of rubber they could find, and citizens were asked to turn in items such as old tires, garden hoses, and rubber shoes for recycling. Jesse "Junior" Honeycutt, of Walnut Ridge, was unable to serve due to childhood polio but still did his part. The sign on his truck states "Your Help Needed— Salvage Scrap Rubber—This Truck Will Haul It For You." (JBW.)

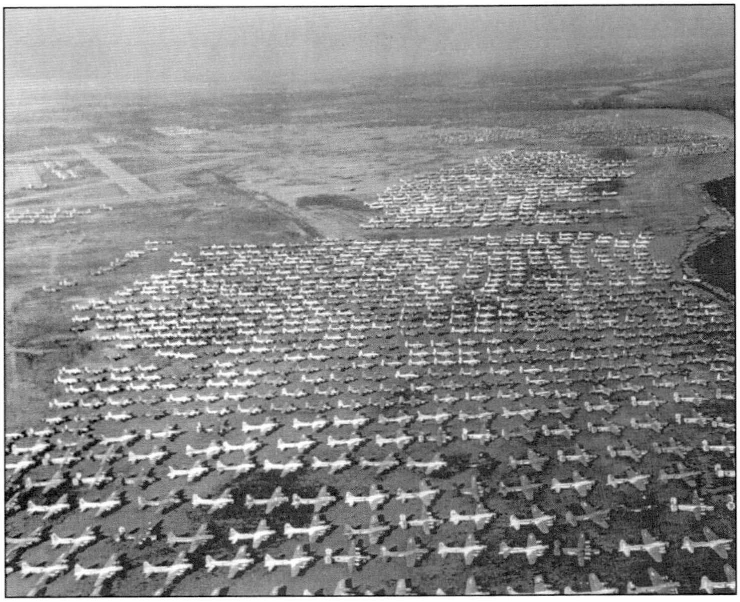

At the end of the war, the airfield was designated as a salvage depot for surplus aircraft from all over the world. Over 10,000 huge bombers, transports, trainers, fighters, and other types of aircraft were flown to Walnut Ridge for disposal. It was the largest number of aircraft ever assembled in one place on the face of the earth. (WOH.)

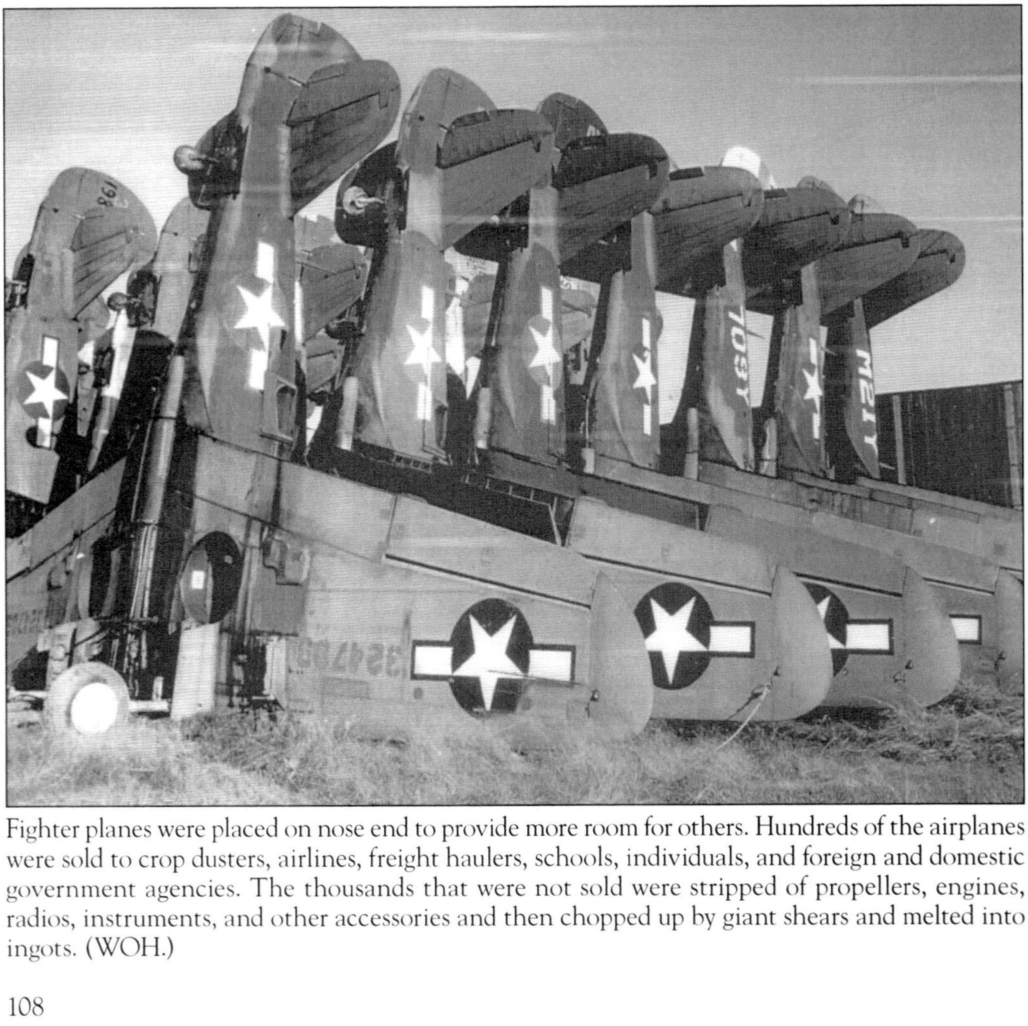

Fighter planes were placed on nose end to provide more room for others. Hundreds of the airplanes were sold to crop dusters, airlines, freight haulers, schools, individuals, and foreign and domestic government agencies. The thousands that were not sold were stripped of propellers, engines, radios, instruments, and other accessories and then chopped up by giant shears and melted into ingots. (WOH.)

Seven

Disasters

Ice storms, floods, droughts, tornadoes, fires, railroad strikes, the Great Depression—Walnut Ridge and Hoxie have had more than their fair share of disasters, acts of God, and just plain old hard times. Rather than wallow in self-pity, though, the citizens of both towns have a long history of brushing off the dirt, finding an alternative path, and rebuilding better than before.

The first fire on record in Walnut Ridge destroyed over six businesses and houses in 1888 on Northeast Front Street. This was followed in 1893 by the worst fire in the history of Walnut Ridge, destroying 13 businesses covering two blocks of Northwest Front Street. The seven-year-old son of W.D. Davidson, the proprietor of the Star Hotel, was killed in the blaze. An Irishman, learning the boy was still in the building, ran back inside to save him and also perished. Ad Kane was arrested and confessed that he started the fire, claiming he was paid $25 and given two suits. He named several prominent people as conspirators, but no one was arrested. In just a matter of months, the entire two blocks were replaced with brick buildings.

Hoxie and Walnut Ridge Schools were both damaged by fires and tornadoes. In all cases, the community rallied to help; classes were held in churches and even private homes, and buildings were either remodeled or eventually replaced with new ones.

The 1920s and 1930s were the worst decades for both towns, but Hoxie was hit especially hard. It all started on July 1, 1922, when 400,000 railroad workers went on strike nationwide, including 300 in Hoxie. In possible retaliation, the Missouri Pacific abandoned the passenger and freight terminal in Hoxie on July 12, 1922, making Poplar Bluff the intermediate terminal between Little Rock and St. Louis. The strike was over by August, but the jobs did not return. The Union Station in Hoxie burned in 1924 and was rebuilt in 1925. A tornado devastated Hoxie in 1927, the same year that the Missouri Pacific moved the remaining railroad shops to Poplar Bluff and abandoned the roundhouse. Two years later, the Great Depression started, crippling anything left of Hoxie's economy.

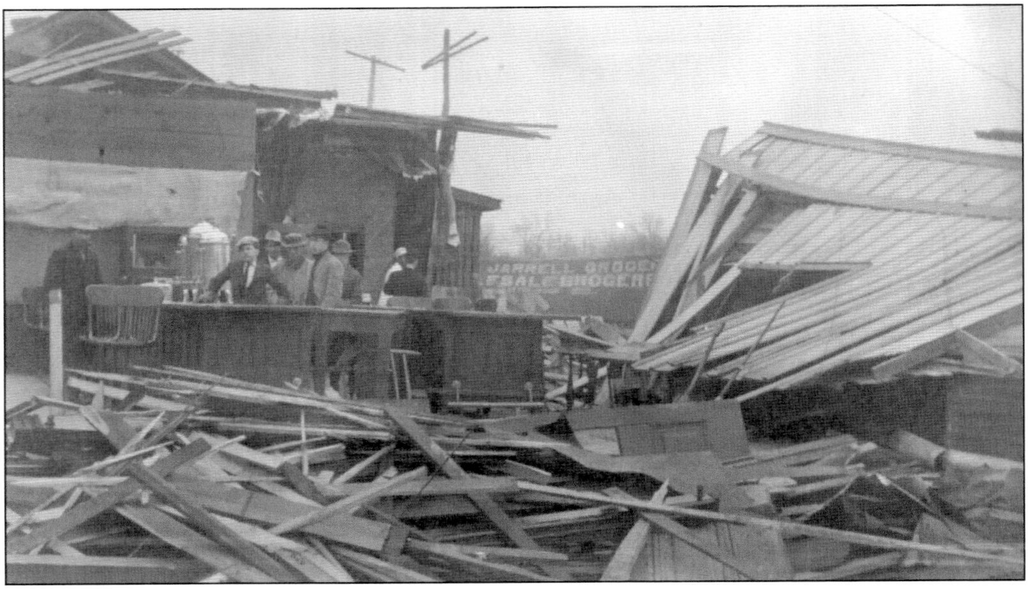

Hoxie was hit hardest when both towns were visited by a devastating tornado on March 20, 1913. Luckily, no lives were lost. The Van Noy restaurant, part of a chain that served the railroads, was completely destroyed, except for the bar area, which seems virtually untouched, with coffee urns set up and bar stools still standing. It was adjacent to the Hoxie Union Station, partially seen on the left. (JBW.)

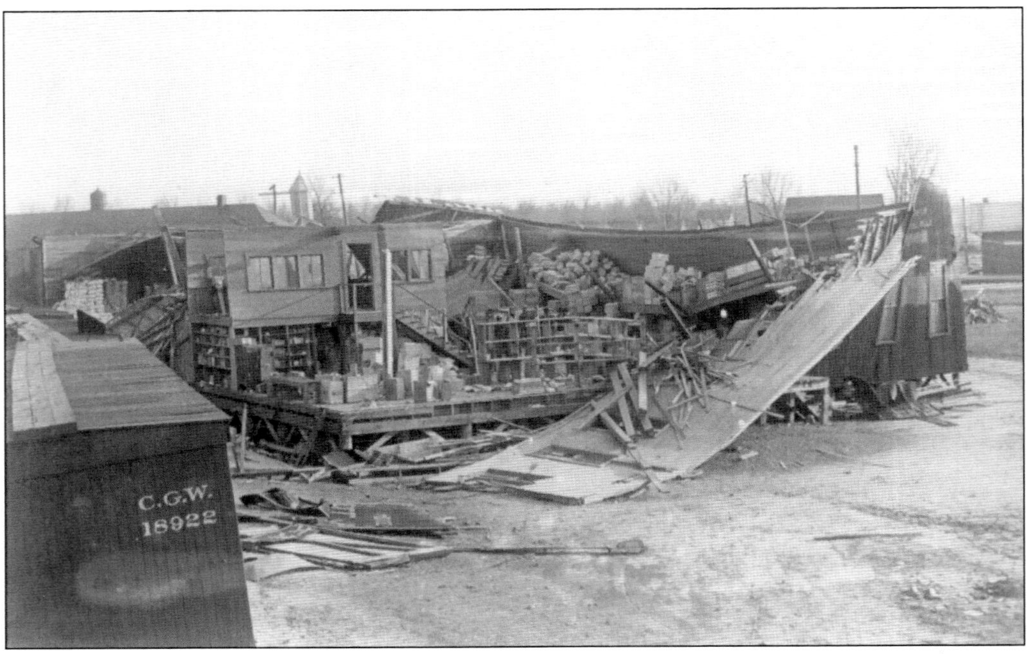

The Plunkett-Jarrell Wholesale Grocer received the heaviest damage in 1913, estimated at $20,000. Three wooden boxcars, the nearest from the Chicago Great Western Railroad, are on a sidetrack next to the loading platform. The top of the damaged Frisco freight depot is visible on the left. Behind it are two silos from the Modern Gin Company, also heavily damaged. Both towns, still in their boom period, recovered quickly. (JBW.)

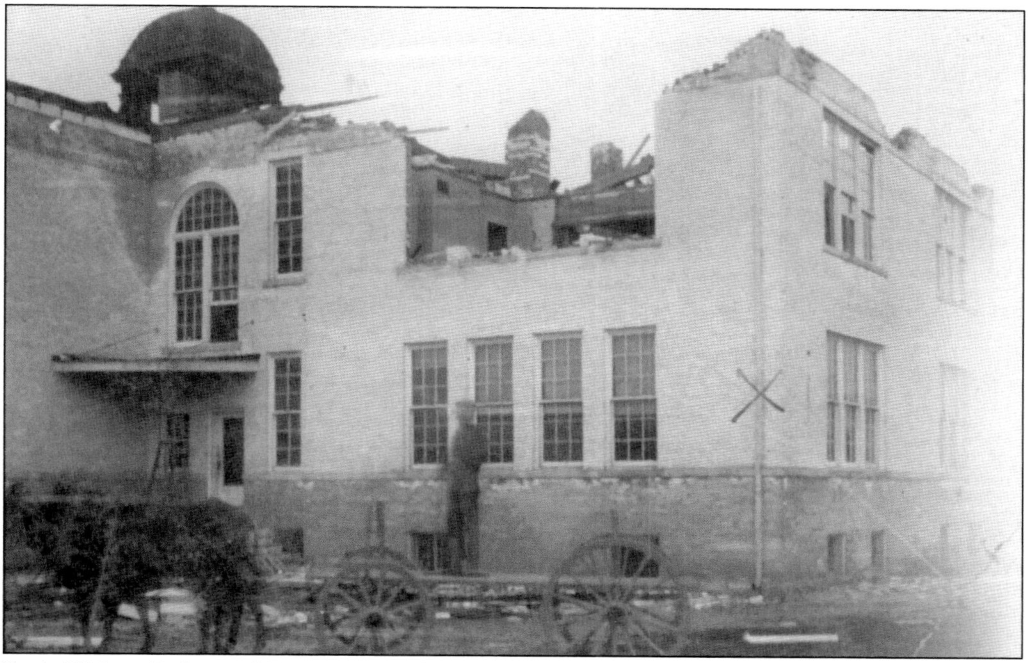

Both Walnut Ridge and Hoxie received extensive damage to their public school buildings. The tornado hit around 9:00 p.m., so school was not in session. Hoxie School, built in 1908, was located at the corner of Lindsey and Lawrence Streets. Children then attended classes in several churches and lodge halls. Adding insult to injury, a heavy snow blanketed both towns a few days later, with most citizens still with no electricity. (JBW.)

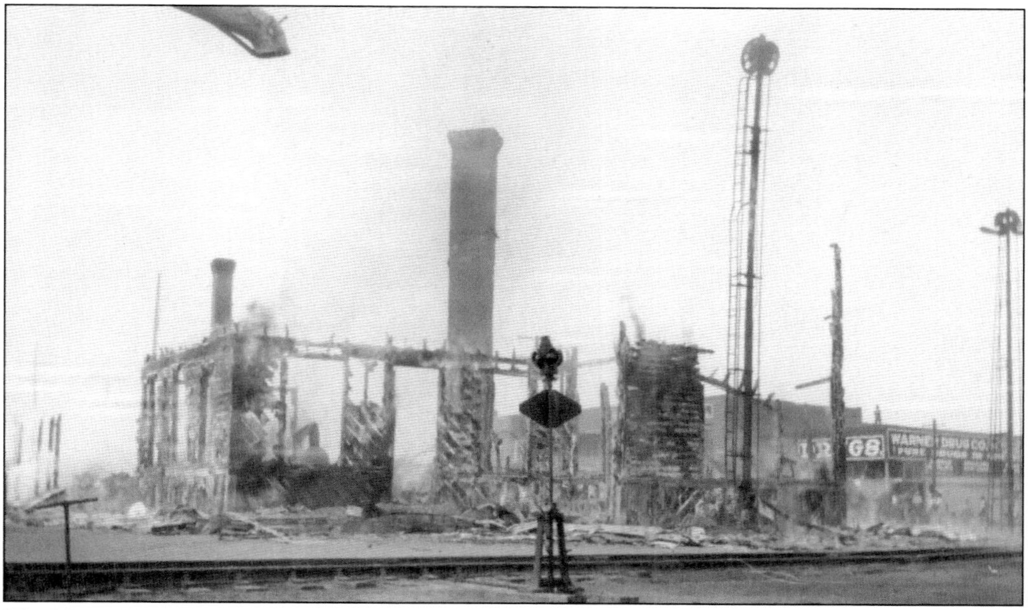

The Hoxie Union Station was completely destroyed by fire on October 9, 1924. The fire originated in the adjacent Liberty Café, formerly the Van Noy restaurant, when a waitress mistook gasoline for coal oil while filling a coffee urn lamp. With no waterworks, both buildings quickly burned. The plate-glass windows of Warner Drug Store, seen across the street at right, burst due to the excessive heat. (JBW.)

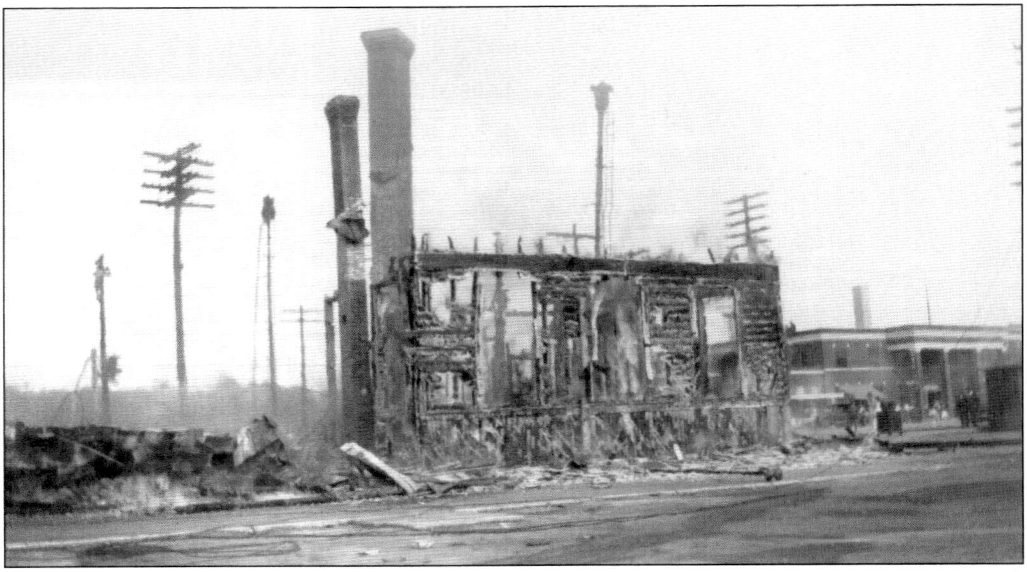

Another angle of the remains of the Hoxie Union Station shows the two-story brick Boas Hotel, across the street on the right. Ironically, plans had already been made to build a new depot in Hoxie. Railroad representatives had just visited the day before the fire, taking pictures of the old depot and recording measurements for the new structure. The new brick depot was opened in 1925. (JBW.)

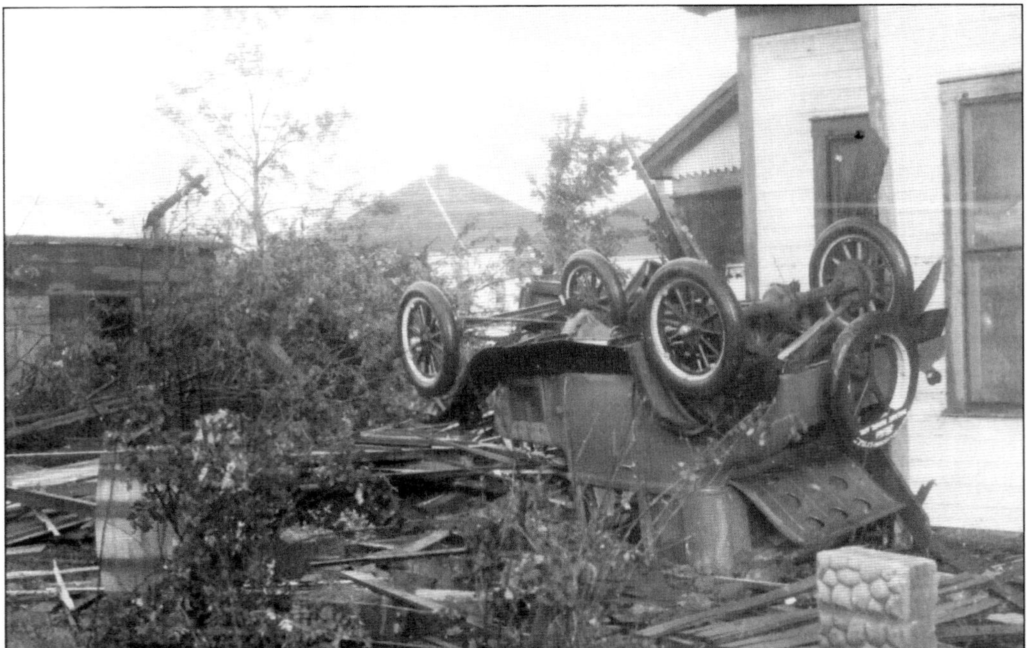

People still talk of the tornado of May 9, 1927. Over 800 people lost their lives that day in the southern United States. Two were killed in Hoxie, eight in Walnut Ridge, and 18 others within a 10-mile radius. The tornado cut a quarter-mile swath, destroying 51 homes in Walnut Ridge and 20 in Hoxie. The spare tire on this overturned car is stamped Snapp-Robinson-Lytle Ford, Walnut Ridge. (JAG.)

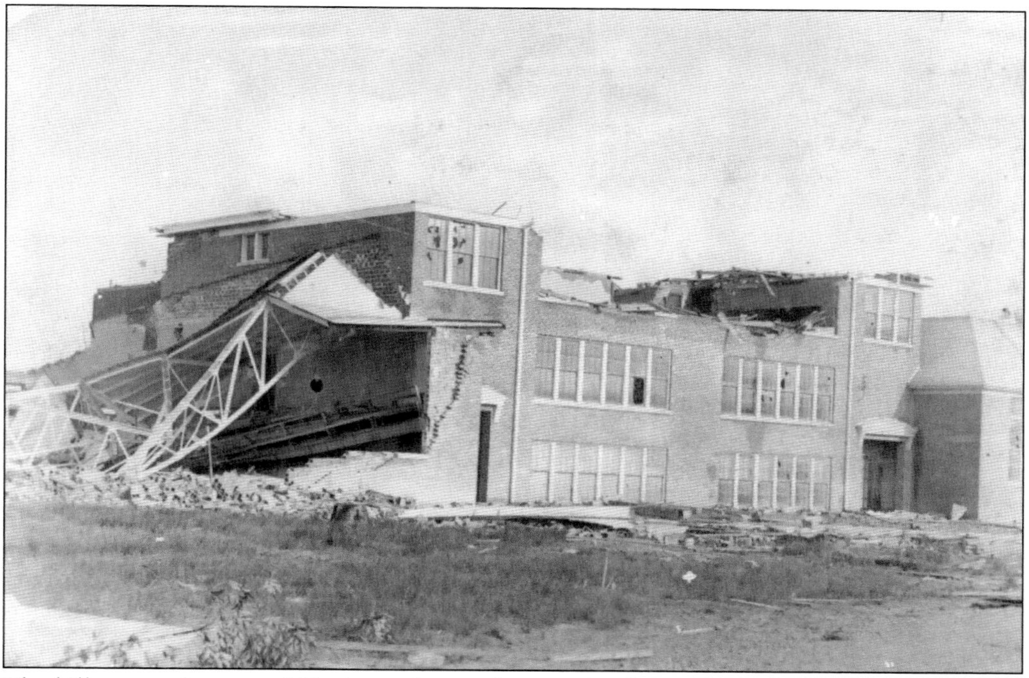

The killer tornado entered Hoxie on the southwest side of town around 3:00 p.m. First hit was the new high school building, which had just opened four months prior. The top floor of the three-story school building was destroyed, and the gym on the south side of the building was demolished. Two girls, Louise Hatley and Imogene East, were killed instantly, and several others were injured. (HW.)

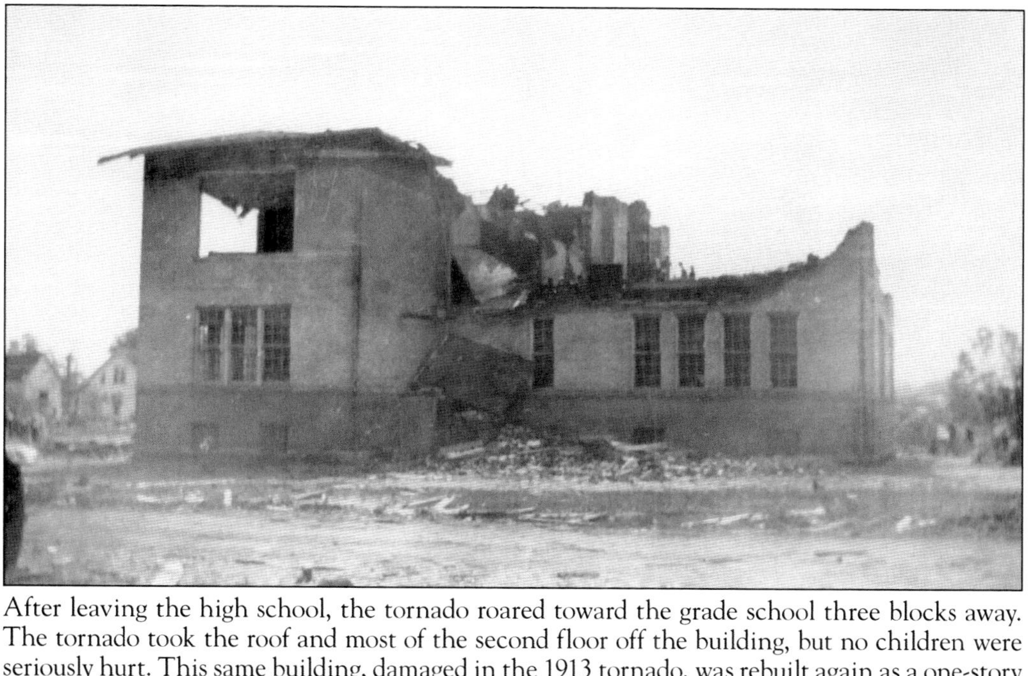

After leaving the high school, the tornado roared toward the grade school three blocks away. The tornado took the roof and most of the second floor off the building, but no children were seriously hurt. This same building, damaged in the 1913 tornado, was rebuilt again as a one-story stucco building. It, along with the rebuilt high school, was destroyed by a fire of suspicious causes in 1941. (HW.)

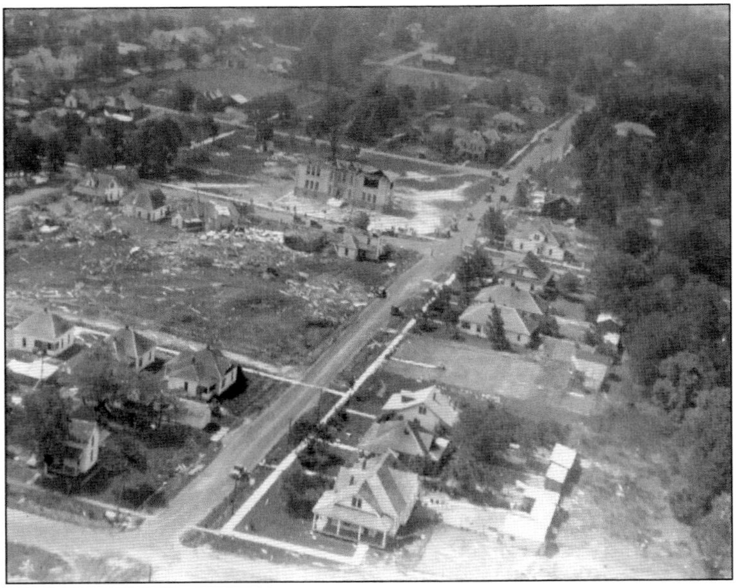

Intersecting with Memphis Street in the lower left, Lawrence Street divides this aerial view of Hoxie after the 1927 tornado. The destroyed grade school is visible on the corner of Lindsey and Lawrence Streets, near the center of the image. Strewn debris and lumber mark the storm's path from right to left. From here, the tornado crossed Memphis Street and the Frisco tracks on its way to Walnut Ridge. (JBW.)

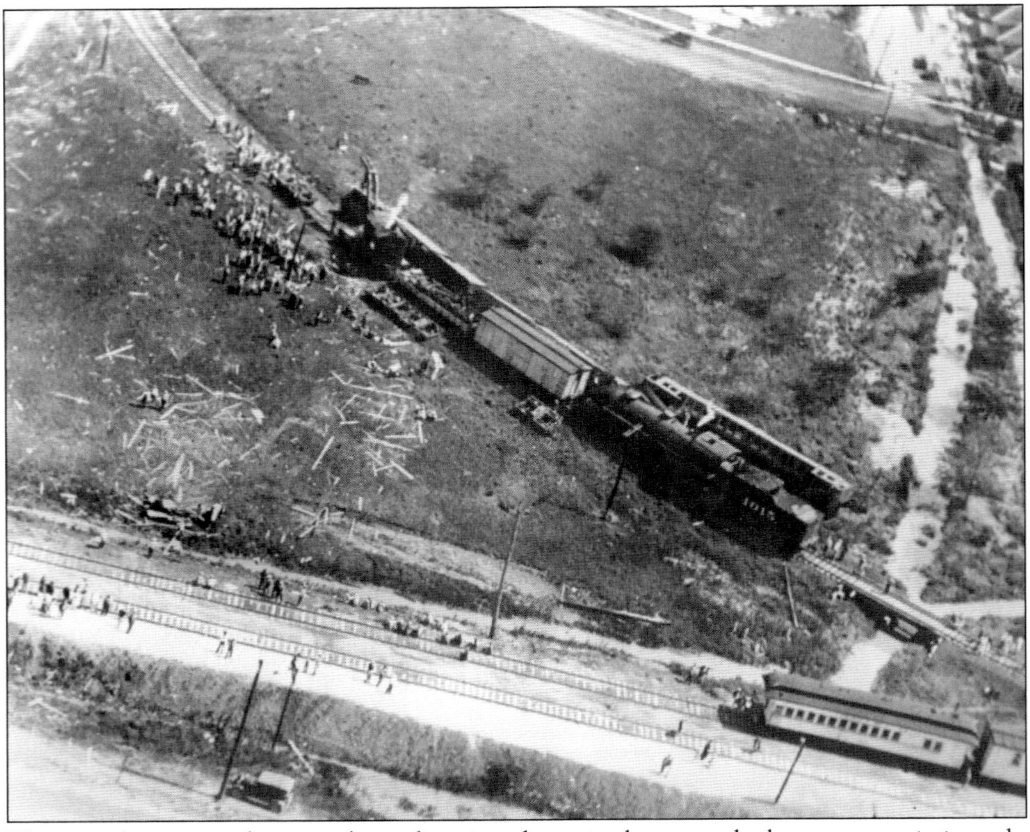

The tornado continued in a northeast direction, damaging houses and other structures in its path. It crossed the Frisco Railway tracks about two blocks west of the Hoxie Depot, where a Frisco train waiting to make its run to Cape Girardeau, Missouri, was blown on its side. The back fence of the Boas Hotel property is visible on the far right, just past Turkey Creek. (JBW.)

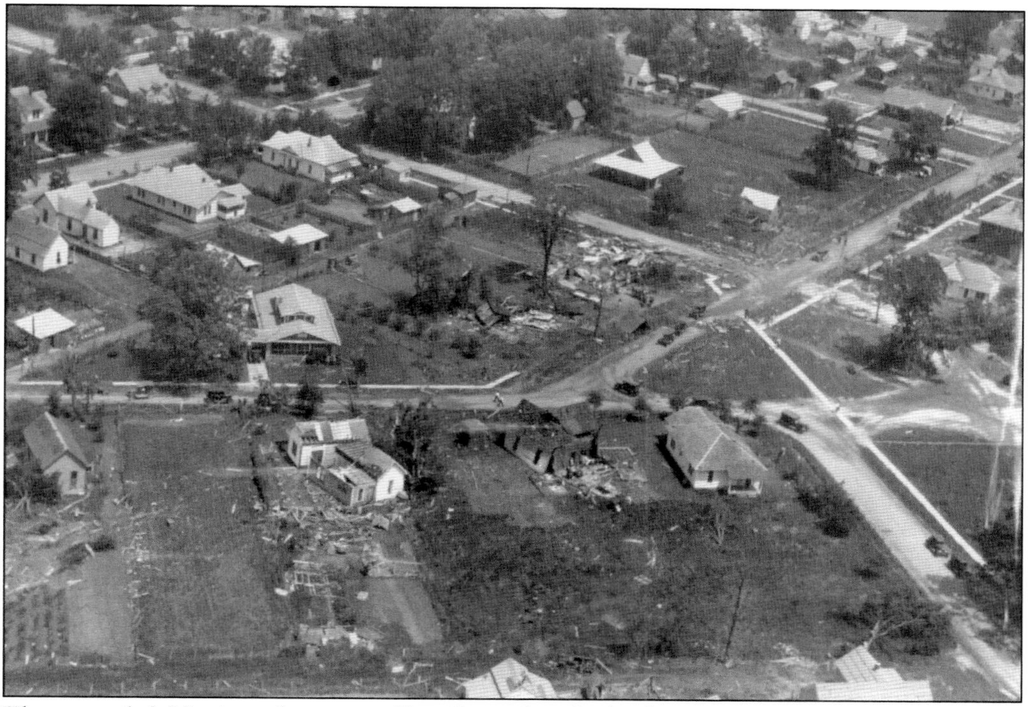

The storm left Hoxie and swept up East Second and Third Streets in Walnut Ridge, causing substantial material damage. Fifty-one homes were leveled or blown over. This aerial view shows these two streets, near the Walnut Ridge High School, out of view. The school had 30 broken windows, and a portion of the roof was torn away. (JBW.)

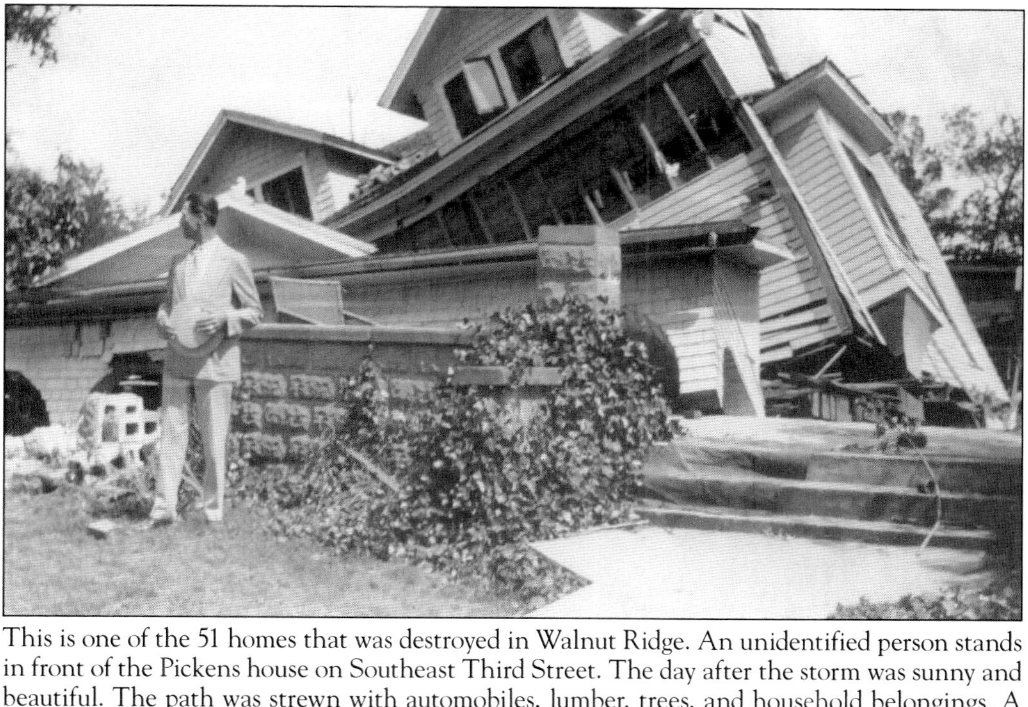

This is one of the 51 homes that was destroyed in Walnut Ridge. An unidentified person stands in front of the Pickens house on Southeast Third Street. The day after the storm was sunny and beautiful. The path was strewn with automobiles, lumber, trees, and household belongings. A local hotel was taken over by the Red Cross and served as a hospital. (JK.)

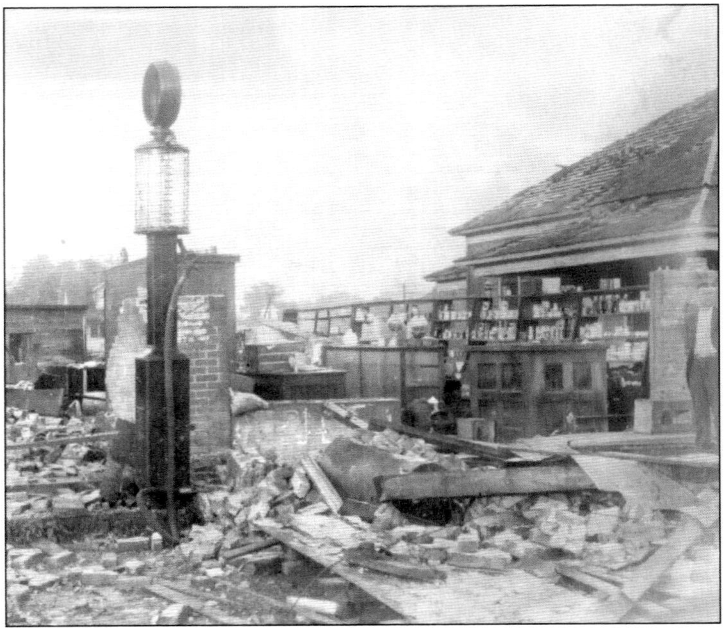

The store belonging to Hoxie's Henry Downing was totally demolished. Downing was hit by an electric fan and injured. T.C. McNairy, a salesman for Plunkett-Jarrell Grocer, was also inside the store but escaped unharmed. All four walls and the roof were lifted by the storm and carried away. Downing stands in the aftermath, shown with shelves and items on the bar literally untouched. (JAG.)

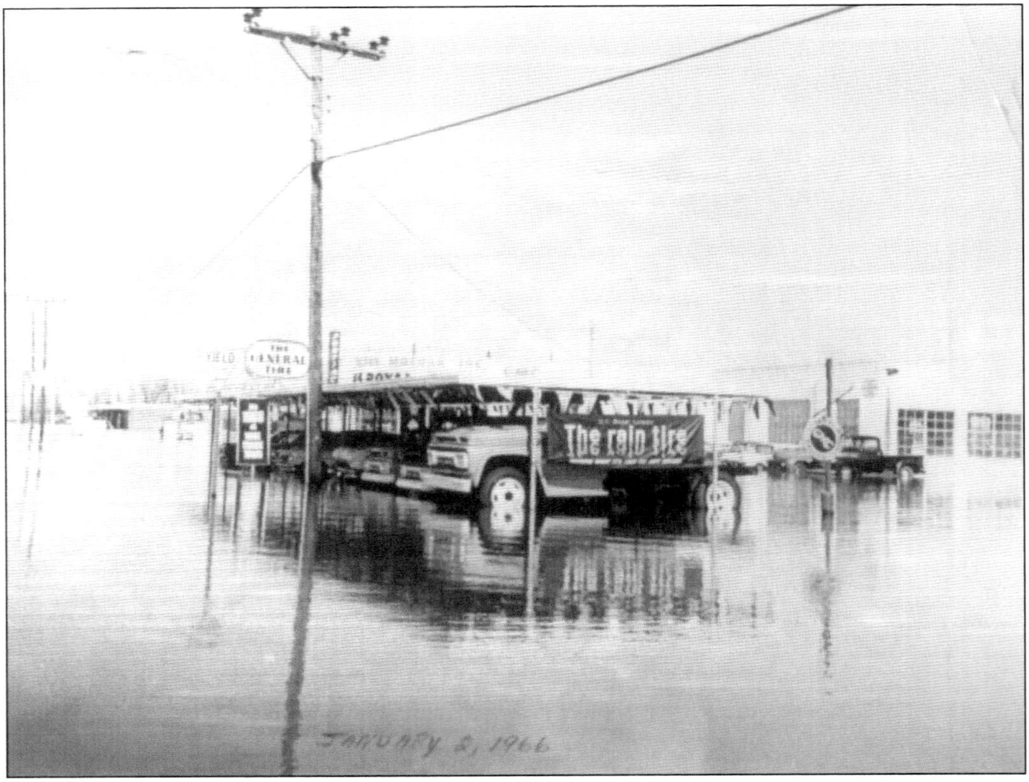

Nine inches of rain on January 1, 1966, caused Village Creek to flood, causing $500,000 in damages in Walnut Ridge. Many said this was worse than similar floods in 1927 and 1935. Tolson Motor Company, pictured here, reported 16 inches of water in its offices. Fifty families were forced to evacuate, 200 homes were surrounded by water, and there was flood damage to over 20 businesses. (TB.)

A disastrous fire destroyed the Sharum Gymnasium and the Walnut Ridge High School building on December 12, 1957. The annual invitational basketball tournament was in progress, and three games were played the previous night; the gym was vacated by 11:00 p.m. Within a few hours, the gym was completely engulfed in flames, which spread to the high school. Speculation was that a cigarette dropped under the bleachers had started the fire. (AHC.)

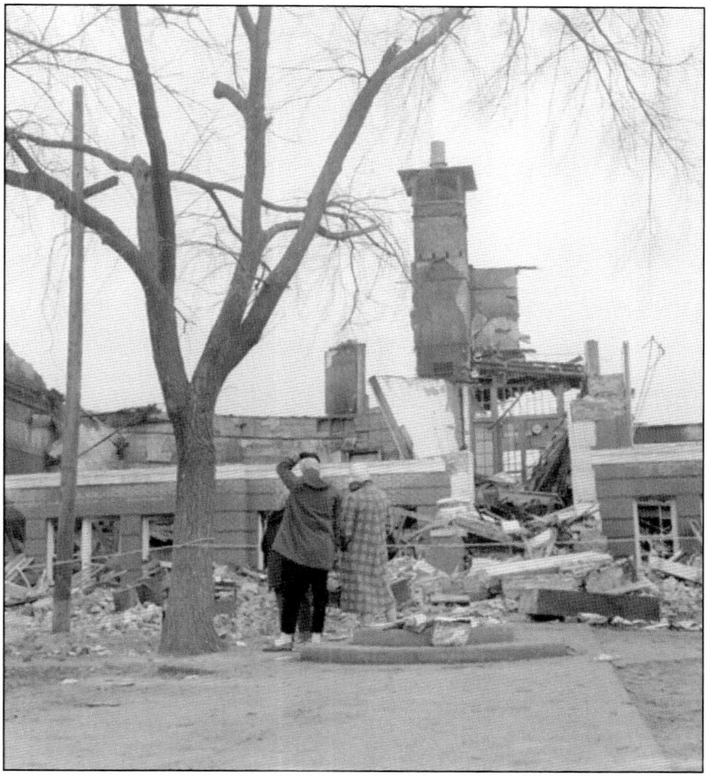

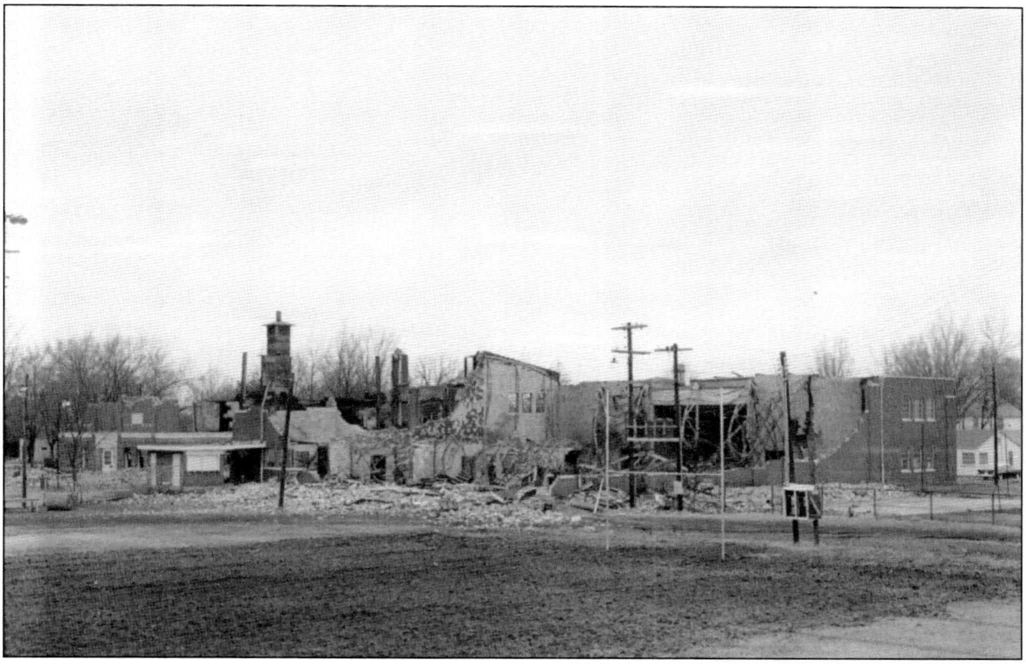

This view from the football field shows the destroyed gymnasium and Walnut Ridge High School building. Cost of the fire exceeded $300,000 in damages. Reporters at the time said it was the biggest loss in the history of the town. It definitely was a devastating loss, but was no comparison to the fire of 1893, which literally destroyed half of downtown Walnut Ridge. (AHC.)

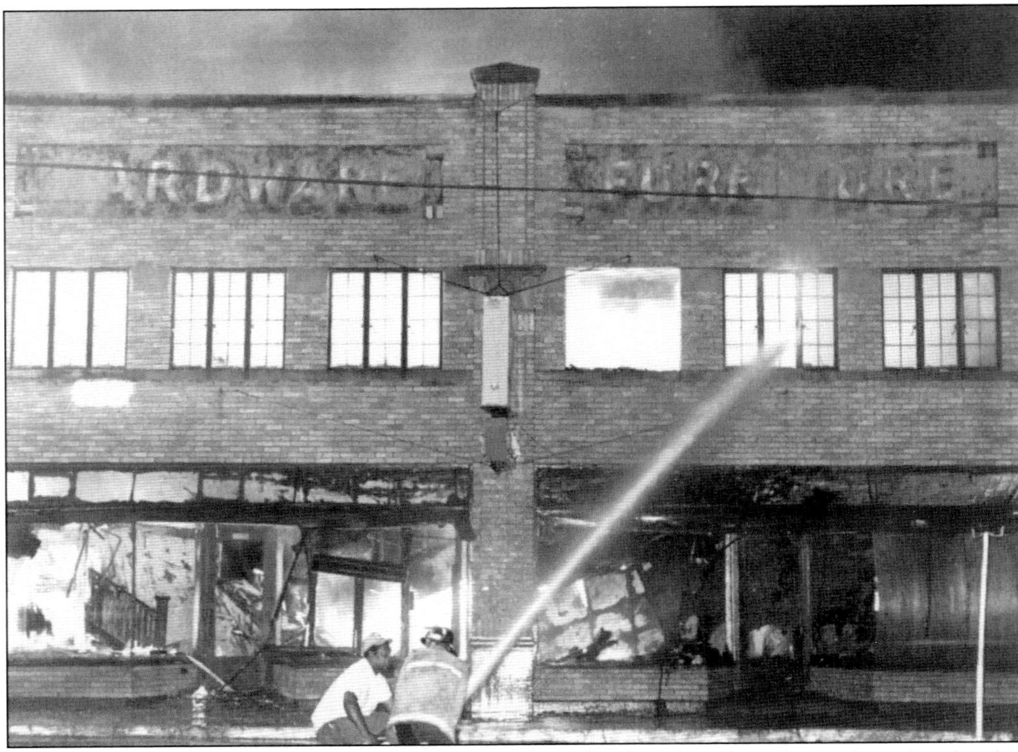

Previously using volunteers, the City of Walnut Ridge hired and paid members for the fire department in the late 1940s. After the armory was built in the mid-1950s, the old USO building on East Main Street became the department's home. Here, Walnut Ridge firefighters battle a blaze on Main Street at the old Burrow Hardware store in 1984. Police determined the fire to be arson, but no suspects were ever charged. (CR.)

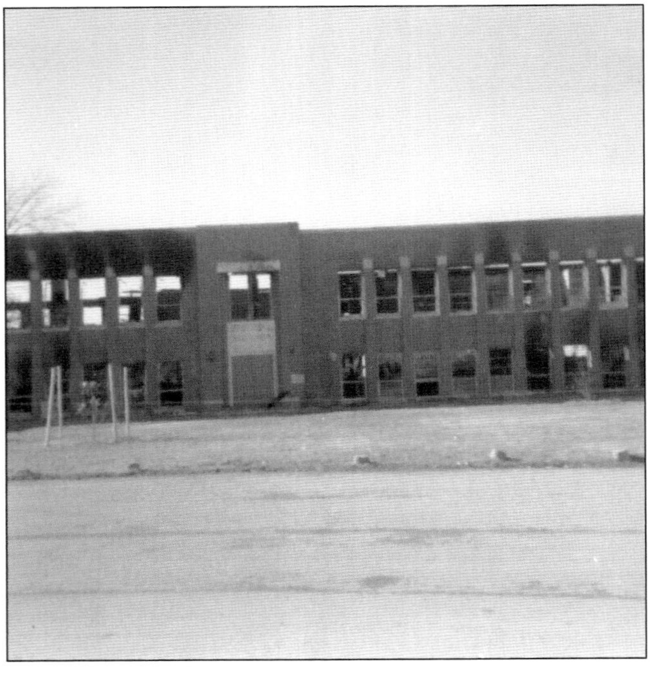

A brand-new Hoxie High School building was constructed in 1971, and the old two-story high school building was repurposed for junior high classes. Just a year later, in December 1972, the junior high school building was decimated by fire. Fire had struck in the exact same spot in December 1941, when the three-story high school building was burned to the ground and replaced with this now-destroyed two-story building. (LPL.)

Eight

Local Culture

Early Walnut Ridge and Hoxie were basically like towns out of an old Western movie set. Saloons were abundant, and the nightlife was rough. A February 1884 newspaper article mentions that John A. Rhea, early leader and first Walnut Ridge marshal, mortally wounded James Bottoms in the neck with a penknife. Articles like these were commonplace and included fights, killings, and even train and bank robberies. Hoxie, at this time, had a very large hobo camp and was known nationwide as the most dangerous town in the country.

Churches had a slow start but were finally able to bring stability to the reckless towns. Lawless and unstable at first, Walnut Ridge and Hoxie banned alcohol by 1915, even before Prohibition. By the 1920s, they were sterling examples of Bible Belt communities. Walnut Ridge's founder, W.M. Ponder, was a Presbyterian. Hoxie's founders, Henry and Mary Boas, were Catholic. So, it made sense that the Presbyterian church was the first founded in Walnut Ridge in 1878, and the Catholic church was the first founded in Hoxie in 1883. The Methodists and Baptists quickly followed in both towns in the late 1800s and early 1900s. Freewill Baptist, Pentecost, Church of Christ, and others followed later. Religion is still a very important part of both communities.

Politically, the majority of both towns have historically consisted of Yellow Dog Democrats, none prouder than when Arkansas's own Bill Clinton was sworn in as president of the United States in 1993. The Republican Party has become more populous in the past decade.

Both towns are community-minded, support many clubs and charities, and love their music, theater, sports, hunting, outdoor activities, and festivals. The Freemasons, Knights of Pythias, Odd Fellows, and Order of the Eastern Star were early charitable organizations in both towns, followed by the Lions Club and Jaycees. The Kiwanis Club, Rotary Club, Circle of Friends, and Junior Auxiliary are the most active today. There have been too many clubs to mention all, but a few included sewing, rug hooking, garden, music, china painters, bridge, extension homemakers, and historical. There were several opera houses and an open-air theater in Walnut Ridge and early silent film theaters in both towns. Baseball has been played here since the 1890s and football since the 1920s. Hunting and fishing have always been favorite pastimes.

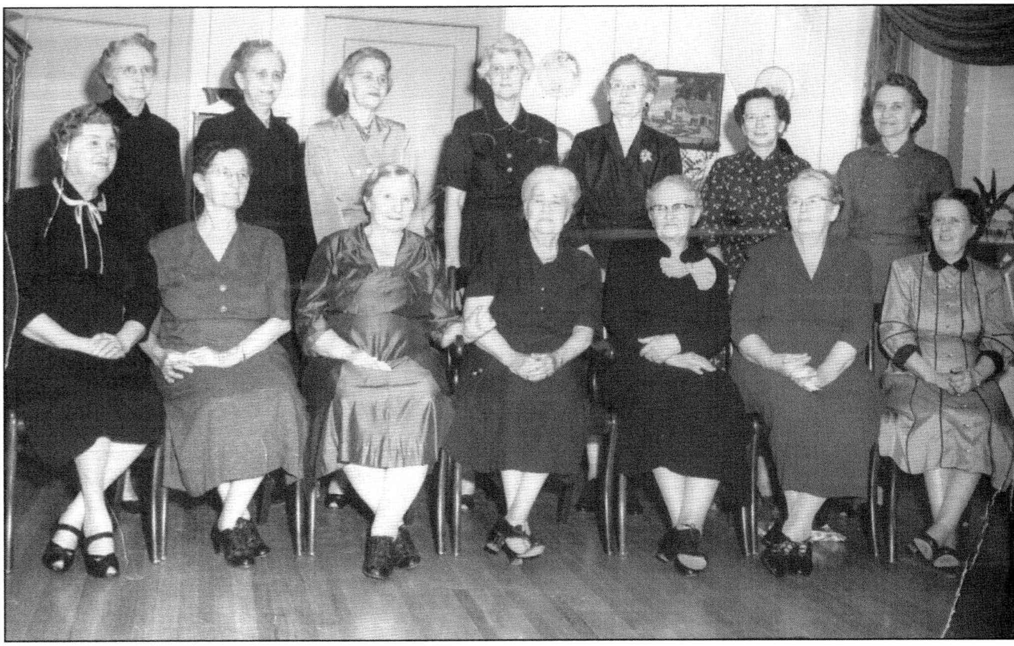

The Walnut Ridge Sunshine Sewing Club, founded in 1933, was one of the most popular women's groups in town for many years. Pictured at a 1950 Christmas dinner are, from left to right, (first row) Lizzie Rainwater, Laura Nemrick Grimes, Hannah Moore, Flora Bassett, Pearl McCarroll, Mable Johnson, and Mary Bassett Belk; (second row) Virgie Raney, Ruth Baker, Hazel Followwill Moore, Ethel Followwill Rainwater, Laura McCarroll, Lena Fender Rainwater, and Virgie Cravens Jung. (JMS.)

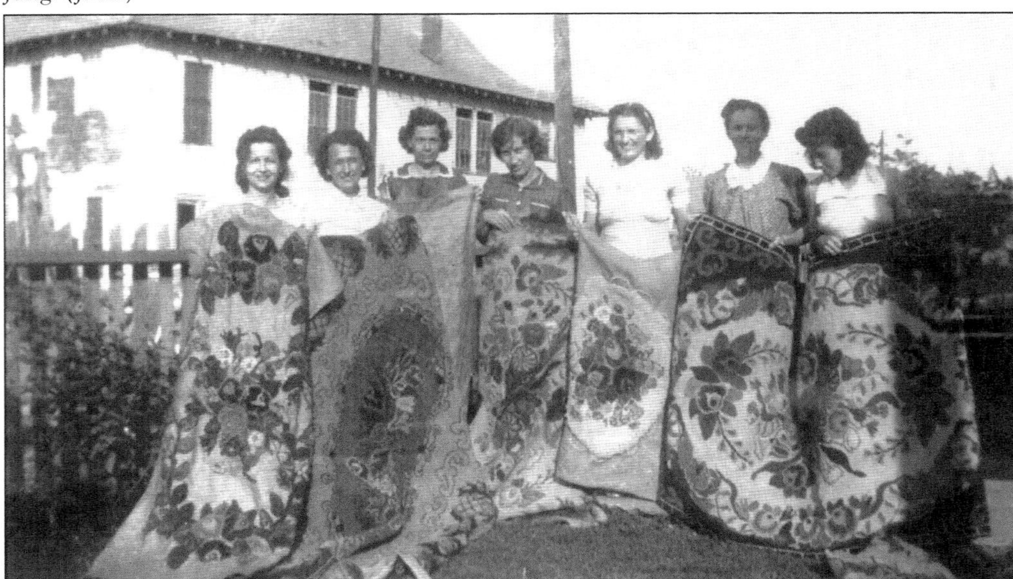

Inspired by the wife of a Methodist minister, Mrs. Harry King, the Hoxie Hooking Club was chartered in the late 1930s. Known at first as the Happy Hookers, the club's name was changed later for obvious reasons. There were seven original Hookers. From left to right are Gracia Judkins, Buna Cooper, Evelyn Weir, Mary Andrews, Ruby Woodyard, Julia Mae Green, and Lenore Doyle. The rug hooking club was active for several decades. (LBD.)

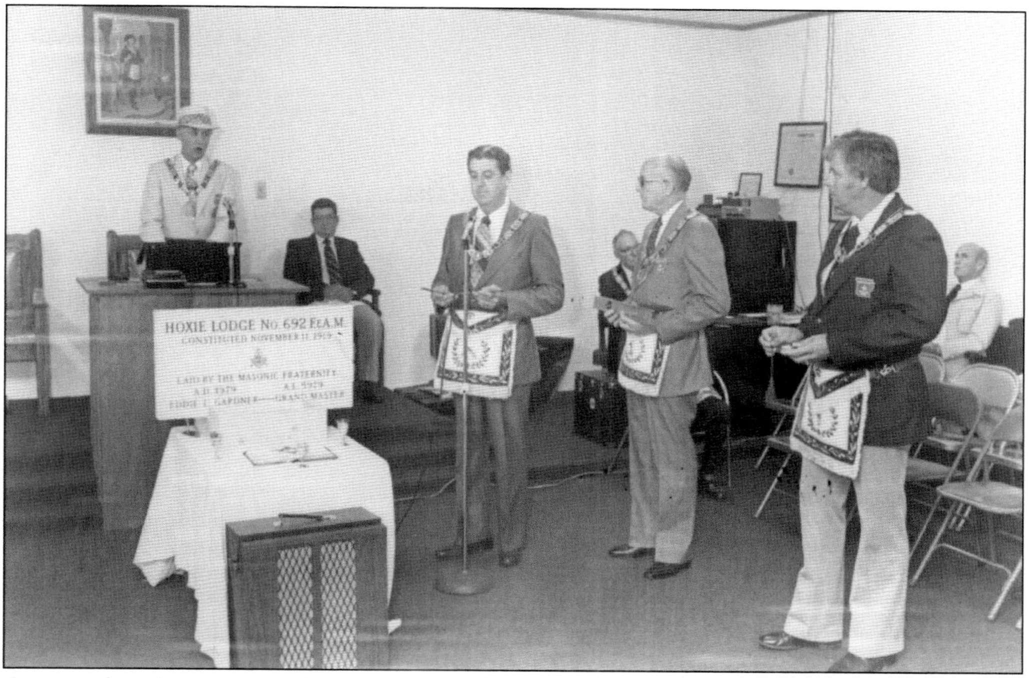

George Thornburgh, a member of Aurora Lodge No. 423 in Walnut Ridge, was the grand master of Free and Accepted Masons of Arkansas in 1879. Eddie Gardner, a member of Hoxie Lodge No. 692 held the same position 100 years later. Standing at the podium, Gardner leads a cornerstone dedication at the Hoxie lodge on its 60th anniversary in 1979. Seated to his immediate right is Bert Walter and seated at far right is Ted Riggs. (JCW.)

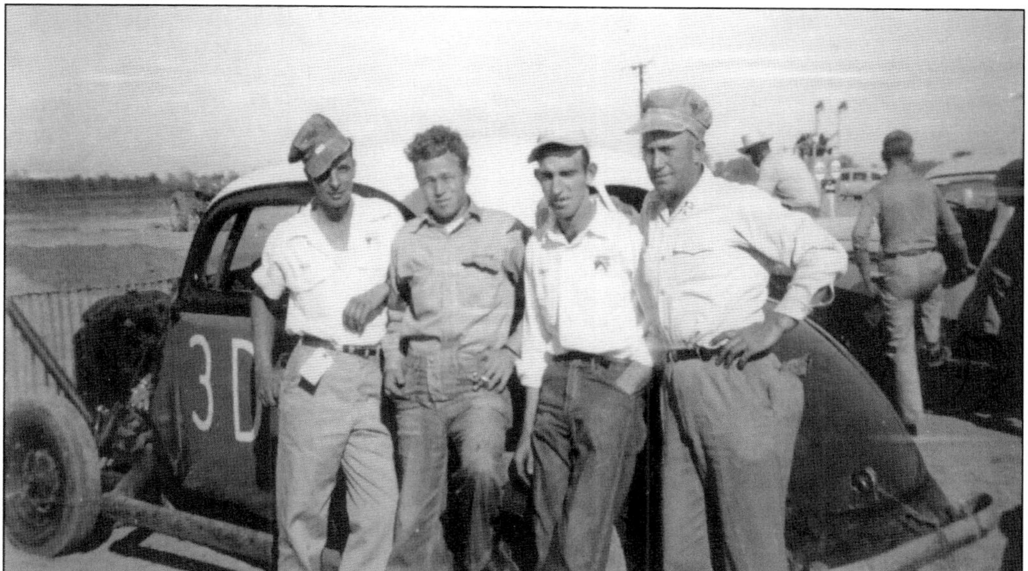

Pictured from left to right, Mac McComb, Curly Downs, Lloyd Ashlock, and Austin Smith are standing in front of their *3 D* race car in the mid-1950s. Ashlock started Ashlock's Tire Service in Hoxie, later moving to Walnut Ridge. Smith owned a service station on East Main Street in Walnut Ridge, and McComb worked the parts desk at Snapp Motor Company. Racing is still a popular sport in northeast Arkansas. (SSM.)

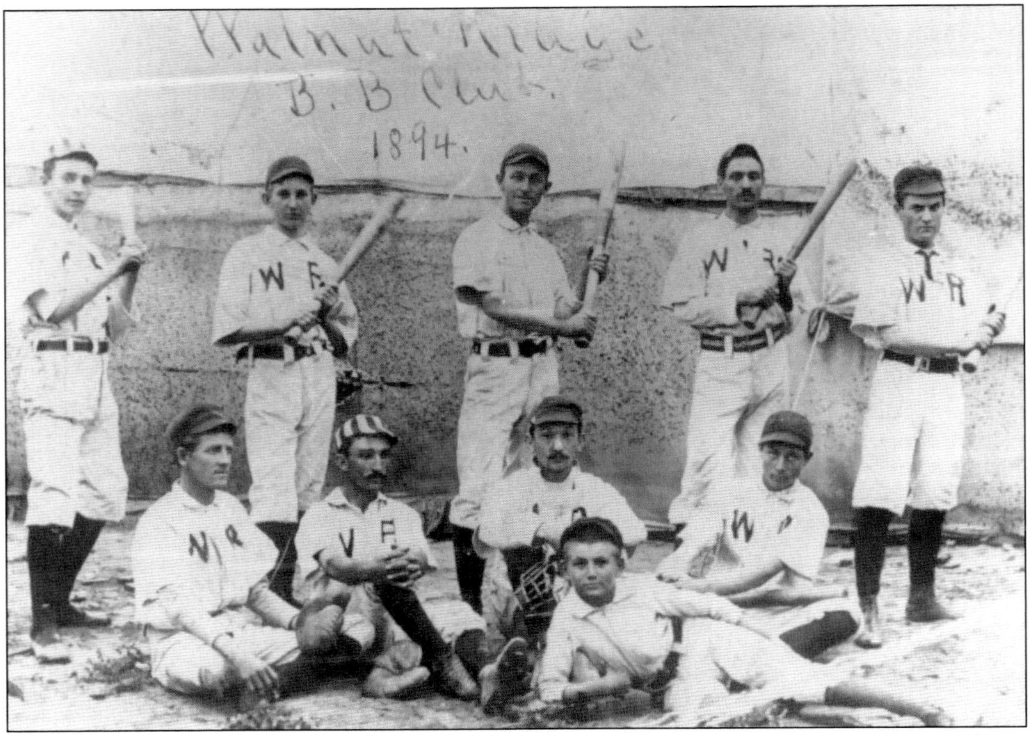

This is the Walnut Ridge Baseball Club in 1894. Pictured, from left to right, are (first row) Dr. Clinton Meriwether, Montie Sharum, David Bloom, Carroll McCarroll, and Solon Crook; (second row) Bert Israel, George Ponder, Berg Israel, C.W. Cooper, and Bob Cooper. Meriwether was a prominent physician, Bloom started Bloom's Department Store with two of his brothers, and Bob Cooper and his brother Moses each owned successful drugstores. (AHC.)

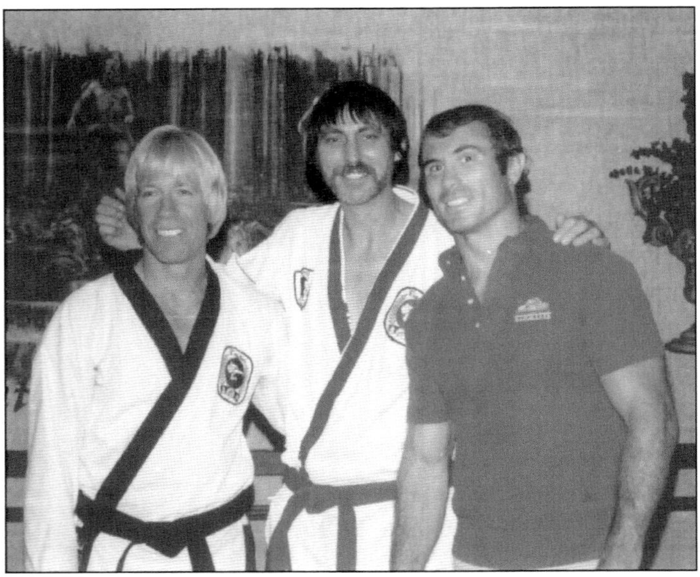

Fred Weeks (center), a native of Hoxie, stands with Chuck Norris (left) and Bill "Superfoot" Wallace in 1978, when Weeks received his black belt from Norris. Weeks formed the Allied Tang Soo Do Federation in 1980 in Walnut Ridge, which is still a thriving martial arts academy to this day. Over $45,000 has been raised for selected charities by the academy's annual board-breaking demonstrations. (FW.)

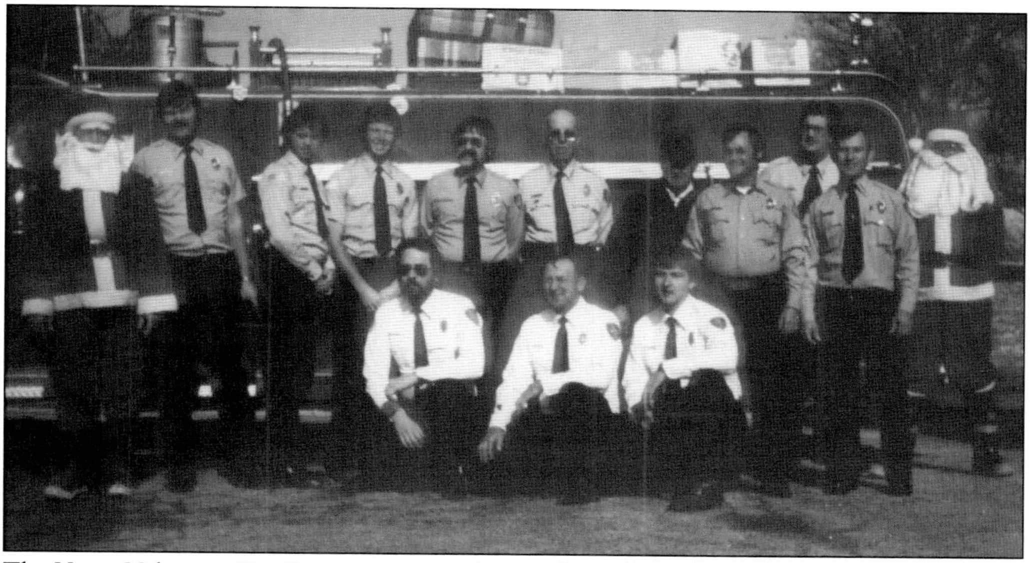

The Hoxie Volunteer Fire Department was chartered in July 1954 with 16 members under Chief Merle Woods. Zack Lawhon, kneeling in center, is the fire chief in this December 1982 photograph. Leonard Ringle Jr., sixth from left on the second row, is the only charter member still enlisted. A long-standing and much-anticipated Christmas tradition involved Santa Claus riding the fire truck through Hoxie and passing out candy to children. (MT.)

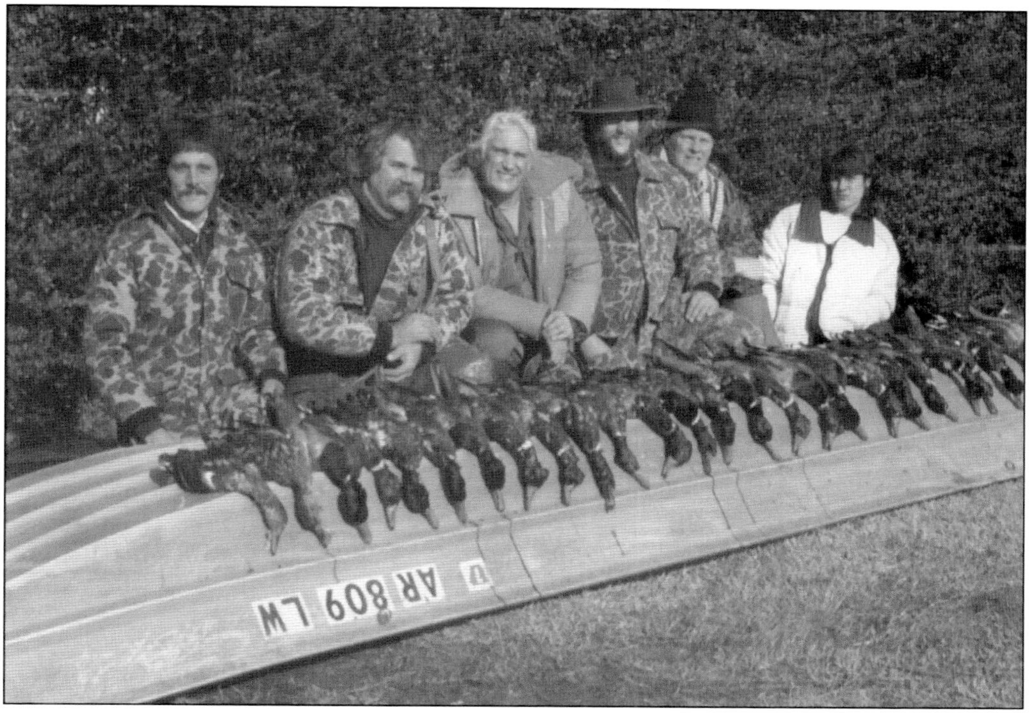

Migratory waterfowl are drawn annually to the numerous rice fields and flooded timber area nearby, making Walnut Ridge and Hoxie the duck-hunting mecca of the world. Country music star Charlie Rich is one of several famous personalities who have hunted here. Rich (third from left) is shown with local hunting guides Charles Snapp (to his left) and Stan Jones (to his right) after a successful hunt in the early 1980s. (CS.)

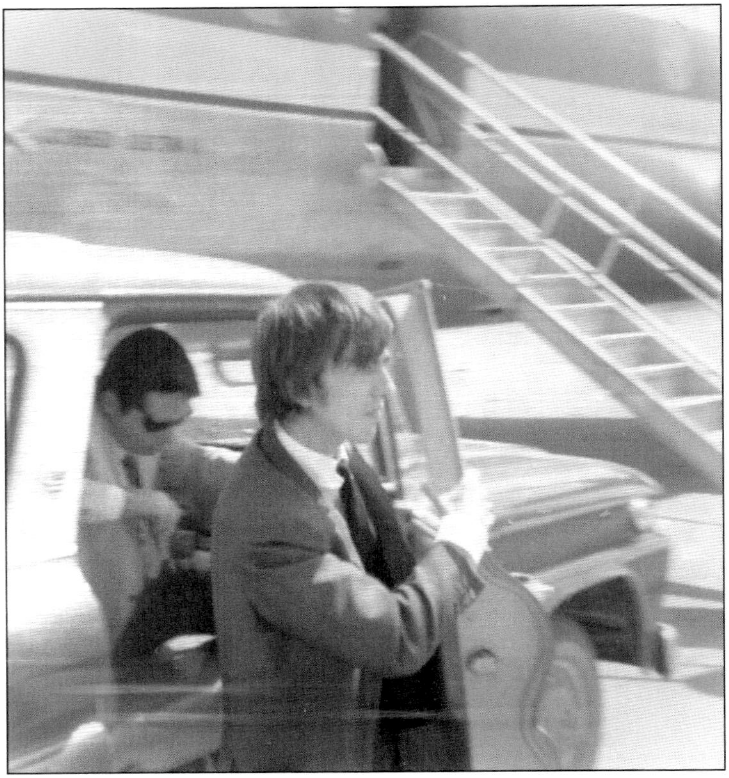

A quiet night in 1964 was interrupted by the unusual sound of an airliner approaching Walnut Ridge Airport. Its arrival sparked enough interest that three local teenagers went to investigate, only to discover that the Beatles had landed in Walnut Ridge en route to a weekend vacation at a dude ranch in Missouri. Paul McCartney and George Harrison returned to Walnut Ridge in a GMC Suburban. Harrison is seen making his way back to their plane. (CMS.)

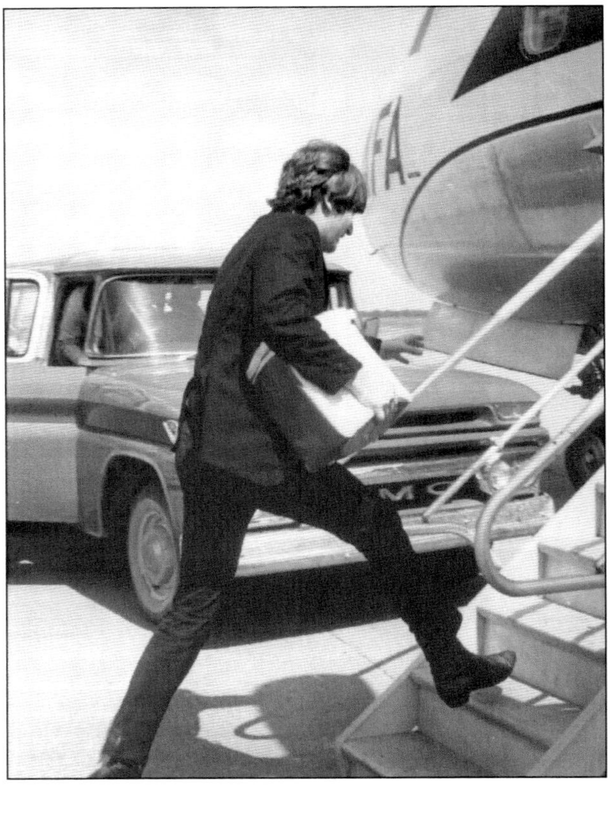

The ranch, located in Altus, Missouri, was owned by Reed Pigman Sr., who operated the charter airline that the Beatles were using. Walnut Ridge had the closest airport that would accommodate such a large plane. After a concert in Dallas, the Beatles secretly landed in Walnut Ridge on September 18, 1964, with plans to depart for New York the following Sunday. The secret did not last long. John Lennon is shown hustling to their plane after their return. Lennon and Ringo Starr had flown back from Missouri in a small aircraft. (SR.)

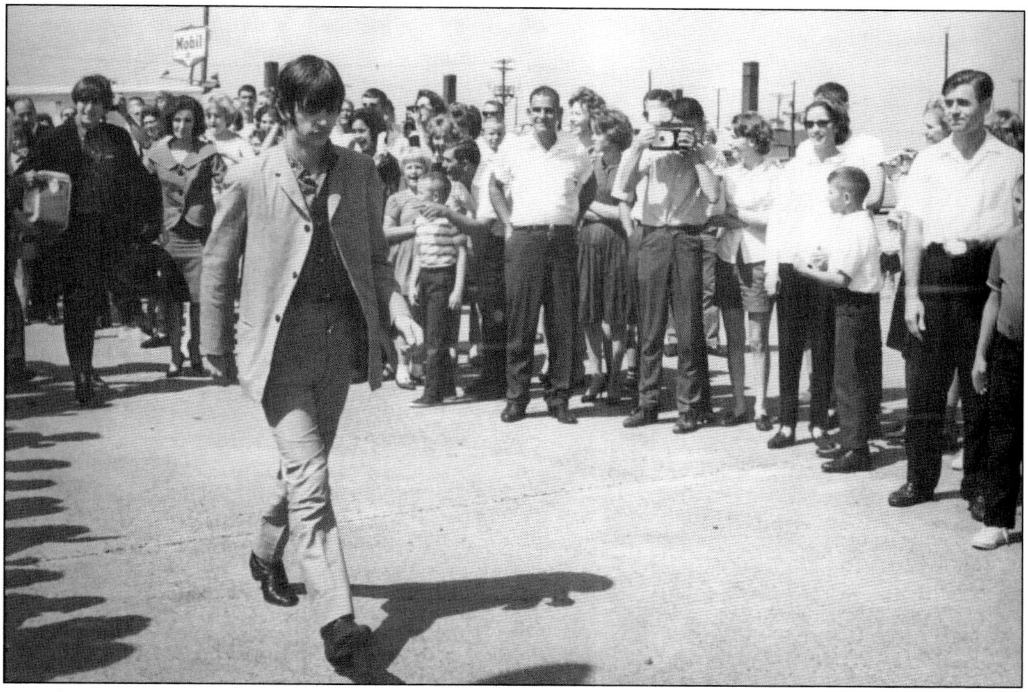

Word spread quickly around town, especially among teenagers. A crowd of several hundred was gathered at the airport by Sunday morning, September 20, 1964, to greet the Beatles. Ringo Starr, in the foreground, and John Lennon, on the far left, are seen making their way through the crowd to their airplane. (SR.)

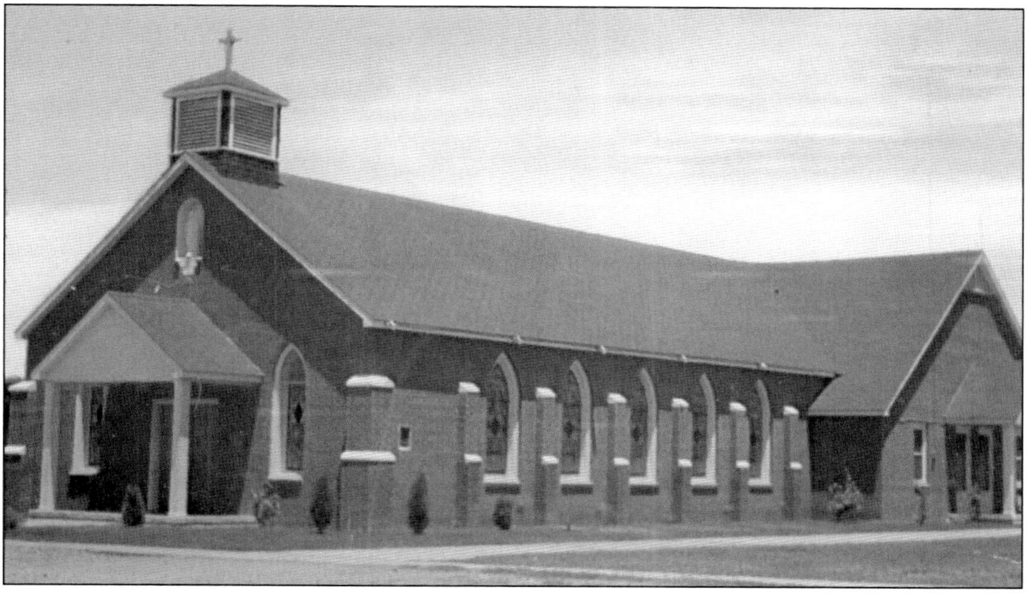

The first church built in Hoxie was a Catholic church, located at the corner of Lindsey and Texas Streets, in 1886. After burning in 1913, it was replaced with another between Ruth and Jackson Streets. When the parish outgrew this, a third was built in 1925 in Hoxie between Towne and Cleveland Streets, where it served until 1950, when the Catholics built a new sanctuary on Free Street in Walnut Ridge, pictured here. (JBW.)

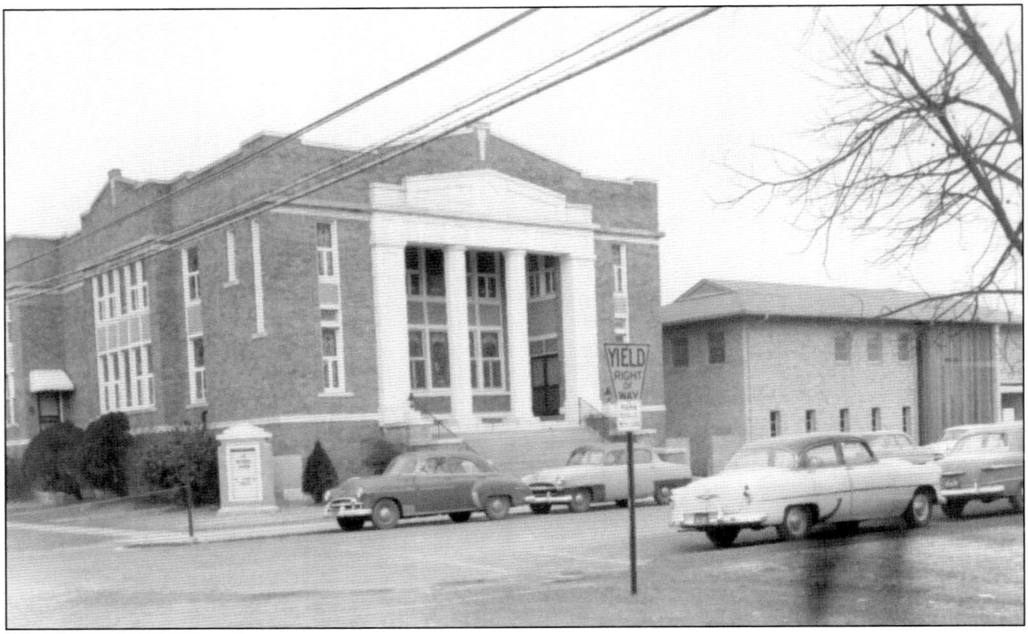

First United Methodist Church of Walnut Ridge was established in 1885 by Rev. S.D. Evans. The Methodists shared a building with the Presbyterians at first and then erected their own building in 1886—a one-room, frame structure located at the corner of Walnut and Northeast Third Streets. The present church, built in 1922, is pictured here in the 1950s at the corner of Vine and Southwest Second Streets. (JBW.)

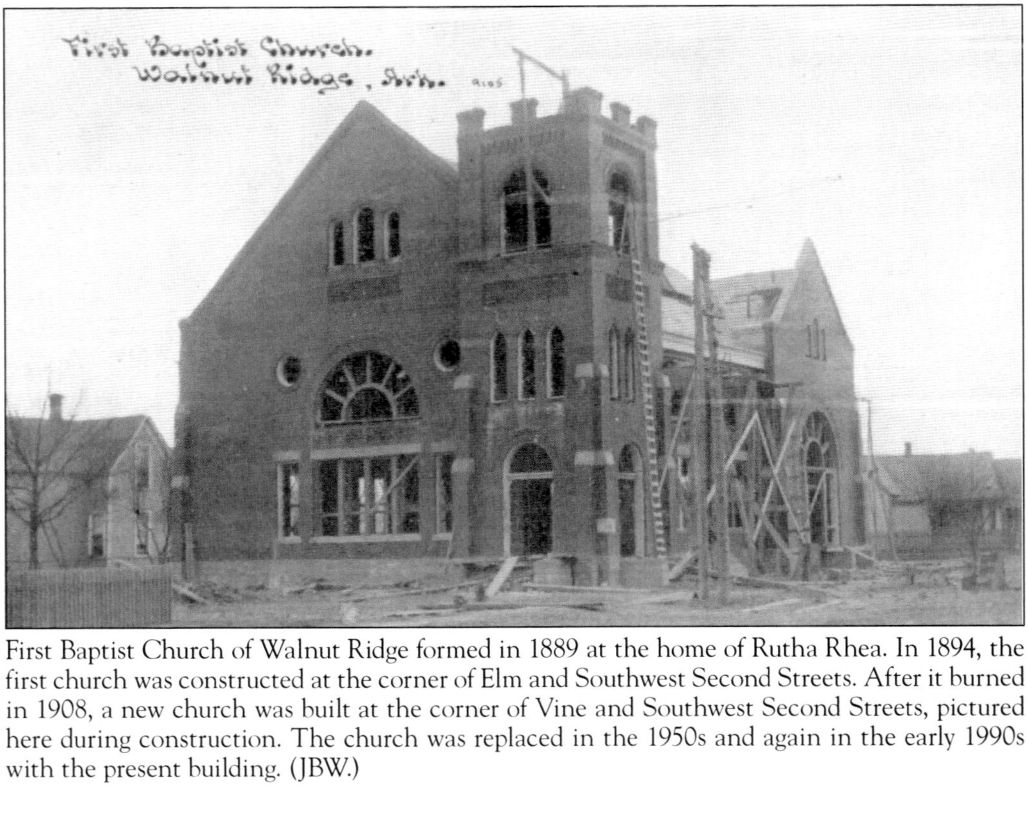

First Baptist Church of Walnut Ridge formed in 1889 at the home of Rutha Rhea. In 1894, the first church was constructed at the corner of Elm and Southwest Second Streets. After it burned in 1908, a new church was built at the corner of Vine and Southwest Second Streets, pictured here during construction. The church was replaced in the 1950s and again in the early 1990s with the present building. (JBW.)

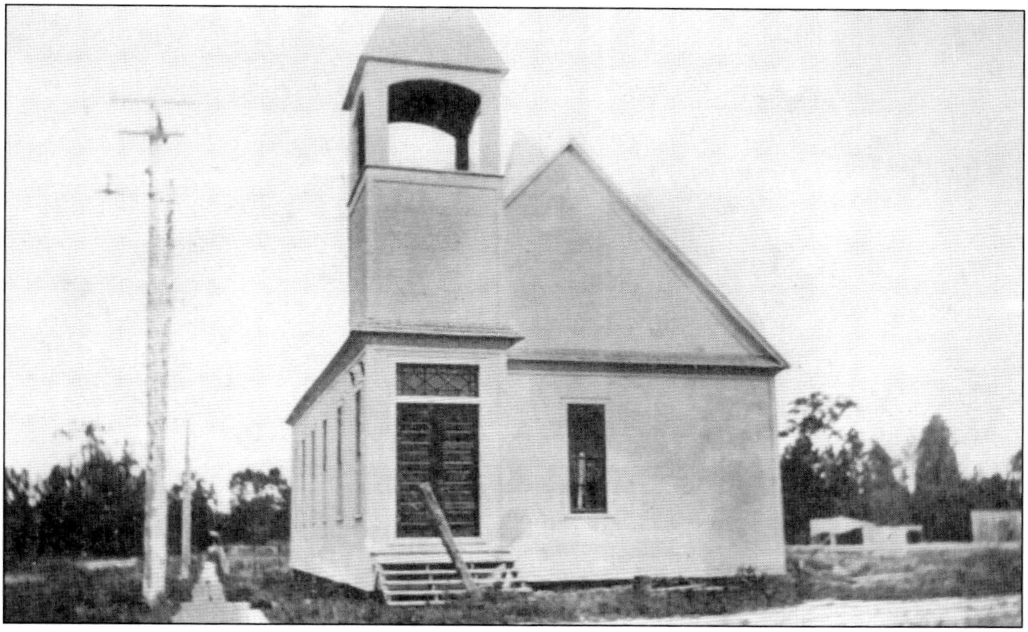

Hoxie Methodist Church was organized in 1903. First meeting in the old red school building at Annie and Lawrence Streets and then sharing a building with the Presbyterians, the Methodists built their first church in 1908, pictured here. Located at the corner of Broad and Gibson Streets, it survived damage during the 1913 tornado but was destroyed by fire in 1927. Their current brick sanctuary is at the same location. (LD.)

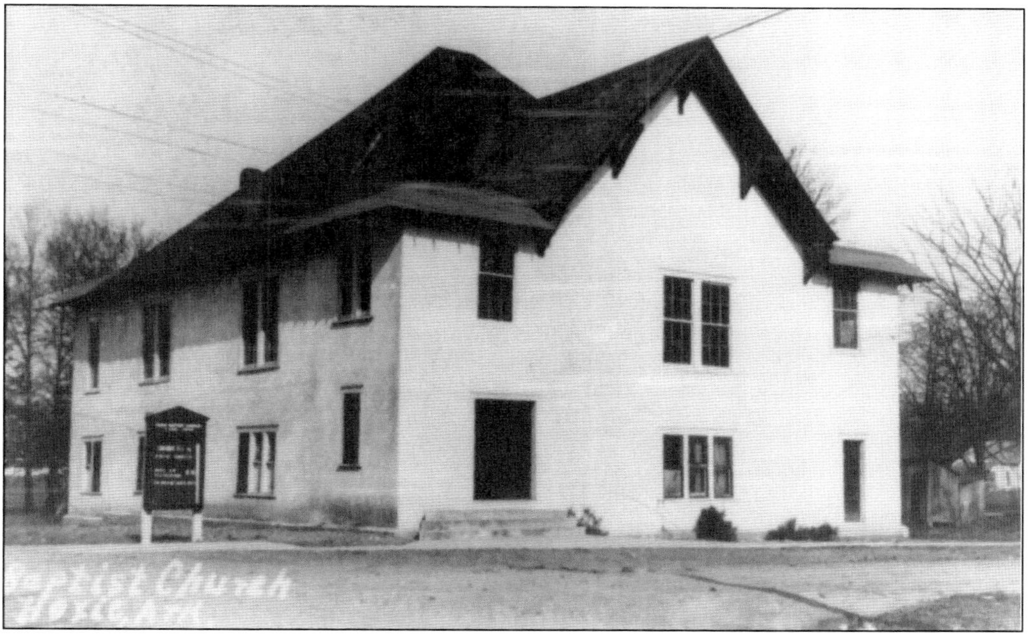

Hoxie Baptist Church was organized in 1907, with nine charter members. Its first building was at the corner of Broad and Lindsey Streets. Damaged by the 1927 tornado, the original structure was remodeled and looked slightly different than it does in this picture, taken later. This building was used until the present sanctuary was erected in 1954 at the same location. Classrooms were added in 1956. (FBCH.)

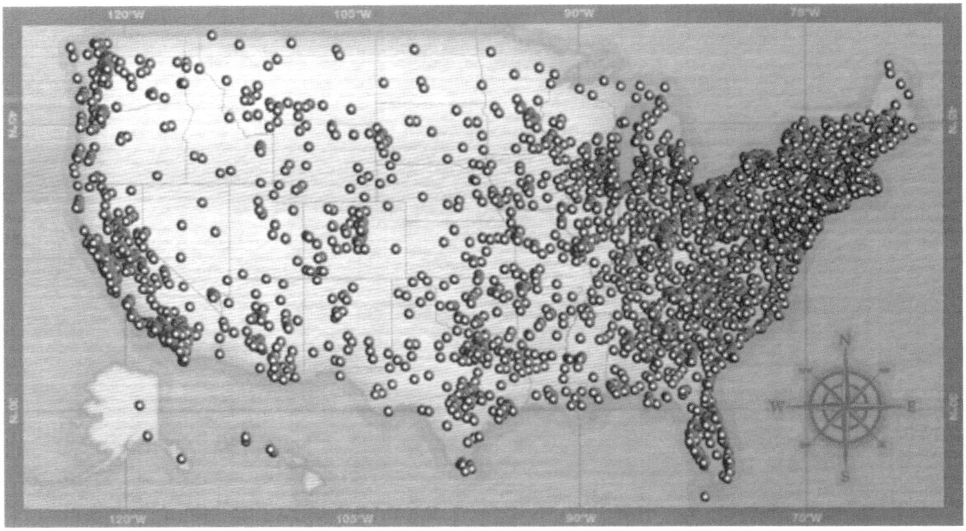